A Guide for
OLD
TESTAMENT
STUDY

A Guide for
OLD TESTAMENT STUDY

William W. Stevens

BROADMAN PRESS
Nashville, Tennessee

4212–10
ISBN: 0–8054–1210–7

Dewey Decimal Classification: 221
Library of Congress Catalog Card Number: 73–91606
Printed in the United States of America

To my wife, Dorothy,
whose inspiration and cooperation
have made this work possible.

Contents

Illustrations and Maps

Preface

Though many books have been written to give the reader a rapid survey of the entire Old Testament period—a sort of pen-and-ink sketch of the high points of Israel's history—this work is sent forth with a special hope that a simple presentation of the story of the Hebrew people might show clearly how God dealt with this peculiar nation. Perhaps the Nebo-like vista of those mighty acts of God found in these pages may inspire the reader to delve further into the wondrous revelation of God in the Hebrew Scriptures.

Much recent study and research has helped the Old Testament to acquire a fresh significance for present-day Christians, thus emphasizing its vital importance for a true understanding of the New Testament. Old Testament history has been made to glow anew with the recent marvelous archaeological discoveries in Bible lands; for characters and events that were once considered remote and prosaic have now been enhanced by the light cast upon them by the artifacts and ruins recovered from a bygone age. Tiny Israel, nestled between mighty nations to the north and to the south, is discerned to have been part of a pulsating world movement and international intrigue, yet playing a highly significant role on the scene of the historic stage of the pre-Christian era.

This book assumes a limited knowledge of the Old Testament on the part of the reader. It should be helpful to Sunday School teachers who are trying to present Old Testament facts and meanings to their pupils. Pastors could also use it as a manual for special classes in Old Testament study. The book is primarily intended as a textbook for schools or for instruction by correspondence. Wherever it is used, the pupils should be urged to read the Scripture passages cited at the beginning of each chapter to get acquainted with the biblical text for each chapter.

All Scripture quotations in the book are from the American Standard Version. Since this translation is now in public domain, no permission is needed to quote from it; but I am still grateful to its translators and publishers. Also, I offer deep gratitude to all who in any way have helped in my compiling and writing. May this book meet the needs of many who want to understand the Old Testament as a whole and thus enrich their appreciation and use of the whole Bible.

W. W. S.

Photographs 11 and 19 were furnished generously by the Israel Government Tourist Office. All others are by Fon Scofield, Jr., Foreign Mission Board, and are used by permission.

The Significance of the Bible

1. The Bible, *the* Book

The Christian religion bases its authority upon a book, and that book is called the Bible. The word Bible comes from the Greek word *biblos,* which at first meant the bark of the papyrus plant and later the pith of the papyrus plant, then the paper made from the plant itself. The word *biblion* meant a papyrus roll on which the Bible was originally copied. The Latin term *biblia* also means book, and it is through the Latin that the term came into the English language as Bible. To say "the Bible" is to say "*the* Book."

The Bible is a large book, in fact it is a collection of books—66 in number. It is composed of two parts: the Old Testament, consisting of 39 books, and the New Testament, consisting of 27 books. It is a book that has had a tremendous influence in the making of our nation and is deeply ingrained in our religious heritage. George Washington said, "It is impossible to rightfully govern the world without God and the Bible." John Adams called the Bible "the best book in the world," and Lincoln declared: "Take all of this book upon reason that you can and the balance by faith and you will live and die a better man."

Church people have heard it preached and taught Sunday after Sunday, yet many of them possess only a meager knowledge of its contents. They tend to praise it more than they study it. They would say the Bible contains all of life's answers, but they are not usually able to give directions for locating those answers. Of course on the part of nonchurch people the Bible is unexplored or wholly ignored. Yet, in spite of the dearth of biblical knowledge, the Bible has continued to exert a significant influence in our cultural heritage. Laws, architecture, painting, sculpture, literature, music, education, business, domestic life—all have felt the mighty impact of God's Word.

2. Divinely Inspired

There are three pertinent factors to be noted when viewing the miraculous nature of the Bible. The earliest writing of any part of the Bible was about 1300 B.C.; the latest writing was A.D. 100, a span of approximately fourteen centuries. Most scholars believe about thirty men had a part, either great or small, in writing the various components of the Bible. Also, the varied manuscripts were written in localities covering a broad geographical territory, from Persia and Mesopotamia in the northeast, to Egypt in the south, and on over to Rome in the northwest. Yet, in spite of this immense span of time, the large number of contributing writers, and the vast geographical area involved, there is a remarkable unity in the purpose and content of the Holy Scriptures. One great theme can be found like a scarlet thread from Genesis through Revelation: the redeeming love and activity of God offering rebellious man a means of atonement and the gift of pardoning grace and everlasting fellowship. Only a book guided by the providential hand of God could evolve from such overwhelming obstacles and emerge as the authoritative voice of God.

Coupled with this line of reasoning is the added factor that the various biblical documents, collected and preserved through the changing fortunes and attitudes of the 1,400 productive years, have persisted through nearly twenty centuries to contemporary times, despite often fierce opposition. All this would attest to the miraculous nature of this Book of books.

The authority of the Bible speaks to its divine nature; so we say it was divinely inspired. The record of God's revelation to man came about because God inspired, or "breathed into," the writings. This is the root meaning of the English word "inspired," which had its origin in the Latin language. God's revelation is the disclosure, or unveiling, of himself to man, whereby he made himself known to man. This God did through mighty acts in history dealing with the great personalities in both the Old and the New Testaments. Then God supremely revealed himself in the advent of his Son, Christ Jesus, in flesh; Christ is the ultimate revelation. As revelation is the truth or concept of and about God that emerges from his

dealings with man, so inspiration is the faithful proclaiming or record-
ing under divine guidance of the truth received in revelation. Revelation has to do with the "what"; inspiration has to do with the "how."
The messages Isaiah preached in the streets of Jerusalem were just
as inspired as the ones he wrote down on a scroll. As Jesus stood
before the multitudes and taught winsomely, he *was* the revelation.
"And the Word became flesh, and dwelt among us and we beheld
his glory" (John 1:14). The Bible is the record of this revelation,
written through divine inspiration that all men might read.

The *fact* of inspiration is found on page after page of Scripture.
Every "Thus saith the Lord" of the Old Testament prophets was
a declaration of inspiration. Paul states, "Every scripture inspired
of God is also profitable for teaching, for reproof, for correction,
for instruction which is in righteousness" (2 Tim. 3:16). Jeremiah's
statement "Jehovah appeared of old unto me, saying . . ." (Jer.
31:3) has its parallel in many other places in the Scriptures. But
how God inspired is another matter, for no biblical writer saw fit
to explain to his future readers just how God psychologically dealt
with the mind of the writer so as to produce a record that would
be considered the oracle of God—"God breathed into." He was
so intent on relating "what" God had revealed that he took no
time to tell just "how" God "controlled" him, or "took him in
hand," or "breathed into" him so that his message would be faithfully
recorded and true to that which he had experienced at the time
of God's revealing activity.

As a result of various opinions relative to inspiration three views,
or theories, of inspiration have evolved. (1) An extreme view, held
by liberal scholars, is that the original writers of the biblical documents were inspired in the same sense that any writer, or poet,
is inspired to do his best work. According to such a view, a man
like Tennyson, Browning, or Milton was inspired in a sense equal
to Isaiah, Jeremiah, or Matthew. The inspiration for the one was
the same as for the other. (2) Another extreme view, held by ultra-
conservative scholars, is that the biblical writers were inspired to
the degree that every minute detail of their work was dictated, or
automatically directed, by divine guidance. The writers became
automatic transcribers. In the former view man is everything and

God is left out. In the latter view God is everything and man is left out.

(3) A third view is that the task of writing was assigned to men who were moved and directed by the Spirit of God. Both man and God were involved, for God did not bypass human experience. He has never done so in any of his dealings with man. Isaiah had a tremendous experience with God one day in the temple and penned his experience, or God-given revelation, under the guidance of the Spirit in what is now the sixth chapter of his book. From the experience came the writing, all under the direct influence of God. This third view accounts for the differing styles of the various writers in the Bible; it seems the most reasonable from every angle. At the same time, however, it must be maintained that controversies over inspiration are both futile and pointless. All the theories maintain that the Bible is inspired; it is merely the psychological method that is disputed, and this is due much to the fact that the Scriptures reveal very little upon which an opinion can be based.

3. Two Main Divisions

The Bible is divided into two divisions: the Old Testament and the New Testament. The first and longer division has to do with God's dealings with people and events prior to the coming of Christ. The second division concerns the events connected with the life, death, and resurrection of Christ and the great movement that evolved from them. The Jew accepts only the first division, not the second. The Christian accepts both as God's divine Word and believes that the first leads up to and is fulfilled in the second. Without the second the first is incomplete.

The word "testament" is not a good term to use to depict the main idea in each of these divisions. The term "covenant" is a better word with which to translate the Hebrew and Greek terms that are involved, the word "testament" unfortunately having come into English usage by way of the Latin Vulgate of Jerome. The first English translations were translations of Jerome's Latin, where *testamentum* was translated "testament." It would be much better today to speak of "Old Covenant" and "New Covenant" instead of "Old Testament" and "New Testament."

The covenant idea is extremely important in the proper under-standing of the Bible. In the old, God made an agreement, or cove-nant, with Israel at Sinai whereby they became his chosen people, called to that capacity with certain responsibilities and purposes. But Israel did not live up to the covenant. So Jeremiah said that God would make a new covenant with his people, an inner and spiritual one (Jer. 31:31 ff.). Christ came and established the new covenant with his life, death, and resurrection. All who accept this new covenant—the Christians—constitute the "new Israel." The writer of Hebrews states twice that Christ brings into being the new covenant foretold by Jeremiah. Therefore, Christians are the people of the covenant, the new covenant that fulfills the old covenant; for the old covenant finds its highest significance and "reason for being" in the new covenant. In speaking of the cup at the Last Supper Jesus said, "This cup is the new covenant in my blood, even that which is poured out for you" (Luke 22:20). So the idea of the covenant is basic to both Old and New Testaments. It is unfortunate that the word "testament" has covered it up.

4. Unity of the Bible

The Bible is not just a collection of religious writings brought together in a haphazard manner. It is not an anthology of stories loosely gathered under one cover. Rather it is a history, a history with a purpose. It is "salvation history," or "faith history." It is the history of the mighty acts of God, performed here on earth, in time, as he revealed himself to his people, and always with a very significant purpose in mind: that man might walk and talk in fellowship with God eternally. We say that the Bible has unity because all its various parts to some degree contribute to this major theme. What God began at creation he completed at the cross. But the Bible also looks forward to a completion, or consummation, of God's work, when all the loose ends of history will be tied together in one great event on one great day. This story of redemption, "redemption history," is conveyed by the whole Bible; both Testa-ments, Old and New, have vital roles. The Old makes sense when read in the light of the New, and the New is richer and more meaning-ful when it is discerned as the complement—not just supplement—of the Old. Truly there is unity in the Bible, a unity that stems from the central theme of redemption; God's providential guidance hovers over every page.

5. A Religious Book

Since the theme of the Bible concerns the relationship of man to God, it is a religious book. It contains history, but it was not written just to record history. Its history is religious history. History is the stage on which the revelation of God took place. God communicated with man through great acts, mighty deeds, events through which he was seen or felt or heard. The Bible is a record of selected events in which God has acted on behalf of man; it is not a printed message handed down from heaven giving the state of affairs there. The Bible is deeply set in human history.

The Bible contains biographies of great personalities, but these biographies are not ends in themselves. Each is presented to show the hand of God moving in and through his people. The life stories concern real people who lived, and breathed, and experienced the directive effect of God's purpose among them.

The Bible deals with the environmental world about us, but it does not purport to be a book of science. We live in a science-oriented world, a world highly influenced by the modern scientific method and by scientific data. Whatever "science" may be found in the Bible is couched in the thought forms of that period, as would be expected. To endeavor to make the Bible conform to the inductive scientific method of today is to do it an injustice. The Bible deals with ultimate realities, values, and spiritual truths which must be accepted on faith, not scientific observation. To suppose that the Bible is the source of all knowledge, both scientific and religious, would never enter the mind of most biblical scholars. They realize that at God's own discretion man has been permitted to make tremendous scientific discoveries, both in and out of the laboratory. The fact that the biblical writers were inspired of God did not necessitate that they reveal all the modern discoveries back in their period and in their writings. Inspiration did not provide them with technical knowledge in a prescientific age. The Bible is a religious book and it achieved its religious purpose with stupendous success.

6. Archaeology and the Bible

Archaeology pertains to the study of old things and ways of living. It is the science that discovers, evaluates, and interprets relics and artifacts of the distant past. Pottery, sculpture, weapons, written documents on clay, stone, or papyrus paper—all tell their story of ancient cultures. Even where there is no written history, the belongings of a nation can reveal its way of life. The interest of the Bible scholar focuses on the archaeology of the biblical lands. For more than a century scholars have been recovering valuable relics left by the people of the Bible and their neighbors, all of which has thrown considerable light upon the way of life of God's peculiar people. We should not think of archaeology as a means of "proving" what the Bible says; the Bible does not need such verification. Its truth is both authoritative and self-evident. However, the "finds" of archaeology have confirmed time and again what is stated in the Scriptures. Therefore the science of archaeology has become a very valuable tool in making possible the reconstruction of the living conditions under which the Bible was written and produced.

These are some of the most important archaeological finds:

(1) The Tell-el-Amarna Tablets were letters written in Babylonian cuneiform on clay tablets by some officials in Palestine addressed to the Pharaohs of Egypt describing living conditions in Palestine about 1300 B.C., a little before the Exodus. They spoke of a people called the Habiri, who were probably the Hebrews.

(2) The Rosetta Stone was discovered by some scholars working in Egypt under Napoleon of France. It contains an inscription in three languages: Egyptian Hieroglyphic, Egyptian Demotic, and Greek. Since scholars were already familiar with the Greek, they were able to decipher the Egyptian language and present their discovery to all other interested people.

(3) The Code of Hammurabi was uncovered in 1901–1902 at Susa, a city of ancient Persia. It is written in Babylonian cuneiform and contains 247 laws of King Hammurabi who lived about 1900 B.C., the approximate date of Abraham. These laws are very similar to the laws of Moses.

(4) The Moabite Stone was found in what was the territory of ancient Moab. It was erected by Mesha, king of Moab, about 850 B.C. telling of his success in throwing off the yoke of Israel. The story is in 2 Kings 3.

(5) The Siloam Inscription was discovered in 1880 by a schoolboy in an ancient passageway under the walls of old Jerusalem. Written on the wall in the tunnel, it proved to be the record of how the workmen cut the tunnel back in the days of Hezekiah, king of Judah, to provide a water supply for the city in time of siege. It is the oldest piece of Hebrew writing in existence. Second Kings 20 tells about the tunnel, cut in the eighth century B.C.

(6) The Behistun Rock of Persia was inscribed with three languages: Old Persian, Akkadian or Babylonian, and Elamite. Since this rock-hewn memorial of Darius' victory was carved on rock 500 feet above the plain, it was not read for over 2,000 years. In 1835 it was copied and deciphered, leading to the deciphering of the Babylonian language and to a greater knowledge of the Persian.

(7) The Black Obelisk of Shalmaneser III is an Assyrian monument revealing the only known likeness of a king of Israel. It depicts Jehu paying tribute to Shalmaneser III, the Assyrian king.

(8) The Cylinder of Sargon II, king of Assyria about 722–705 B.C., tells of the conquest of the city of Samaria by Sargon in 722–721 B.C. This record corroborates the statements found in the Bible in 2 Kings 17.

(9) The Dead Sea Scrolls, ancient manuscripts found in 1947 in caves near the Dead Sea seven miles south of Jericho, constitute the most remarkable archaeological discovery of modern times. Altogether nearly 100 manuscripts of the Old Testament books have been recovered, with every Old Testament book except Esther represented in the collection. These scrolls were placed in the caves by the Qumran community, which was dispersed prior to the destruction of Jerusalem in A.D. 70. Up to this discovery the oldest manuscript of the Old Testament was dated about A.D. 900. Therefore, these Dead Sea Scrolls are about 1,000 years older than any Old Testament manuscripts possessed by scholars prior to their discovery.

7. The Canon

The word "canon" is derived from a Greek word, which in turn came from a Semitic word meaning reed. This reed, a very early measuring instrument, gave to the term the added meaning of "rule," "standard," or "norm." When applied to the Scriptures, it denotes those books considered divinely inspired as set over against those not so considered. So there is the canon of the Old Testament, the canon of the New Testament, and the canon of the Bible. The word was so used as early as the third century A.D., for the eminent scholar Origen employed it at that time to designate the divinely inspired books. The process by which a canon is derived and established is called canonization.

The Old Testament was of course canonized by the Jews and accepted also by the Christians as God's inspired word. But where the Jews consider the Old Testament (known by them simply as the Hebrew Scriptures) to be final and complete, the Christians see the Old Testament as the record of the revelation preparatory to the coming of Christ; its true meaning is found in its fulfillment in him. Before the New Testament was written, with its material being dispersed as oral tradition, the only written Word the Christians possessed was the Old Testament. This they used wonderfully well in propagating the gospel, as is seen in the story of Philip and the Ethiopian treasurer on the road to Gaza (Acts 8:26–40).

A consideration of the Old Testament canon must take into account that all the religious writings of Israel were not thought of as Scripture. The following references show an ample amount of writings that failed to be included in the canon: Numbers 21:14; Joshua 10:13; 2 Samuel 1:18; 1 Kings 11:41; 14:19, 29. It must also be kept in mind that the Old Testament did not simply "drop from the sky" ready-made, or "fly together" book by book until it evolved as it is today. Nor did all the books of the Old Testament meet with a general approval right from the start; some won immediate acceptance, while others were weighed and considered for many years. Most of the books included in the final canon were written long before their inclusion in the list considered as "the oracles of God." This process required centuries of experience.

The first books of the Old Testament to become "canonized" were Genesis, Exodus, Leviticus, Numbers, and Deuteronomy, which collectively are known as the Torah. Torah means law, being derived from the Hebrew word for that term. These first five books are also called the Pentateuch, which is a work meaning "five fifths," the five fifths of the law.

The second section to win approval was the prophetic section, which the Jews divided into Former Prophets and Latter Prophets. Their Former Prophets are what are now known as the historical books (Joshua, Judges, 1 and 2 Samuel, and 1 and 2 Kings). Their Latter Prophets include Isaiah, Jeremiah, Ezekiel, and the twelve minor prophets. This prophetic section was included in the canon after the Babylonian exile.

The third section of the Old Testament to be considered as the authoritative word of God, and therefore as part of the canon (about A.D. 90), was termed the Writings, and included Psalms, Proverbs, Job, Song of Solomon, Ruth, Lamentations, Ecclesiastes, Esther, Daniel, Ezra-Nehemiah, and 1 and 2 Chronicles. It is readily seen that the Jews divided their Scriptures into these three main divisions: Law, Prophets, and Writings.

Jesus quoted from the Hebrew Scriptures time and again; it is clear that he loved them, considered them as authoritative, and directed men to them as the spiritual guide for their lives. To the Sadducees he said, "Ye do err, not knowing the scriptures, nor the power of God" (Matt. 22:29). And to the Jews he admonished, "Ye search the scriptures, because ye think that in them ye have eternal life; and these are they which bear witness of me; and ye will not come to me, that ye may have life" (John 5:39–40).

The New Testament canon also did not spring into being immediately but was the result of a long process. Many of Paul's epistles, written first, were not at first considered as divinely inspired. Then the Synoptic Gospels were produced, probably around A.D. 70–75. Then Revelation came around A.D. 95, with the Gospel of John about this same date to possibly five years later. These different books were circulated among the various churches as independent units, or documents, before they began to be collected into larger units, and at last into one large body, or corpus, to become known as the New Covenant.

As was the case with the Hebrew Scriptures, not all the writings about Jesus and the early church were included in the canon. When Luke began his Gospel, he informed his readers that many had "taken in hand to draw up a narrative concerning those matters which have been fulfilled among us," but that he wanted to trace "all things accurately from the first" (Luke 1:1–3). What happened to these "many" other documents? For some reason or other, they seem to have disappeared. Some of them may have been fantastical, some heretical, and others quite valuable. Through the years there was a sifting and a "proving" of those writings that were valuable and that answered the spiritual needs of the early Christians. These were copied and recopied, for they were the ones read and reread. When church councils began to meet and to draw up lists of books for a canon, they were merely recognizing the ones that had the most widespread usage.

Therefore, it was under the guidance of the Holy Spirit that the early Christians collected a group of documents which witnessed with a sense of authority to the reality of the incarnation of Christ and of his meaning to believers. Canonization of the New Testament was a long process, one in which the church councils merely vindicated the selection of books already made by the people. The earliest section of the New Testament to circulate as a group was the Gospels, then the Pauline letters, then the remaining parts. Their acceptance into the canon was more or less in this order. The first list of books of the New Testament that was identical to the one we have now was made in A.D. 367 by Bishop Athanasius of Alexandria. Therefore this date could possibly be used as the date of canonization of the New Testament. An important church council meeting in A.D. 397 drew up the same list, after which all debate concerning the inclusion or exclusion of any book ceased.

8. Septuagint and Apocrypha

The Hebrew Scriptures were written in the Hebrew language, the language of Palestine up to the Babylonian captivity. While in exile in Mesopotamia in the area of the Euphrates River, the Hebrew exiles took up the Aramaic language, bringing it home to Palestine when they returned three or four generations later under Zerubbabel, Ezra, and Nehemiah. The Aramaic replaced the Hebrew as the language of Palestine in the home, the street, and the marketplace; but the sacred writings used in the Temple and in the Palestinian synagogues were still in Hebrew.

The number of Jews outside of Palestine, known as the Jews of the Dispersion, was tremendous. Of course they spoke the language of the land where they lived, and one of the most common of these languages was Greek, the language so successfully dispersed by Alexander the Great and his followers. In Alexandria, a very significant city at the mouth of the Nile River, lived a large contingent of Jews who spoke Greek and who wished copies of the Hebrew Scriptures in that language. Ptolemy Philadelphus, ruler of Egypt, and his successors (about 285–200 B.C.) arranged for the translation, which was named Septuagint, from the Greek word for seventy. It goes by the symbol LXX, from the Roman numerals for 70. Seventy learned Jewish rabbis were supposed to have produced it, but actually seventy-two men did the work. The Septuagint is important to Christians because it is the book quoted by the New Testament writers. Also it became the Bible of the early Christians, prior to the writing of the New Testament documents, as they pushed out in the great missionary movement of the apostolic age. When the Christians made use of this Septuagint to prove Jesus the Messiah foretold by the Hebrew prophets and writers, the Jews tended to reject the translation and began to produce other Greek translations.

Because the Septuagint was widely distributed throughout the Roman world, the Jews of Alexandria accepted it as their canon, but they added to that canon fourteen other books known as the Apocrypha, which is a Greek word meaning hidden. These fourteen books, written in the period 200 B.C. to A.D. 100, are as follows: 1 Esdras, 2 Esdras, Tobit, Judith, the Rest of Esther, Wisdom of Solomon, Ecclesiasticus, Baruch, Song of the Three Holy Children, Susanna, Bel and the Dragon, Prayer of Manasseh, 1 Maccabees, 2 Maccabees. The Greek-speaking Jews considered these books inspired, but the Aramaic-speaking Jews of Palestine did not; consequently those books were not in their canon. Protestants, following the Hebrew canon, do not accept the Apocrypha as inspired. Roman Catholics, following the Greek Alexandrian canon, do include these books in their Bible. Josephus, the Jewish historian, and Philo, the Jewish philosopher, never quote from them. No New Testament writer quotes directly from them, nor did Jesus ever refer to them. Even though Protestants do not consider these books as inspired, they do recognize their value for information concerning the history of the Jews in the interbiblical period, especially 1 and 2 Maccabees.

9. Old Testament World

The entire territory in which the events of Old Testament history took place comprised less than one half the land area of the United States, and one third of this was desert. It included Mesopotamia (modern Iraq), Syria, Palestine, and Egypt. Most of the events took place in Palestine, the promised land of the Hebrews.

Mesopotamia, meaning "between the rivers," consisted of all the land between the Tigris and the Euphrates Rivers. Here was the seat of both the Assyrian and Babylonian empires. West of Mesopotamia and bordering the Mediterranean Sea (called Great Sea in the Bible) lay Syria, with the Lebanon and Anti-Lebanon mountains and the Orontes and Leontes rivers. The capital of Syria was Damascus. South of Syria was Palestine, known in the Old Testament as the land of Canaan and the land of promise. Palestine and Holy Land are late names, the former probably being derived from the term Philistia and the latter from the fact that it is holy to Jews, Muslims, and Christians. East of Palestine was the desert of Arabia and south of it was the Sinaitic peninsula, steeped in the tradition of Moses and the Israelite wanderings. Southwest of Palestine was Egypt, famous for the great Nile River and the place of Hebrew bondage.

The climate of Palestine varies from extremely hot at times in the coastal plains and in the Jordan valley to very cold on Mount Hermon, a peak 9,200 feet high, which is snow-covered most of the year. The rainy season is in the winter (October through March) and the dry season is in the summer (April through September). Soon after the rains come in October, plowing can be started and the wheat and barley crops sowed. These are winter crops, with

the reaping and harvesting coming in March and April. Whenever
this regularity failed, a drought occurred (1 Kings 17; Ruth 1).

10. Natural Divisions of Palestine

There are four natural divisions in geographical Palestine, all running north and south. (1) Next to the Mediterranean Sea is the
Maritime Plain, a low, sandy, fertile plain divided into three sections:
the plain of Acre and Tyre in the north, the plain of Sharon in
the center, and the plain of Philistia in the south. These plains are
very fertile, noted for both grain and fruits. (2) Parallel to the
Maritime Plain is the second division, the Western Highlands, a
long high ridge varying in height from 1,000 to 2,500 feet. Beginning
in the Lebanon mountains and running south to the desert of Arabia,
it is divided into Galilee in the north, Samaria in the center, and
Judah (or Judea) in the south. Between Galilee and Samaria there
is a break in the ridge, the famous plain of Esdraelon (or valley
of Jezreel). Located in Judah is Jerusalem, most famous city of
all Palestine. Three religions revere it: Judaism, Islam, and Christianity. (3) Parallel to the Western Highlands is the Jordan River
Valley, a ravine that varies from one to fourteen miles in width.
The river has its beginning near Mount Hermon, flows to the Lake
of Galilee, and then through the valley to the Dead Sea. The Lake
of Galilee is also called Sea of Gennesaret and Sea of Tiberias.
In the Old Testament it is called Sea of Chinneroth and lies about
685 feet below the level of the Mediterranean. In the Bible the
Dead Sea is called Salt Sea, Sea of the Arabah, and Sea of the
Plain, and is about 1,290 feet below the Mediterranean. It is readily
discerned why the river is called Jordan, "Descender." Of course,
the Dead Sea is very salty, containing about 25% solid matter. (4)
The fourth section, and parallel to the Jordan, is the Eastern Highlands, now called Transjordania. It is much like the Western Highlands and is noted as an agricultural and pastoral country. Bashan
and Gilead are in its northern section.

11. Cities

Most of the cities occupied by the Hebrews were previously built
by the Canaanites or other inhabitants of Palestine, with the Hebrews

rebuilding and enlarging them. Some of the cities were walled and were used for defense; other cities were not walled. The walled cities were never large, since they were strongholds constructed into as small a space as possible. In early times the walls were simple, but later they were made of cut stone, even dressed stone. There were towers and gates, sometimes at regular intervals. The streets were narrow and usually crooked, and in early times not paved. They were not sanitary, for garbage was dumped into them and left for the scavenger dogs. Shops were built along the streets for the display of goods for sale. The bazaar was a covered arcade with rows of shops on both sides; here "bargaining" was the order of the day.

The Creation and Early Happenings
(Genesis 1—2)

1. God the Creator

The first eleven chapters of Genesis form an introduction to the history of the Hebrew nation. Genesis means "beginning," and this is exactly what the book unfolds for the reader—the beginning of the whole created order. God is presented as the creator of all things, thus inspiring in the Hebrews an awe and reverence for their guide and sustainer. He, being almighty and all powerful, was able to lead his chosen ones into a noble destiny.

"In the beginning God created the heavens and the earth" (Gen. 1:1). With these dramatic words starts the history found in the Hebrew Scriptures, our Old Testament. There are two significant things about the word "create." In the Scriptures it is found only with God as the subject, never man. Therefore only God can "create." Also "create" means to bring into existence that which is nonexistent. It means to make from nothing, or to produce something without using material existing prior to that time. Creation is not just an idea of God; it is that idea made objective. It is God's creative energy becoming force. It is the beginning of what we call time. Creation is not necessary to God: he did not have to create, but chose to do so. Therefore it is the act of the free will of God. Psalm 104 and Job 38 are poetic descriptions of God's creation, corresponding to what is found in Genesis 1 and 2.

2. Days of Creation

The creation was not instantaneous but progressive, taking place in six periods of time. Six beautiful paragraphs in Genesis 1 show how God, as a creative Spirit, acted through successive periods and prepared the world for the highest point in his creative work, man. In this first chapter of Genesis the phrase "and God" is found thirty times; thus every statement is what God did or said. The important fact in creation is not "how" God did it, or "how long" it required. The significant thing is that the eternal God was the sole creator. Matter is not eternal; God is eternal.

The six periods were as follows: (1) light was created and divided from darkness; (2) the firmament or atmosphere surrounding the earth was created; (3) water was separated from land and the earth was covered with vegetation; (4) sun, moon, and stars were created to give light; (5) marine life and winged fowl were created; (6) land animals and man were created. Lower forms were created first, reaching the climax in the production of man. During the course of creation we read repeatedly, "And God saw that it was good." But after the creation of the sum total, including man, we read, "And God saw everything that he had made, and, behold, it was very good" (Gen. 1:31). Thus all received the divine approval.

3. Creation of Man

In all instances except the creation of man God spoke and things came into being. Not so with man. "And God said, Let us make man in our image, after our likeness: and let them have dominion over the fish of the sea, and over the birds of the heavens, and over the cattle, and over all the earth, and over every creeping thing that creepeth upon the earth" (Gen. 1:26). Man, created last, was superior to all other creatures; God breathed into him his Spirit and he became a living soul. Man does not *have* a soul; he *is* a soul. He was made in the "image of God," and this refers to man's spiritual make-up, not physical. This does not refer to hands, arms, legs, etc., but means that he is similar to God in intellectual, moral, and spiritual qualities. He was made to walk and talk with God and to have fellowship with him. He was told to "multiply, and replenish the earth, and subdue it: and have dominion" over all other creatures (Gen. 1:28). He was to exercise lordship over nature and guide it to its intended destiny.

The name "Adam" comes from a Hebrew word meaning "man," which is the reason that throughout these early chapters of Genesis the Hebrew word that is translated "man" is the same word that is translated "Adam." In the King James Version Genesis 2:18 reads, "And the Lord God said, It is not good that the man should be alone; I will make him a help meet for him." Genesis 2:21 reads,

"And the Lord God caused a deep sleep to fall upon Adam, and he slept." The next verse states, "And the rib, which the Lord God had taken from man, made he a woman, and brought her unto the man." The word "Adam" and the word "man" in these verses are the same in the Hebrew. And it must be remembered that the Hebrew alphabet has only one set of letters, not capitals and small letters. So it is hard to determine proper nouns and common nouns in the original language. Therefore to capitalize a word and make it a proper noun, a name, is purely up to the judgment of the translator. This is the reason that sometimes when the King James will say "Adam," the American Standard will say "man." In Genesis 2:19 in the King James where the word "Adam" is used (twice in fact) there is a footnote that says "the man." Also, this word "adam," meaning "man," designates not only a specific man, but mankind in general. There is another Hebrew word meaning only a specific man, the word *ish*. This word is never used in these early chapters of Genesis. The name "Eve" means "living." "And the man called his wife's name Eve; because she was the mother of all living" (Gen. 3:20).

4. Eden

The Bible says that God put created man in a garden in Eden (Gen. 2:8), and that there were four rivers in the garden: Pison, Gihon, Hiddekel, and Euphrates. The third of these is the Tigris River, as it is so-called in the Revised Standard Version (1952). Some scholars think the first two were simply early irrigating canals of central Babylonia. The term "Sippur in Eden" was found imprinted on a clay tablet discovered in Babylon in 1885. Therefore Eden must have been somewhere in Mesopotamia, although there are a few scholars who contend it might have been elsewhere. Mesopotamia means "between the rivers"—between the Tigris and the Euphrates.

Man was told to dress and to keep the garden and to eat of every tree of the garden *except* the tree of the knowledge of good and evil. Thus man was commanded to work, for work is something that in God's sight is always seen as good and honorable. There is dignity to work; it is not to be thought of as punishment for disobedience. Work is not a curse, but a blessing, something essential to the happiness of man. Man's life in Eden was not only one of happiness but one of probation. There was a "Thou shalt not." Failure to heed this negative command would result in death (Gen. 2:17).

From the beginning God has favored monogamy, one wife for every husband. This is the ideal, as seen in the first home, the first institution in society. Later man departed from the ideal and had many wives, which is known as polygamy; but this was not God's intention. In the New Testament Jesus definitely places his stamp of approval on one husband and one wife (Matt. 19:4–6) and brings us back to God's original intent.

5. Sabbath

"And on the seventh day God ended his work which he had made; and he rested on the seventh day from all his work which he had made. . . . And God blessed the seventh day, and hallowed it; because that in it he rested from all his work which God had created and made" (Gen. 2:2–3). The word "sabbath" does not mean "seventh." It comes from a Hebrew verb meaning "to cease." The sabbath goes from sundown Friday to sundown Saturday. In Exodus 20:8–11 God commanded man to rest on the sabbath. Thus, with God's sanctifying or making it holy, plus his command to use it for rest, two ideas were connected with the sabbath in the mind of the Hebrew: holiness and rest. Man is so made that he needs one day out of seven to rest and recover his physical and mental strength. Along with this, he needs a day dedicated to the worship and homage of God.

6. Temptation and Fall

How did sin and evil enter into the world? This is the question that man has been asking for centuries. The vivid experience found in the third chapter of Genesis has an eternal interest for mankind. Here then was the presence of an evil power with an evil motive, namely, the overthrow of the work of God and the instilling of doubt in man's mind in regard to God's goodness and favor. The tempter wished to cause man to question the integrity and love of God. His appeal to the couple was based on three things normally thought of as good: the desire for food, the desire for the beautiful, and the desire for knowledge. "And when the woman saw that the tree was good for food, and that it was a delight to the eyes, and that the tree was to be desired to make one wise, she took of the fruit thereof, and did eat; and she gave also unto her husband with her, and he did eat" (Gen. 3:6). The serpent had already informed her, "Ye shall not surely die" (Gen. 3:4), thus denying the truthfulness and righteousness of God. His plea was based on a lie, and his argument to the pair was that God did not want them to be as he is. God had given them much but not enough. It was the temptation to play God, to be themselves God. Eve tasted and ate, then gave to Adam to do the same.

Here there is not only a picture of the origin of sin in the human race; it is also the picture of the inception of sin in every life. Man's transgression brought a change in his whole being and especially in his relation to God. He was conscious of his guilt, as is evidenced in his fleeing from the presence of God. "And they heard the voice of Jehovah God walking in the garden in the cool of the day: and the man and his wife hid themselves from the presence of Jehovah God amongst the trees of the garden" (Gen. 3:8). The close relationship between man and God was broken, for sin was committed. Immediately he endeavored to place the blame upon his wife. "The woman whom thou gavest to be with me, she gave me of the tree, and I did eat" (Gen. 3:12).

7. Punishment

As a result of the disobedience the serpent was to crawl on its belly and to eat the dust of the ground. The woman was henceforth to be subordinate to her husband and to endure great suffering in childbirth. The man was to be subject to a life of extreme toil and suffering. The "thorns" and "thistles" of Genesis 3:18 and "the sweat of thy face" of Genesis 3:19 are symbols of the great pain and extreme hardship to be encountered by all mankind from that time on. Disaster, disease, trials, sickness, loneliness, sorrow, pain, tears, and heartaches are before him. But the most fearful result of man's sin was death, both physical and spiritual. "For dust thou art, and unto dust shalt thou return'' (Gen. 3:19). God had taken dust and breathed into it his Spirit, and man had become a living soul (Gen. 2:7). Now man was to return to that dust. He died spiritually, for the image of God was marred. His physical days were numbered. Death stalked his way. "And now, lest he put forth his hand, and take also of the tree of life, and eat, and live for ever—therefore Jehovah God sent him forth from the garden of Eden, to till the ground from whence he was taken" (Gen. 3:22–23).

God made man a free moral agent, which means he has the power of choosing good or evil. If only good lies before him, and he has only that course, he does not have this right of choice. Good is inevitable. God will not take away this important feature of man, that he has the right to choose. To do so would make him less than man. Adam had that choice; every individual today has the same privilege. But God threw out a ray of hope to fallen man, as recorded in Genesis 3:15. "And I will put enmity between thee and the woman, and between thy seed and her seed: he shall bruise thy head, and thou shalt bruise his heel." (The word "bruise" here means "lie in wait for.") This statement is fulfilled in Christ, for Christ is the seed of the woman, Mary. By his life, death, and resurrection he destroyed the power of Satan. But in so doing he himself was "bruised" at Calvary. Here is the first messianic passage in the Old Testament. Man shall not be forsaken of God. The ensuing struggle shall be long and hard, but victory will ultimately come through one born of woman, yet without sin.

8. Adam's Sons

To Adam and Eve were born Cain and Abel. Little is said of these two concerning their physical and spiritual make-up. Cain seems to have been characterized by jealousy and wickedness; Abel seems to have been reverent and lovable. Cain means "begotten" or "acquired," while Abel means "breath" or "transitoriness." Both of the boys brought a sacrifice to Jehovah, Cain one from the field, and Abel one from the flock. Cain's may have been a sheaf of wheat, while Abel may have brought a sheep. Cain's offering was rejected of God, while Abel's was accepted. From the words recorded in the Bible it is perfectly apparent that Cain's attitude was bad and his spirit wrong, while Abel's offering was made in the spirit of true worship. Being jealous, Cain slew his brother and became the first murderer in recorded history. God immediately banished Cain to the land of Nod, where he married and began a race noted for city-building, arts, crafts, and industries.

But God did not wish that his purpose for man should come down through such a one as Cain; therefore he gave to Adam another offspring, Seth, meaning "substituted." From this son came the line finally to produce the Hebrews, God's chosen ones. "Then began men to call upon the name of Jehovah" (Gen. 4:26). In this line are found Enoch, of whom it was said, "And Enoch walked with God: and he was not; for God took him" (Gen. 5:24), and Noah, of whom it was said, "But Noah found favor in the eyes of Jehovah" (Gen. 6:8).

9. Long Life

The length of the lives of the people of the period prior to the flood has been a problem to scholars for many years. Adam lived to be 930, Seth to be 912, Methuselah to be 969. What is the answer to these many examples of prolonged life? Various explanations have been given. (1) Some hold that a name used, such as Jared, refers not to an individual but to a tribe over which he was the original head. (2) Some hold that there was a difference in ways of measuring time, counting moons or seasons as years. (3) Some hold that man's strong original body yielded slowly to the aging process. The people actually lived that long. Adding weight to this theory is that the same Hebrew word for "year" is used after the Flood, when the lives were much shorter, as is used prior to the Flood when they are longer. This explanation seems to be the most reasonable.

10. Noah and the Flood

The Bible is brief about the condition of the earth just prior to the Flood, yet it does say that there is the vivid combination of men of renown and men of wickedness. It speaks of "the mighty men that were of old, the men of renown" (Gen. 6:4). This is immediately followed by a contrasting statement: "And Jehovah saw that the wickedness of man was great in the earth, and that every imagination of the thoughts of his heart was only evil continually'' (Gen. 6:5). Renowned in the eyes of men and lawless in the eyes of God—this was the sordid state of things. God determined to blot man from the face of the earth and then start again, only retracting that decision in the saving of the family of Noah. Noah, a man of righteousness, was to be God's agent during this time of destruction. ''But Noah found favor in the eyes of Jehovah'' (Gen. 6:8). Also, ''Noah was a righteous man, and perfect in his generations: Noah walked with God'' (Gen. 6:9).

God announced to Noah that he was going to destroy the earth by a flood; therefore he commanded him to build a boat, or ark, along the best lines of that day. In it were to be preserved his family of eight people plus specimens of the clean and unclean animals and birds. Noah and his wife, plus his three sons, Shem, Ham, and Japheth, born to Noah when he was 500 years old, plus their three wives, constituted the eight people.

One week was required to load the cargo, after which God himself sealed the door. ''And Jehovah shut him in'' (Gen. 7:16). At 600 years of age Noah was experiencing an unusual happening. The rains descended ''and the windows of heaven were opened'' (Gen. 7:11). For forty days and nights it continued.

The Bible does not depict the struggling mob of drowning humanity in this dreadful disaster. The waters became more and more, ''and all the high mountains that were under the whole heaven were covered. Fifteen cubits upward did the waters prevail; and the mountains were covered'' (Gen. 7:19–20). ''And every living thing was destroyed that was upon the face of the ground . . . and Noah only was left, and they that were with him in the ark'' (Gen. 7:23).

After floating for nearly seven months the ark came to rest on Mount Ararat. Noah then used two birds to check on the condition of the earth. On her second flight the dove plucked an olive leaf, but she did not return the third time. After more than a year since embarking, the whole cargo was unloaded. Noah immediately built an altar and offered sacrifice to God. ''And Jehovah smelled the sweet savor; and Jehovah said in his heart, I will not again curse the ground any more for man's sake'' (Gen. 8:21).

God then made a covenant with Noah not to destroy the earth again with a flood. "And I will establish my covenant with you; neither shall all flesh be cut off any more by the waters of the flood; neither shall there any more be a flood to destroy the earth" (Gen. 9:11). Then God established the rainbow as a visible sign of his covenant with Noah for all future generations. God blessed Noah and his sons and commanded them to multiply.

Noah's righteousness momentarily waned, for he became drunk with the wine from his own vineyard. Being drunken and in an exposed condition there occurred an episode for which Canaan, the son of Ham, was to receive the curse of servitude. It is believed by some scholars that Canaan may have been a partaker of Ham in mocking Noah. Shem and Japheth received blessings instead of curses (Gen. 9:20–27).

11. The Table of Nations

The tenth chapter of Genesis is what has been termed "The Table of Nations." Genesis 9:18 states, "And the sons of Noah, that went forth from the ark, were Shem, and Ham, and Japheth: and Ham is the father of Canaan. These three were the sons of Noah: and of these was the whole earth overspread." Shem means "name"; Ham means "heat"; Japheth means "enlargement." In this "table" the writer gives the generations descending from these three sons and the geographical areas inhabited by their descendants. When a Hebrew word ends in im, it is in the plural, which is the case several times for the final syllable of the names of certain people. This would imply that that name in the table would not be for an individual but for a nation.

The descendants of Shem spread to central Asia, thence in an easterly and westerly direction. The descendants of Ham spread to the whole of Africa and the southern peninsulas of Asia, India, and Arabia. The descendants of Japheth occupied the coasts of the Mediterranean Sea in Asia Minor and Europe, and from there spread over Europe and much of Asia.

12. The Tower of Babel

The story of the tower in the eleventh chapter of Genesis is the

cause of the spreading of Noah's descendants as found in the tenth
chapter. The writer gave the results, then the cause. Scholars do
not agree as to the reason for the building of this tower. However,
Genesis 11:4 seems to indicate that the purpose was that of providing
a great name for men and of preventing a spreading of men over
the earth. "And they said, Come, let us build a city, and a tower,
whose top may reach unto heaven, and let us make a name; lest
we be scattered abroad upon the face of the whole earth." Would
not this be the opposite to God's command to Noah after the flood?
Here he stated, "Be fruitful, and multiply, and replenish the earth"
(Gen. 9:1). But this would require hardships, arduous tasks, and
moving to distant areas. Therefore God never permitted their proud
structure to be completed; for he confused their common speech
and scattered them abroad. God said, "Come, let us go down, and
there confound their language, that they may not understand one
another's speech. So Jehovah scattered them abroad from thence
upon the face of all the earth: and they left off building the city"
(Gen. 11:7–8). How appropriate that it should have been called Tower
of Babel, for "Babel" means confusion. The writer is endeavoring
to show us that this rebellion against God's wish was both futile
and disastrous to the best interests of mankind.

Abraham and Isaac
(Genesis 12—26)

1. Survey of the Period

The first eleven chapters of Genesis form an introduction to the history of the Hebrews as a nation. Genesis 12—50 starts with the call of Abraham and closes with the death of Joseph in Egypt. All the ancient biblical countries are included in this dramatic story: the Mesopotamian Valley, Syria, Palestine, and Egypt. This involves the Fertile Crescent, a term made popular by the noted archaeologist J. H. Breasted. We are on sure ground geographically when we study the cities and the areas involved, for archeaology has shown these locations to be real and authentic places. The writer has preserved for us a winsome and picturesque account of the deeds, activities, achievements, customs, and worship of the Hebrews of the patriarchal age.

The word "patriarch" means "ruling father." The oldest male member of the tribe virtually ruled the tribe; when he died, the eldest son took over. It was also the age of nomadic living, for they lived in tents and moved frequently. They counted their wealth in gold, silver, flocks, herds, tents, jewels, sons, and daughters—never lands. Read Job 1:1-3, where all the possessions of Job, "the greatest of all the children of the east," are listed. Nothing is said of pasture and land. When all the grass of one area was gone they moved to another. These people are not to be thought of as gypsies, for they were generally wealthy and prosperous. It was an honored and respected way of life, unlike the fixed habitation found later during the days of the kingdom.

2. Mesopotamia

Abraham was originally involved with two great cities in Mesopotamia, Ur and Haran. Mesopotamia is a geographical term, not a national one, for it involved the whole Tigris-Euphrates valley. In this area there was a common language making communication

1. Euphrates River

easy. This was not an alphabetical written language, but one in which wedge-shaped marks were made on a clay tablet with a stylus, or sharp instrument. This tablet was then baked till it was hard. Time does not alter them, so that these records, if found, can be easily read.

There were many irrigation canals connecting the Tigris with the Euphrates, thus insuring more than one crop per year. There were skilled workmen and artisans in metals, ornaments, jewelry, and fabrics. There were huge libraries, some volumes of which have been translated into modern languages. Astronomy, mathematics, and science were taught. Architects and engineers of that day amaze us with their technical skill manifested by the buildings erected. Banking, law, and government were on a highly civilized level. The measurement of time was calculated to the minute and second of today. There was a calendar for the solar year. The famous Code of Hammurabi, with its many laws and legal requirements, dated about 1900 B.C., gives a vivid insight into the civic and social life of these people.

3. Ur of the Chaldees

This is the city where Abraham lived when the biblical narrative first mentions him. It was located on the west bank of the Euphrates River and was one of the most prosperous cities of southwest Babylonia at the time of Abraham, 1900 B.C. Most scholars think it can be identified with the modern city of Mugheir, about 130 miles from the mouth of the Euphrates on the Persian Gulf. At that time, however, it was not far from the shore of the gulf. The patron god of Ur was the moon-god Sin (or Nannar). There were other gods also, for Joshua in the book that bears his name (24:2) informed the children of Israel that their forefathers, even Terah, served other gods while living in this valley of the Euphrates River.

The noted archaeologist Woolley has made extensive excavations at Ur, where he found royal palaces, tombs, cuneiform tablets, a ziggurat, and a temple of Nebuchadnezzar. Down at a certain level he found a deep deposit of silt, which indicates that at one time there must have been deep water and an interruption in civilization. Some scholars consider this as an indication of the flood, others

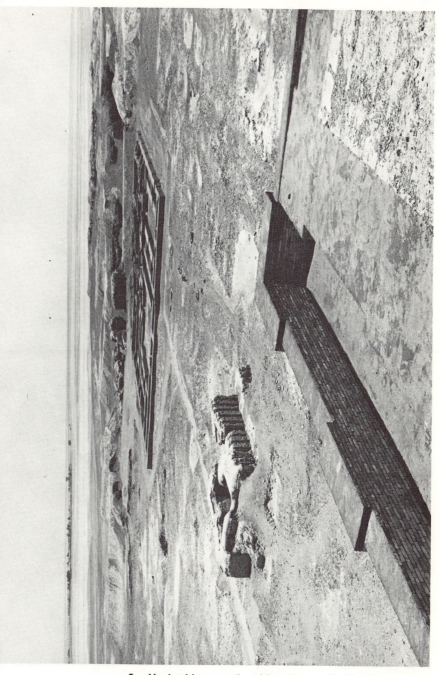

2. Ur, looking south, with palace ruins in the center

are not so certain. The temple of the moon-god Sin was uncovered and deposits of jewelry, carvings, and many other things discovered. The tomb of Queen Shub-ad was uncovered, leading to rich evidence of the culture of that day.

4. Abraham's Early Life

This great character's name was at first Abram, meaning "exalted father," which was later changed to Abraham, "father of a multitude." His wife was Sarai, meaning "contentious." Genesis 20:12 tells us she was also his half sister, having the same father but a different mother. The father of Abram was Terah, who had two other sons, Nahor and Haran. Nahor's wife was Milcah. Haran had a son Lot, the nephew of Abram who was associated with him closely over the years. Haran died before Terah and his family migrated from Ur.

Terah took Abram, Sarai, and Lot and departed from Ur with the intention of going to the land of Canaan. On the way they stopped at Haran, located in the northwestern part of Mesopotamia on a small river flowing south for sixty miles into the Euphrates. It was a great commercial center on an important trade route. The moon-god Sin was also an important god of this locality. This upper part of Mesopotamia was called Paddan-aram. Here Terah died; and, as it appears in Genesis 24:15, Nahor arrived later with his wife Milcah to settle down and raise a family. It was from Nahor's family that Rebekah, and Rachel, and Leah were to come. These immigrants from Ur would be at home here in both culture and worship; even the language was the same.

5. Abraham's Call and Response

"Now Jehovah said unto Abram, Get thee out of thy country, and from thy kindred, and from thy father's house, unto the land that I will show thee: and I will make of thee a great nation, and I will bless thee, and make thy name great; and be thou a blessing: and I will bless them that bless thee, and him that curseth thee will I curse: and in thee shall all the families of the earth be blessed" (Gen. 12:1–3). According to Genesis it appears that Abram received his call while living in Haran; according to Stephen's great defense

in the seventh chapter of Acts he received it before he lived in
Haran (Acts 7:2). He was to get up and depart to a land that God
would indicate.

So Abram, Sarai, and Lot departed to the Land of Promise (Heb.
11:9). The other name for this territory as found in the Bible is
the Land of Canaan, so named because of the people already dwelling
there. To these two biblical names the world has added two more
names, Palestine and Holy Land. Palestine is probably derived from
the name Philistines, the people living on the coast. Holy Land
is a later designation given to the land because of its association
with our Lord. These two names are not found in the Bible but
are the most common ones used today. The area now includes
Israel and Jordan, with the Gaza Strip administered by Egypt.

God's statement to Abram was both a command and a promise.
It was a command to get up and, on faith in God, go to a new
land that would be pointed out to him. Consider the courage and
the trust that such an undertaking would involve! His friends would
probably consider him foolish and impractical. Travel in those days
was difficult and arduous. It would require days! All his possessions,
his flocks and herds, must be taken along. Family ties must be
severed. Barren and desert country must be passed through. "By
faith Abraham, when he was called, obeyed to go out unto a place
which he was to receive for an inheritance; and he went out, not
knowing whither he went" (Heb. 11:8).

God's statement was not just a command; it was also a promise,
a promise containing several distinct features. (1) God would make
of him a great nation. This was fulfilled in that he was the father
of the Hebrews. (2) God would give to him a great name. Jews,
Christians, and Muhammadans all look back to him in a religious
sense. (3) He would be a blessing to all nations. The great gift
of the Hebrews to the world lies not in the realm of the artistic,
the legalistic, the musical, the military—but in the realm of the moral
and spiritual. (4) He would receive a land for all his descendants.
This was Canaan.

So Abram, Sarai, and Lot moved south to the Land of Canaan,
the very center of the activity of the ancient world, the land "in
the midst of the nations" (Ezek. 5:5).

6. At Shechem and Bethel

Abram was led by faith to the very center of Canaan before he made his first stop. Passing across the Jordan he proceeded to Shechem, which means "shoulder," or "ridge." It received its name from being situated between Mount Ebal and Mount Gerizim, the twin peaks of Samaria. Water falling on the west goes to the Great Sea (as the Mediterranean is called in the Bible); water falling on the east flows to the Jordan River valley. It is now the modern city of Nablus. Here, at the famous oak of Moreh, God spoke to Abram and said, "Unto thy seed will I give this land" (Gen. 12:7). Abram built an altar and worshiped the Lord.

But Abram did not tarry long at Shechem, even though it was noted for its fountains, rills, and watercourses—a perfect pasture-land. He moved on to the south and came to Bethel, then known by the Canaanite name of Luz, also a marvelous area for pasturage. Here Abram also erected an altar "and called upon the name of Jehovah" (Gen. 12:8). Yet he was not to stay here for long either, for he journeyed on toward the south, or Negeb, the extreme southern portion of Palestine just below the Salt Sea. (The term Dead Sea is a late name for this body of water. The three biblical names are Salt Sea, Sea of the Arabah, and Sea of the Plain.)

7. In Egypt

Due to a famine in southern Canaan Abram departed for Egypt. With the overflowing of the Nile famines were scarce there; therefore Egypt became a source of food for suffering neighbors. So to the fertile Nile valley Abram, Sarai, and Lot journeyed, and while here Abram stooped to deception.

There was a vicious practice among ancient lands. Kings and ruling monarchs were despotic in their dealings with their subjects. If one saw a beautiful woman and wanted her, he would have the husband killed and then add the newly made widow to his harem. There is an old papyrus entitled "Story of Two Brothers" which gives an account of how a pharaoh took into his harem the wife of a man and then had the man killed. Did not David do exactly this concerning Bathsheba and her husband Uriah? The surprising thing is that "the man after God's own heart" would stoop to such a degrading act.

Because of Sarai's beauty Abram feared just this. So he conceived a scheme that would, if such became the case, at least protect him and spare his life. He told Sarai to pose as his sister. In fact, she was his half sister, having the same father but a different mother. She agreed; but as was feared, the news of her beauty soon reached Pharaoh's ears, and he sent for her to add her to his harem. Immediately God sent plagues upon Pharaoh, who, upon learning the truth, requested that Abram and Sarai leave his land and go their way.

8. Again at Bethel

Abram, Sarai, and Lot returned by way of the south to Bethel, or Luz, where Abram again called upon the name of the Lord. Here Abram was to be plagued with more trouble. Due to the enormous flock and herds of both him and Lot their herdsmen quarreled. "And there was a strife between the herdsmen of Abram's cattle and the herdsmen of Lot's cattle" (Gen. 13:7). Since the possessions of Abram and Lot were so great, and since "the land was not able to bear them, that they might dwell together" (Gen. 13:6), Abram made a generous offer. He invited Lot to look over the whole land and to select the area where he wished to live.

Lot chose the beautiful and open Jordan valley, while Abram remained in the hill country. Lot went to the "cities of the plain," even as far as Sodom, a most wicked and evil place. God gave his promise to Abram for the third time. "Lift up now thine eyes, and look from the place where thou art, northward and southward and eastward and westward: for all the land which thou seest, to thee will I give it, and to thy seed for ever. And I will make thy seed as the dust of the earth: so that if man can number the dust of the earth, then may thy seed also be numbered. Arise, walk through the land in the length of it and in the breadth of it; for unto thee will I give it" (Gen. 13:14–17).

Abram journeyed south to Hebron, to the oaks of Mamre, and dwelt there. Again, as usual, he built an altar to worship Jehovah. This was to be his home for the rest of his career, and not only his home but the home of Isaac and Jacob after him.

9. At Hebron

This ancient city, noted for its fine pastures and fruitful vineyards, holds a very prominent place in Old Testament history. On many maps it will be named Kiriatharba, meaning "City of Arba." It is 3,029 feet above sea level, higher by far than the mountains in Galilee, higher even than Jerusalem (2,610 feet above sea level.) Here Abram made friends with three brothers: Mamre, Aner, and Eshcol, local chieftains. At the oaks of Mamre he built an altar and experienced several visitations from Jehovah.

10. Rescue of Lot

Lot was living at Sodom when there was an invasion of that territory by allies from Mesopotamia. Five kings from the territory of the Tigris and Euphrates came down and made war against the five kings of the five cities of the plain, the plain of the lower Jordan. These five cities were Sodom, Gomorrah, Admah, Zeboiim, and Bela (or Zoar, as it was also called). The leader of the four invading kings was Chedorlaomer, king of Elam, a city east of the Tigris in the territory near the Persian Gulf. The five Canaanite kings had been vassals of the four kings to the north, serving them for twelve years. In the thirteenth year they rebelled; so Chedorlaomer and his allies marched down upon them arrayed for battle. After defeating many native chieftains east of the Jordan and south of the Dead Sea, they defeated the five Canaanite kings in the lower Jordan at the vale of Siddim. They plundered their cities and carried off many captives, including Lot and his family.

This news soon reached Abram, who hastily gathered up his 318 trained servants and went in pursuit of the returning Mesopotamian army. Genesis 14:13 states that the three Amorite brothers, Mamre, Aner, and Eshcol "were confederate with Abram," which tells us that they aided him in this venture. Genesis 14:24 confirms this fact. Abram defeated Chedorlaomer and his allies far to the north in the region of Damascus, recovered Lot, the captive men and women, and the goods, and returned to the lower Jordan. Here they were met by the king of Sodom and by Melchizedek, king of Salem and priest of the most high God. This man's name means "king of righteousness." He blessed Abram, after which Abram gave him a tenth of all the goods he had recovered. Abram asked nothing for himself, but requested that portions be given to the three men that had helped him (Gen. 14:13–24).

11. Renewal of the Promise

God soon appeared to Abram and renewed the covenant promise of future blessings. Abram and Sarai had no son, though married for many years. Abram reminded God of this fact, and that "he that shall be possessor of my house is Eliezer of Damascus" (Gen. 15:2). God had promised Abram that he would become the head of a great race; but how could this be, seeing he had no son? Would not Eliezer, one of his own home-born slaves, inherit all his possessions? Therefore God, after stating that Eliezer would not be his heir, led Abram out by night so he could view the brilliant Palestinian sky. "Look now toward heaven, and number the stars, if thou be able to number them: and he said unto him, So shall thy seed be" (Gen. 15:5). Abram believed God, and God accepted his belief (Gen. 15:6).

After an animal offering to God a deep sleep came upon Abram, during which he had a terrific experience and reassurance from God that these things would be. However, to the promise God added the dread prediction that his descendants would be afflicted and serve a foreign people in a foreign land for 400 years, "and afterward they shall come out with great substance" (Gen. 15:13,14). God added that the land to be given the Hebrews would extend "from the river of Egypt unto the great river, the river Euphrates" (Gen. 15:18), quite a vast territory. The "river of Egypt" mentioned here is not the Nile. It is a river flowing into the Mediterranean between the Nile and the land of Canaan.

12. Birth of Ishmael

After this incident in the life of Abram many years passed, and still there was no son. Therefore Sarai suggested to Abram that he take her Egyptian handmaid, Hagar, and have a child by her. Hagar, then given to Abram for a wife, conceived and brought forth a son. She named the child Ishmael, having been instructed of God to do this while in the wilderness where she had been driven by Sarai. Ishmael means "God heareth," so named because God heard her affliction. The angel also told her that he would be the father of a people that "shall not be numbered for multitude" (Gen. 16:10). He became the father of the Ishmaelites, Abram being eighty-six when the child was born.

13. Promise of Isaac

God again appeared to Abram and again renewed the covenant promise that he would make of him a great nation. At this time God changed his name from Abram, exalted father, to Abraham, father of a multitude. "And I will make thee exceeding fruitful, and I will make nations of thee, and kings shall come out of thee" (Gen. 17:6). To this was added other statements of the great blessings of the covenant relationship. Then God established the rite of circumcision as a sign and token of the covenant relationship, ordaining that all males to be born from that time on were to be circumcised on the eighth day after birth. This later became a part of the Mosaic law, with circumcision becoming a symbol of the bond that should bind every Hebrew to Jehovah. Even slaves of the household were to submit to this rite, and failure to do so meant death or expulsion from the Hebrew clan (Gen. 17:14). Abraham and all the males of his household submitted to the rite.

God changed Sarai's name to Sarah, meaning "princess." From "contentious" to "princess"—quite a step-up for Abraham's wife! When God announced to Abraham that he should have a son by Sarah, he "laughed, and said in his heart, Shall a child be born unto him that is a hundred years old? and shall Sarah, that is ninety years old, bear?" (Gen. 17:17). Therefore God told him to name the boy that would be born Isaac, meaning "laughter."

14. Sodom and Gomorrah

Abraham entertained angels and did not realize it. Three strangers appeared to him as he sat at the entrance to his tent at the oaks of Mamre, to whom he gave true oriental hospitality, feeding them well with a veritable banquet. One announced to Abraham that

Sarah would bear a son, which Sarah overheard in the tent door. She too laughed, for she had been barren all her life and was now past the age of bearing a child. But the promise was only repeated. One of the three who did the speaking seems to have been Jehovah himself (Gen. 18:1–5).

Abraham escorted them as they left, at which time Jehovah told Abraham that he wanted to visit Sodom, that the sin of Sodom and Gomorrah was very great. Abraham, filled with fear for Sodom, made a plea that it be spared destruction. Was not Lot his nephew living there? Jehovah promised that if even ten righteous people could be found in the city it would be spared.

Genesis 19 presents the sordid picture of what the three messengers found at Sodom. Therefore the destruction was inevitable; even Lot's two sons-in-law could not be warned. Lot was informed to take his wife and two daughters and flee and not look behind. "But his wife looked back from behind him, and she became a pillar of salt" (Gen. 19:26). Lot and his daughters fled to Zoar (meaning "little"), for it was to be spared. "Then Jehovah rained upon Sodom and upon Gomorrah brimstone and fire from Jehovah out of heaven; and he overthrew those cities, and all the Plain, and all the inhabitants of the cities, and that which grew upon the ground" (Gen. 19:24–25).

15. Moabites and Ammonites

Lot and his two daughters went out from Zoar and lived in a cave. The girls, thinking there would now be no heir for their father, made him drunk with wine. The older had a son by her father and called his name Moab. This was the father of the Moabites. The second had a son by her father and called his name Ben-ammi. This was the father of the Ammonites. Here is a vivid example of the fact that the Old Testament pictures frankly and openly the sordid events as well as the beautiful ones.

16. Birth of Isaac

Abraham went south and dwelt at Gerar, a Philistine city, whose king was named Abimelech, a hereditary title meaning "father-king." Here Abraham practiced the same deception he had engaged in while down in Egypt, saying that Sarah was his sister. Abimelech sent for Sarah, as Abraham had feared; but God revealed the truth to Abimelech in a dream. Immediately he restored Sarah to Abraham, plus sheep, oxen, men and women servants, as well as a thousand pieces of silver.

Sarah now conceived and bore to Abraham a son, named Isaac. He was one hundred and she ninety-one when the birth occurred. When the child was weaned, Abraham made a feast; and when Sarah saw the child playing with Ishmael she demanded of Abraham that Hagar and Ishmael be ejected from the family. This Abraham reluctantly did, sending them away into the wilderness of Beersheba with only some food and a skin of water. God spoke to Hagar, telling her that the boy would become the father of a great nation. He became an archer, married an Egyptian, and became the founder of the Ishmaelites, living in the wilderness of Paran. He became the father of twelve sons and one daughter.

Abraham then made a covenant with Abimelech at Beersheba, the most southern city in Palestine. Beersheba means "well of the oath." Abraham "sojourned in the land of the Philistines many days" (Gen 21:34).

17. A Test of Faith

God now subjected the faith of Abraham to a supreme test, saying to him, "Take now thy son, thine only son, whom thou lovest, even Isaac, and get thee into the land of Moriah; and offer him there for a burnt-offering upon one of the mountains which I will tell thee of" (Gen. 22:2). Human sacrifice, as devotion to a god, was well known in that primitive age; but this was commanded of Abraham by Jehovah as the acid test. He had had many trials. There was the call to leave his homeland. There was the famine that drove him to Egypt, the deserting of Lot, and the destruction of Sodom. Then there was the long-deferring of the promised heir, followed by the expulsion of Ishmael and Hagar. Now he was commanded to take his only son Isaac a three-days' journey and to offer him as a burnt offering on a mountaintop there. But Abraham's faith did not falter. The writer of Hebrews years later said, "By faith Abraham, being tried, offered up Isaac: yea, he that had gladly received the promises was offering up his only begotten son; even he to whom it was said, In Isaac shall thy seed be called: accounting that God is able to raise up, even from the dead; from whence he did also in a figure receive him back" (Heb. 11:17–19).

Genesis 22 portrays in simple pathetic language the preparation, the journey, the dialogue between the father and the son, the building of the altar, the binding of Isaac, and the raising of the knife to slay him. One of the most touching incidents occurred when the boy said, "Behold, the fire and the wood: but where is the lamb for a burnt-offering?" To this Abraham replied, "God will provide himself the lamb for a burnt-offering, my son" (Gen. 22:7–8). The young boy even carried the wood intended for his own sacrifice. When Abraham raised the knife to slay his bound son, an angel of Jehovah called to him out of heaven and told him to stay his hand, that God now knew that he feared him, for he had not withheld his only son. Abraham looked and saw a ram in a thicket, caught by its horns. This he sacrificed instead and called the place Jehovah-jireh, meaning "Jehovah will provide." God again stated to Abraham the covenant promise, just as many times before. Abraham returned and lived for a while at Beersheba, but soon went back to Hebron.

18. Death of Sarah

While living here under the oaks of Mamre, Sarah died at the age of 127. Abraham made what was evidently his first purchase of a piece of land, the famous cave of Machpelah and the surrounding field. This purchase was made from Ephron the Hittite for 400 sheckels of silver. Ephron first offered the land free; but Abraham insisted upon paying for it, thus avoiding any dispute later. This cave was used to bury Sarah, and later on Abraham, Isaac, Rebekah, Jacob, and Leah. Today the Mosque of Hebron stands over the cave.

19. Marriage of Isaac

Abraham took the initiative in the marriage of his young son Isaac, a custom strange to us today. He did not want the wife of Isaac to come from the wicked Canaanites, but from the family of Nahor his brother left many years ago up in Haran in the northeastern part of Mesopotamia. Therefore Abraham sent Eliezer, his faithful servant, to Haran to secure a wife for Isaac. Eliezer traveled to

Haran and stopped outside the city at the time young ladies would come to the well to draw water, asking God for a sign indicating to him the girl whom he desired for Isaac. Rebekah, the daughter of Bethuel, the son of Nahor, fulfilled the condition. Rebekah's brother was named Laban. Eliezer went to the home of Bethuel and Laban and Rebekah and revealed the nature of his visit and all that God had done for Abraham, and they willingly permitted Rebekah to return with Eliezer to become the wife of Isaac. "And Isaac brought her into his mother Sarah's tent, and took Rebekah, and she became his wife; and he loved her" (Gen. 24:67).

20. Death of Abraham

After the death of Sarah Abraham took another wife, Keturah, who bore him six sons: Zimran, Jokshan, Medan, Midian, Ishbak, and Shuah. These sons, along with Ishmael, became the ancestors of the Arabian tribes of today. Midian became the father of the Midianites, mentioned several times later in the Old Testament. But Abraham, prior to his death, gave all that he had unto Isaac (Gen. 25:5).

At the age of 175 Abraham died and was buried by both Isaac and Ishmael in the cave of Machpelah. The "friend of God," as he is so-called in James 2:23, came to the end of a notable career. He has been termed also the father of the Hebrew people and the father of all believers. The only monotheistic people in the world —the Jews, the Muhammadans, and the Christians—all look back to Father Abraham. All the nations of the earth have truly been blessed through him.

21. Birth of Esau and Jacob

Rebekah was barren and could have no children. But Isaac prayed to Jehovah that this would be changed. God heard his prayer; she conceived and had twin sons: Esau and Jacob. God told her before the boys were born that there were two nations within her, but that one was stronger than the other and would be served by the weaker. The stronger would be the younger. Esau was born first, but during the birth Jacob was holding to Esau's heel. Esau means "hairy" or "rough"; Jacob means "he that holds by the heel" or "supplanter." The difference between the two boys was foreshadowed even in their births. Esau became a mighty hunter and the favorite of his father; Jacob was of a quiet, domestic turn and was the favorite of his mother. As young men this difference was vividly seen. Esau came in from a hunt, very tired and hungry. He asked Jacob to feed him with some red pottage that he had made. This was a stew made from red lentils, or red beans, still a favorite food in the East. He replied that he would do so if Esau sold him his birthright, all the privileges of being the eldest son. Esau agreed, to which also Jacob made him give him his oath that it would be so. To this he also agreed. Then Esau ate, drank, and went on his way.

22. Isaac and Abimelech

Due to a famine in the land Isaac went to Gerar, land of Abimelech. Here he did exactly as his father had done: he lied about Rebekah his wife, saying that she was his sister. Abimelech later realized the truth that she was his wife, and rebuked him for his deception. While here Isaac tried his hand at agriculture and was very successful. Likewise his flocks and herds increased greatly, for Jehovah generously blessed him. And Isaac digged again the wells of water that Abraham had dug; for the Philistines had filled them up.

Finally Isaac left Gerar and went to Beersheba, where God appeared to him and restated the covenant promise. There he built an altar and dug a well. When Esau was forty years old, he married two Hittite girls, Judith and Basemath. "They were a grief of mind unto Isaac and to Rebekah" (Gen. 26:35). Later he married Mahalath, an Ishmaelite girl (Gen. 28:9).

Jacob and Joseph
(Genesis 27—50)

1. Jacob and the Blessing

When they were still young men, Jacob gained Esau's birthright in exchange for a dish of red stew. Later there was even a more definite transfer of the right of the firstborn son from Esau to Jacob, an event involving the entire family. According to the custom of that time, Isaac wished to bless his firstborn Esau before he died. Rebekah overheard Isaac's request that Esau prepare for him the venison that he loved so well. Calling Jacob to her, Rebekah informed him of the scheme she had conceived to divert the blessing of her aged and almost-blind husband from Esau to Jacob. Accordingly, Jacob secured two kids from the herd, and his mother delicately cooked them for Isaac. Then, putting the skins of the animals over the hands and neck of Jacob so that he would feel like Esau, and giving him the savory dish, she sent him into the presence of his father. He was reluctant to go, fearing that if his father detected the deception, it might end in a curse rather than a blessing. His mother assured him that in that case she herself would take the curse.

The scheme worked; and Jacob received the blessing intended for Esau, for his bold lies were accepted. "I am Esau thy first-born; I have done according as thou badest me: arise, I pray thee, sit and eat of my venison, that thy soul may bless me" (Gen. 27:19). After feeling his son, Isaac uttered the dramatic saying, "The voice is Jacob's voice, but the hands are the hands of Esau" (Gen. 27:22). But he failed to note definitely the deceit. The old man even came near enough to him to smell the odor of the open field on Esau's clothes that Rebekah had given Jacob to wear. Jacob received the blessing intended for the firstborn Esau (Gen. 27:1–29).

No sooner had Jacob left the presence of his father than Esau returned with the venison, and the deed was known to both Isaac and Esau. Esau said, "Is not he rightly named Jacob? for he hath supplanted me these two times: he took away my birthright; and, behold, now he hath taken away my blessing" (Gen. 27:36). The blessing Esau received from his father, after his pathetic appeal for *some* blessing at least, was almost a curse compared to the blessing Jacob had received—the irrevocable one. He would live in the deserts of the earth and be a servant to his brother. Here is seen an example of the power of the blessing and the power of the curse as found throughout the Old Testament. That which is blessed stays blessed, and that which is cursed stays cursed.

Esau's anger boiled; he vowed to kill his brother. Rebekah, learning of the danger lying over the head of her favorite Jacob, sent him away to Haran, to her people, till Esau's wrath could cool. Isaac also, fearing that Jacob might take a wife from one of the Canaanite girls from in and around Beersheba where the family at that time was living, called Jacob to him for the express purpose of sending him up to Haran in Paddan-aram to secure a wife from among his mother's people. "Arise, go to Paddan-aram, to the house of Bethuel thy mother's father; and take thee a wife from thence of the daughters of Laban thy mother's brother." After this he again blessed Jacob with words similar to the ones used previously.

2. Jacob at Bethel

Jacob began the long journey to the eastern highlands of Aram, where he was to encounter someone just as crafty as he himself. Here there would be measured to him just as he had measured to his brother. His first stop was at the stony ground near Luz, a Canaanite town, where he built a pillow of stones and slept. He dreamed of a ladder going from earth to heaven, with the angels of God ascending and descending the ladder. God spoke to him, renewing the covenant promise, assuring him of his protection, and encouraging him with the hope of a future return. Jacob awoke trembling. "Surely Jehovah is in this place; and I knew it not." He added, "How dreadful is this place! this is none other than the house of God, and this is the gate of heaven" (Gen. 28:16–17). So he called the place Bethel, meaning "house of God," and vowed to give to God a tenth of all he possessed (Gen. 28:10–22).

3. Jacob in Haran

Jacob proceeded on his way till he arrived in Haran, a place where he was to spend the next twenty years of his life. At a certain well he met Rachel, the daughter of his uncle Laban, brother of his mother, with the flocks of Laban. After helping her water the sheep, he kissed her and revealed his identity. Laban welcomed Jacob to his house, where he spent a whole month. Laban had two daughters, Leah, the older, and Rachel, the younger. "And Leah's eyes were tender; but Rachel was beautiful and well-favored" (Gen. 29:17). Jacob made a bargain with Laban to work seven years that he might have Rachel. "And Jacob served seven years for Rachel; and they seemed unto him but a few days, for the love he had to her" (Gen. 29:20). But on the evening of the marriage Laban substituted Leah for Rachel, nor was the deceit discovered till the next morning. Jacob had met someone even more crafty than he. Laban informed Jacob that he must give the older before the younger. Yet, if Jacob would live with Leah for a week he would then give him Rachel, for whom he could work seven more years. To this Jacob agreed and got Rachel at the end of the week, after which he worked for seven more years. This made fourteen of the twenty years Jacob was at Haran, and during this time there were born to Jacob eleven sons and one daughter. Six sons and the daughter were by Leah, and one son, Joseph, was by Rachel. Bilhah, the handmaid of Rachel, gave Jacob two sons; and Zilpah, the handmaid of Leah, gave him also two sons. To Leah were born Reuben, Simeon, Levi, Judah, Issachar, Zebulun, and Dinah. To Bilhah were born Dan and Naphtali. To Zilpah were born Gad and Asher. And to Rachel was born Joseph. Isaac had married his second cousin, Rebekah; but Jacob married his two first cousins, Leah and Rachel.

Jacob proposed to Laban that he send him and his family away, back to Canaan; but Laban knew he himself had been blessed just by the presence of Jacob, so he proposed to Jacob that he continue to work for him further. "Appoint me thy wages, and I will give it," he said to Jacob (Gen. 30:28). Jacob then proposed a partnership arrangement for the flocks, to which Laban agreed. All of the flock reproducing of a certain coloring Jacob was to get, while all of another coloring Laban was to receive. Then Jacob, in his own crafty way, set about to have most of the offspring of the flock to be those he would receive. The hardiest of the animals he used his way, setting aside the weaker for Laban. And Jacob "increased exceedingly, and had large flocks, and maid-servants and men-servants, and camels and asses" (Gen. 30:43).

At the end of six years he realized that Laban and his sons were quite dissatisfied. So he proposed to his wives that they all go to the land of his nativity, the land of Canaan. They agreed; so, while Laban was out sheep-shearing, Jacob and his family, together with the animals and all their substance, stole away toward Canaan. Crossing the Jordan they headed toward Gilead, the land east of the Jordan. "And Rachel stole the teraphim that were her father's" (Gen. 31:19). Teraphim are idols, or family gods.

Laban discovered on the third day that they were gone and went in rapid pursuit. Catching the party of Jacob after a seven-day chase, he rebuked his son-in-law for leaving without informing him. If he had known, they would have been sent off with celebrations. "Wherefore hast thou stolen my gods?" To this question Jacob foolishly replied, "With whomsoever thou findest thy gods, he shall not live." He then told him to search his party (Gen. 31:30–32). Jacob unwittingly placed a curse of death upon his favorite wife Rachel. Laban searched, but without results. Coming to Rachel, who had hidden the gods in the saddle of her camel and sat upon it, she said, "Let not my lord be angry that I cannot rise up before thee; for the manner of women is upon me." Laban did not find the teraphim (Gen. 31:33–35), so became very angry. Nevertheless, he cooled down and made a covenant of peace with Jacob and then returned unto his home. Two men met, each finding in the other his match in cunning and craftiness.

4. Reconciled with Esau

Jacob continued on his way. When angels of God met him, he called the place Mahanaim, meaning "two hosts," or "two companies." He sent messengers to Edom, or Mount Seir, unto Esau informing him of his return with his family and belongings from

Paddan-aram. The messengers returned to Jacob, stating that Esau
was on the way north to meet him with 400 men. Jacob divided
his whole travel party into two companies, for he still feared Esau
greatly, and rightly so. Would twenty years make a difference with
Esau? If Esau came with killing in mind, perchance only half of
Jacob's family would be harmed if he divided his company into
two groups (Gen. 32:7–8).

Jacob was distressed and poured forth his soul to God in prayer,
asking God to protect him. Then, selecting presents from the flocks
and herds, he sent servants on before him and his family with the
presents for Esau. Perhaps these would appease Esau before Jacob
met him. During the night he sent his family and possessions on
across the ford of the Jabbok, a stream of Gilead flowing west
and into the Jordan River fifteen miles above the Dead Sea. He
himself, staying behind, had one of the most remarkable experiences
of his whole career. The Bible states that a "man" wrestled with
him until daybreak. This must mean an angel, for many times angels
are termed "men" in the Bible, both in the Old Testament as well
as in the New Testament. The three angels that came to visit
Abraham are called "men." (Compare also the accounts of the
open tomb of our Lord as found in the Gospels of Matthew and
Mark. Matthew says "angel," while Mark says "man." Hosea 12:4
states that Jacob "had power over the angel, and prevailed.") The
angel asked him his name, to which he replied that it was Jacob.
"Thy name shall be called no more Jacob," he was told, "but Israel:
for thou hast striven with God and with men, and hast prevailed"
(Gen. 32:27–28). Israel means "prince of God." Since all the descendants of Jacob are Hebrews, they are also called Israelites. The
angel touched the hollow of Jacob's thigh so that it was out of
joint, and he limped. Jacob asked the name of the one wrestling
with him, but he refused to give it. Instead, he blessed Jacob. Jacob
called the place Peniel, meaning "face of God," for he said, "I
have seen God face to face, and my life is preserved" (Gen. 32:30).
This whole experience had a profound effect upon the patriarch;
henceforth the weak points in his character began to disappear,
and he was truly a prince of God.

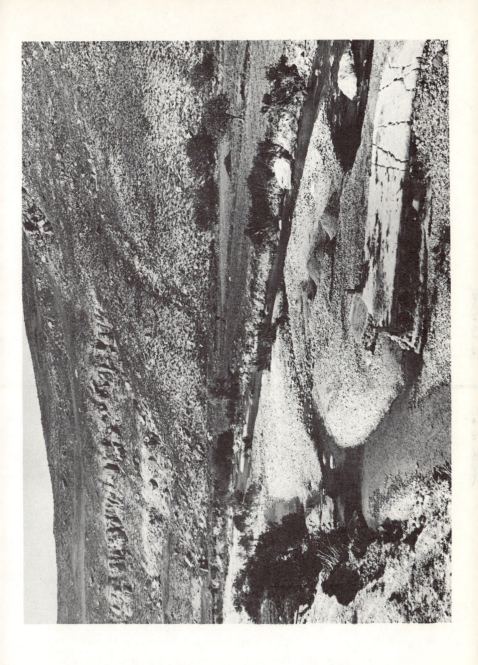

3. Brook Jabbok

The next day he met Esau, Jacob himself leading the way before his wives, handmaidens, and children. He bowed himself to the ground seven times till he came near his brother. "And Esau ran to meet him, and embraced him, and fell on his neck, and kissed him: and they wept" (Gen. 33:4). Esau did not want to accept the gifts offered to him by his brother, but Jacob insisted. So he received them and returned to the rugged mountains of Seir. This country is also known as Edom, meaning "red." The descendants of Esau were known as Edomites, a race of hunters living by the sword.

5. Back to Hebron

Jacob continued on his way home, stopping at a place where he put up booths for his cattle. He named it Succoth, meaning "booths." Then he crossed the Jordan and came to Shechem, buying a piece of ground from Hamor, its chief. Here he settled for a while, building an altar to Jehovah. Here also an unfortunate situation evolved. Dinah, still very young, was dishonored by Shechem, son of Hamor, in whose territory they were living. But Shechem desired the girl very much and offered extensive gifts in order to marry her. An agreement was made, not only for this marriage but for intermarriage in general. Three days after the mutual understanding Simeon and Levi attacked the city, slew all the men, got Dinah, and then left. The sons of Jacob later plundered the city. All this displeased Jacob greatly. Fearing the inhabitants of the land, he was forced to travel on.

Before leaving Shechem, Jacob called for a general purification of his people, demanding that they bring all their foreign gods and their rings for their ears to him. These he buried under an oak tree.

They journeyed to Bethel, where again Jacob had a great experience. He built an altar to God and called the place El-bethel, meaning "God of Bethel." God spoke to him, reassured him of his name Israel, and once again renewed the covenant promise (Gen. 35:1–15).

When they came near Bethlehem, then called by the Canaanite name Ephrath, Rachel gave birth to Benjamin and died. Knowing she was to die she called the child Ben-oni, "son of my sorrow."

But Jacob called him Benjamin, "son of the right hand." Jacob's curse brought death to his beloved Rachel, and she was buried where she died. Jacob erected on her grave a pillar, which is known as "the Pillar of Rachel's grave." Then Jacob had twelve sons and one daughter. Again we see the power of the blessing and the power of the curse. Yet this was not the only trouble that Jacob was to encounter in this area; for Reuben, his firstborn son, had intimate relations with Bilhah, handmaid of Rachel and concubine of Jacob.

Jacob traveled on to Hebron, where Isaac his father was living. Isaac died at 180 years and was buried in the cave of Machpelah by Esau and Jacob.

6. Early Life of Joseph

The life of Joseph has always been inspiring to many people. He was the firstborn son of Jacob and Rachel and full brother to Benjamin. Joseph was the favorite of all the sons of Jacob for we read, "Now Israel loved Joseph more than all his children, because he was the son of his old age" (Gen. 37:3). However, surely the fact that he was the offspring of his favorite wife Rachel must have added to this. (Note the name "Israel" used for "Jacob.")

There were three reasons why his half-brothers became very jealous of him. (1) He tattled on four of his half-brothers, the sons of Bilhah and Zilpah. While shepherding with them he learned of things later related to his father (Gen. 37:2). (2) His father presented to him "a coat of many colors," probably a long coat with sleeves, as used by rich young men. From this his brothers detected a greater love on the part of their father. (3) He had two remarkable dreams, the meaning of which elevated him above his father, mother, and eleven brothers. Their sheaves of wheat in the field made obeisance to his sheaf. And the sun, moon, and eleven stars made obeisance to him. Jacob rebuked Joseph for his self-exaltation, but he remembered the dreams, however (Gen. 37:5–11).

7. Slavery in Egypt

Jacob was living in Hebron, but his older boys took his flocks to far distant parts of Canaan. At one time, when they were near their old home in Shechem, Jacob sent Joseph to them to see how they were fairing. A man directed him on to Dothan ("two wells"), about twelve miles further to the north. When they saw Joseph approach, they said, "Behold, this dreamer cometh. Come now therefore, and let us slay him, and cast him into one of the pits, and we will say, An evil beast hath devoured him: and we shall see what will become of his dreams" (Gen. 37:19–20). But Reuben spoke for him, requesting that they not shed blood, but put him into a pit: for he wished later to get him back to his father. This they did.

While they were eating, a caravan of Ishmaelites (or Midianites, the two names being used interchangeably in the passage) went by. At Judah's suggestion they sold Joseph for twenty pieces of silver, the usual price of a male slave. The merchants then proceeded on to Egypt to sell Joseph, along with their spices and herbs. When Reuben, who at this time was gone, returned, he was greatly distressed at what his brothers had done. The others then dipped Joseph's multicolored coat in the blood of a young goat and brought it to their father, hypocritically asking him if it belonged to Joseph. "It is my son's coat; an evil beast hath devoured him; Joseph is without doubt torn in pieces" (Gen. 37:33). Then Jacob rent his clothes, dressed himself in sackcloth, and sat down to mourn—a custom strange to us but common among Eastern people of that day. The one who had so effectively deceived his father was in turn ruthlessly deceived by his own sons.

Joseph was taken to Egypt and sold to Potiphar, an officer of Pharaoh, captain of the guard. Potiphar noticed that there was something special about Joseph and all that he did, so he put him over his whole household. However, this was not to be of long duration; for Potiphar's wife, becoming infatuated with him, tempted him to commit adultery with her. After relating to her how much Potiphar had done for him and all that he had entrusted to him, he said, "How then can I do this great wickedness, and sin against God?" (Gen. 39:9). This temptation was placed before Joseph day by day, till one day he had to physically escape from her; but in doing so he left his coat in her hand. When her husband returned, she accused Joseph of the sin that she herself had committed. With Joseph's garment to add evidence to her story, Potiphar believed her and immediately had Joseph placed in prison.

8. Interpreter of Dreams

Even in prison all that Joseph did prospered, and Jehovah blessed him. The keeper of the prison depended upon him to help him care for the other prisoners. In time the butler and the baker of Pharaoh were confined there, for they had offended him (Gen. 40:1). The prison where they were all being held was in the very house of Potiphar, the captain of the guard. Each of the two men dreamed a dream during the same night. The butler dreamed of a vine, from which he took grapes and pressed them into Pharaoh's cup; the baker dreamed of three white baskets on his head, the top one of which contained bakemeats for Pharaoh. There the birds ate out of the basket. Joseph interpreted for them their dreams, that the butler (or cupbearer) should in three days be restored to his work and that the baker would in three days be hanged upon a tree, where the birds would eat his flesh. Just as he predicted, it all came to pass. Joseph told the butler his own sad story and asked him to remember him when he was released by interceding on his behalf with Pharaoh. But the butler forgot him entirely.

After two full years Pharaoh became troubled because of two dreams. There were seven fat cows and seven lean cows grazing along the Nile. The seven lean cows ate up the seven fat cows and became no fatter. There was also a second dream, in which there were seven full ears of corn and seven thin ears of corn. The seven thin ears ate up the seven full ears. The following morning Pharaoh was troubled, but all the magicians and wise men of Egypt could not interpret the dreams. When the chief butler informed Pharaoh of Joseph, the imprisoned Hebrew servant, he immediately sent for him that he might see if he could give meaning to his dreams. When brought before Pharaoh, Joseph said, "It is not in me: God will give Pharaoh an answer of peace" (Gen. 41:16). Pharaoh again recounted his dreams, and Joseph gave the true meaning. The seven good cows and the seven good ears represented seven years of plenty; but the seven thin cows and the seven thin ears represented seven years of famine. The doubling of the dream added certainty and imminence to the foretold event. He advised Pharaoh to set over his kingdom a man wise enough to lay up in store one fifth of all the land would yield during the next seven years, as over against the seven years of famine certain to follow them.

9. Release and Promotion

Joseph was appointed by Pharaoh to be the man for the much-needed task. The one who had so ably interpreted his dreams must be the one who could also so successfully put the whole program into effect. Pharaoh said to Joseph, "Forasmuch as God hath showed thee all this, there is none so discreet and wise as thou: thou shalt be over my house, and according unto thy word shall all my people be ruled: only in the throne will I be greater than thou" (Gen. 41:39–40). He gave him his own signet ring, dressed him in fine linen, put a gold chain about his neck, and had him to ride in the second chariot accompanied with the cry "Bow the knee." Very appropriately he changed his name to Zaphenath-paneah, or "revealer of secrets," and gave him for a wife Asenath, the daughter of Potephera, priest at On (later known as Heliopolis), the religious capital of Egypt. At thirty years of age, just thirteen years after entering the country as a slave, Joseph was elevated to a position in Egypt exceeded only by Pharaoh himself.

Joseph immediately went throughout the land making a survey of the crops and the storehouses. During the seven years "the earth brought forth by handfuls." Joseph gathered up the surplus grain and stored it in the cities, even to the extent that he ceased to keep a record of the amount. During this time Asenath gave him two sons; the first was named Manasseh, meaning "forgotten," and the second was named Ephraim, meaning "fruitful."

After the seven years of plenty in Egypt came the seven years of famine—not only in Egypt but "in all the earth." Joseph opened the storehouses and sold to the Egyptians, while at the same time empty caravans came from the surrounding countries to buy food for famished people.

10. The Brothers in Egypt

Jacob, hearing that there was grain in Egypt, sent his sons from Canaan to buy food. But Benjamin he did not send, for he said,

"Lest peradventure harm befall him" (Gen. 42:4). Joseph himself was dispenser and salesman of the grain, so the ten men from Canaan had to deal with their brother himself. Though not known to them, Joseph recognized the ones who had so ruthlessly dealt with him twenty years previously. He dealt with them through an interpreter and spoke roughly to them, even accusing them of being spies. "Nay, my lord, but to buy food are thy servants come. We are all one man's sons; we are true men, thy servants are no spies" (Gen. 42:10–11). They informed him that there was one more at home, the youngest, and that one was dead. Joseph at first said that they would not return home till one went and returned with their youngest brother. So he locked them up.

Three days later he announced to them a second plan. One would stay with him in Egypt as a hostage while the others returned home with the grain. They were then to bring their youngest brother back to Egypt. "So shall your words be verified, and ye shall not die" (Gen. 42:20). Not knowing that the premier of Egypt could understand their conversation with each other, they admitted their sin and acknowledged the fact that this calamity had come upon them by virtue of what they had done to Joseph. After seeing Simeon bound up before their eyes, they retraced their steps to their aged father. On the way home they marveled at the fact that one man's sack contained both the grain and the money.

At home they recounted to Jacob their strange adventure, only to discover immediately that every sack contained both the grain and the money. They informed their father of Simeon's plight and that they must return to Egypt with Benjamin, to which Jacob replied, "Me have ye bereaved of my children: Joseph is not, and Simeon is not, and ye will take Benjamin away: all these things are against me" (Gen. 42:36). Reuben even offered the lives of his two children as a pledge that he would return home with Benjamin, but Jacob refused. "My son shall not go down with you."

Yet hunger is a powerful force. When the food was gone, he was ready for Benjamin to make the trip, but not till after an inner struggle. Judah even offered himself as a surety of Benjamin's return. With a present for "the man," as they referred to Joseph, and with double the money in their sacks they returned to Egypt, bearing

4. Irrigation pump in Goshen

Benjamin with them. They were courteously received, and Simeon was restored to them. They were also informed that Joseph would entertain them with a banquet in his own home. Presenting to him the present, Joseph asked them of their father. When he saw Benjamin, he was forced to leave the room and weep. After his return the banquet proceeded, the brothers being surprised that they were arranged by age. But Joseph ate at a table by himself, and the Egyptians by themselves. "Benjamin's mess was five times so much as any of theirs" (Gen. 43:34).

The next morning they started home, each man with his sack containing grain and his money. But in Benjamin's sack was hidden Joseph's silver cup used for drinking and divining. Not far on their journey they were overtaken by Joseph's steward and accused of stealing the divining cup of his master. They denied the charge; but, if so, they decreed death to the guilty one and bondage for the remaining ones. However, the steward required that only the guilty one be his bondman. Searching the sacks from the oldest on down, he found the cup in the last sack, that of Benjamin.

Back in Joseph's home they were accused by their brother himself. Judah offered bondage for them all, but Joseph reduced this to the servitude of Benjamin only. Judah again spoke for the group, making a tender plea in words of deep pathos to Joseph for mercy. He told of their father and of his reluctance to let Benjamin return with them, and of what all this would do to Jacob. He was willing to remain a hostage, if the others could return to their father.

Joseph, being unable to act his part any longer, asked the Egyptians to leave the room. He then wept so loud that even the Egyptians heard. "I am Joseph; doth my father yet live?" The brothers were so troubled they could not answer, but he reassured them of his peace with them, even interpreting their treacherous act of years ago as God's providential means of preserving the family as his remnant upon earth. They were told to go and to bring their father, his family, and all his goods to Egypt, to dwell in Goshen (meaning "frontier"). There was a scene of utmost rejoicing.

11. Jacob in Egypt

Even Pharaoh was pleased at the news of Joseph's brothers and

gave royal support to Jacob's descent with his family into Egypt.
Returning to Canaan laden down with provision and good things
from Egypt, they informed Jacob of the marvels they had experienced, "And his heart fainted, for he believed them not" (Gen.
45:26). He was overjoyed with the news and the loaded wagons
from Egypt. Journeying by way of Beersheba he stopped, built an
altar, and sacrificed. God reassured him there, that though he
descended to Egypt God would bring him out again (Gen. 46:4).
Jacob, with his party numbering seventy people, went on to arrive
in Goshen. There Joseph met them, and there was much joyous
weeping. Israel said, "Now let me die, since I have seen thy face,
that thou art yet alive" (Gen. 46:30). Joseph appealed to Pharaoh
for Goshen as the land for his family, a land of pastures ideally
equipped for shepherds. Here, in the eastern delta land of the Nile
River, Jacob and his family settled down to live. Jacob was 130
years of age when this occurred, and here he lived for seventeen
years.

12. Death of Jacob and Joseph

Seeing that his father began to weaken, Joseph brought his two
sons to him, that his father might bless them. Jacob informed Joseph
that his sons, Manasseh and Ephraim, were to be considered as
his sons from that time on. He blessed them, giving to Ephraim,
the younger, the firstborn blessing with the right hand. Joseph tried
to correct him, but he stated that the younger would be greater
and his descendants a multitude. Calling to him his other sons he
blessed them one by one, giving to Judah, the fourth son of Leah,
the blessing due the firstborn. Reuben was passed over because
of the event with Bilhah (Gen. 35:22). Simeon and Levi were passed
over due to the Shechemite occurrence (Gen. 34:1–31). However,
each son received the blessing intended for him (Gen. 49:1–27).

Jacob died at 147 years and was buried in the cave of Machpelah
alongside the five already there (Gen. 49:31), having been embalmed
according to the Egyptian method. The long trip was made with
Egyptian help around to the east of Jordan and across into Canaan,
then down to Hebron. Before he died Joseph made them promise

not to bury him in Egypt, so when he finally died at 110 years they embalmed him and placed him in a coffin. Four hundred years later his body was carried out during the Exodus.

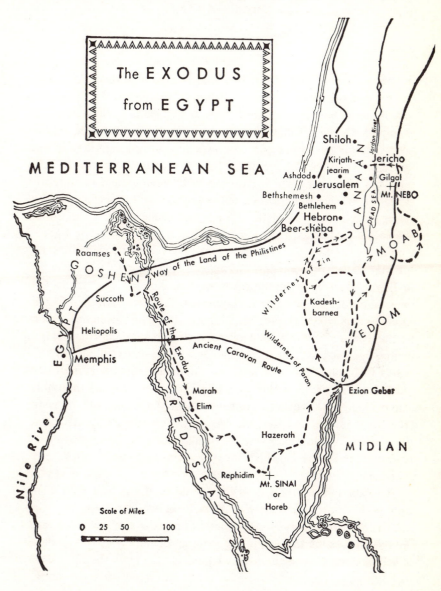

The EXODUS from EGYPT

Moses and the Deliverance
(Exodus 1—18)

1. Introduction

This period extends from the time of Joseph's death down to the time of the Exodus, about 1250 B.C. As the word "Genesis" means "beginning," the word "Exodus" means "going out." It is impossible to speak with authority concerning the date of the great deliverance from Egypt. Some scholars think that it occurred about 1450 B.C., which would be the early date. Others favor 1250 B.C., the later date, which date seems to have gained in support. Since the biblical writers were not prone to date the setting of their writings, we must resort to historical evidence outside the Bible.

Exodus 1:8 states, "Now there arose a new king over Egypt, who knew not Joseph." It is generally believed that Joseph became premier of Egypt sometime during the rule of the Hyksos kings in Egypt, who were foreigners from Asia holding sway from the thirteenth to the seventeenth dynasties (1788–1580 B.C.). These foreign kings would be favorably disposed to other foreigners, such as the Hebrews, and would even be willing to accept a premier of another race. When these alien rulers were expelled and the native Pharaohs were once again in command, they would naturally fear foreign elements within their borders. Many scholars think this "new king" to have been Rameses II of the nineteenth dynasty (1290–1225 B.C.), and that he was therefore the Pharaoh of the oppression. A tablet of Rameses II has been discovered at Beisan in central Palestine in which he states that he built the store city of Rameses in Egypt with Semite slaves from Asia. Rameses II as the Pharaoh of the oppression would conform well with 1250 B.C. as the approximate date of the deliverance from Egypt.

"Every shepherd is an abomination unto the Egyptians" (Gen. 46:34). This helps to explain the locating of the tribes in Goshen, a rich pasture area in the delta of the Nile far from the main part of Egypt. The Egyptians lived a settled life, mostly on small farms.

Most of the people were poor, living in small modest homes, whether on farms or in the cities. Yet there were some wealthy people, residing in elaborate homes lavishly furnished. The lot of the slave was hard, and there were many of them. Thousands and thousands of slaves would have been required to build the pyramids alone, not to mention the many household slaves and those used for other tasks. Due to the yearly overflow of the Nile the land was rich and alluvial, making possible abundant harvests of many crops and various fruits. The Nile was called by the Egyptians Hapi-Mu, "the genius of the waters," and by the Israelites Sihor, or Shihor, "the black" (Jer. 2:18).

There were large cities in which the arts, sciences, and crafts could flourish. The people were of the earliest to know mathematics, especially geometry, and the evidence of their knowledge of physics and engineering is seen in the pyramids and temples they have left. In Acts 7:22 Stephen says that Moses was "instructed in all the wisdom of the Egyptians."

The Egyptians were polytheistic, worshiping many gods. Three of the most ardently worshiped were Ra, the sun god; Opis, the sacred bull of Memphis (or Noph); and Mnevis, the golden calf of On (or Heliopolis). Isis and Osiris were also worshiped in Egypt. Evidently the Hebrews were impressed with this bull and calf worship, for they decided later on that they needed this type of god.

2. The Hebrews in Egypt

"And the children of Israel were fruitful, and increased abundantly, and multiplied, and waxed exceeding mighty; and the land was filled with them" (Ex. 1:7). No wonder the "new king" viewed with alarm this expanding group of Semites in the Nile delta. He voiced this concern to his people and suggested that they "deal wisely with them" before they joined hands with their enemies. Therefore they reduced the people that heretofore had lived the pleasant lives of "colonists" to the status of slaves in the brickyard (Ex. 1:8–11) and laborers in the field (v. 14).

The king of Egypt made three different attempts to curtail the multiplying of the Hebrew population. (1) He endeavored to kill them off with hard and severe labor. Taskmasters were set over them to afflict them with the greatest of oppression. "But the more they afflicted them, the more they multiplied and the more they spread abroad" (Ex. 1:12). (2) An order was given by the king to the Hebrew midwives (Shiphrah and Puah) to kill all Hebrew males as soon as born, but not to kill the females. "But the midwives feared God, and did not as the king of Egypt commanded them, but saved the men-children alive" (Ex. 1:17). So the Hebrews still multiplied. (3) The third attempt to suppress the number of the Hebrews was the king's order to cast into the river every son, but not every daughter (Ex. 1:22). It would be hard to estimate how many Hebrew boys were destroyed due to this order. Years before God had revealed to Abraham in a deep sleep "a horror of great darkness," which was in connection with God's prediction of a 400 years' affliction that would come upon his people (Gen. 15:12–14).

3. Birth and Training of Moses

Amram of the tribe of Levi married Jochebed, his father's sister, also of the tribe of Levi (Ex. 2:1; 6:20). To them were born Miriam and two sons, Aaron and Moses. Aaron was three years older than Moses (Ex. 7:7), with Miriam several years older than Aaron. Moses, "exceeding fair" (Acts 7:20), was hid for three months in his father's house. When his mother was unable further to conceal him, she made for him a small boat of bulrushes, or papyrus stalks. This she sealed with pitch, or bitumen, so it would not leak, and placed it in the reeds by the bank of the river. Miriam, watching the small boat to see what would happen to it, saw that it was discovered by the daughter of Pharaoh, who had come to the river to bathe. She recognized the babe to be a Hebrew, and when the child cried she felt an affection for it. Miriam at once offered to secure for her a nurse from among the Hebrew women to care for the child. When her offer was accepted, she called Jochebed, the child's own mother, to whom the daughter of Pharaoh offered wages to care for the child. So Jochebed cared for her own son, nursing him and finally bringing him back to his foster mother. Pharaoh's daughter named him Moses, which in its Egyptian form is Mo-she. This is from *Mo*, "water" and *Ushe*, "saved" (Ex. 2:10). He was formally reared as the adopted son of Pharaoh's daughter and became "instructed in all the wisdom of the Egyptians; and he was mighty in his words and works" (Acts 7:22). He was probably taught astronomy, mathematics, writing, physics, engineering, medicine, and symbolism from the various pagan religions.

4. Flight to the Midianites

Moses' life naturally divides itself into three periods of forty years each. The first of these is his training and education in Egypt; the second is his life among the Midianites near Mount Sinai; the third involves the years of wandering in the wilderness of the Sinaitic peninsula after the deliverance of the Hebrews from their Egyptian bondage. At the age of forty years a crisis occurred that brought to an end the first of these three periods. Moses went to the territory of his own people, Goshen, and happened to see an Egyptian hitting a Hebrew. Looking in both directions he killed the Egyptian and hid his body in the sand. On the next day, seeing two Hebrews "striving together," he endeavored to determine the cause. Their surly remark revealed the fact that his deed of the preceding day was known. Indeed, even Pharaoh heard; and Moses was forced to flee (Ex. 2:15). This was when he was forty years of age (Acts 7:23).

Striking out in a southeasterly direction he came near Mount Sinai to an area populated by Midianites, a people who were descendants from Abraham and Keturah (Gen. 25:2). Sitting by a well he saw seven sisters that had come to water the flocks of their father. After they had drawn water and filled the watering troughs, they were driven away by unruly shepherds. Moses, in true hero fashion, soon altered the situation and helped the girls with their task. Being invited to their home he met Reuel their father, priest of Midian, also called Jethro. Here he continued to live, for Jethro gave to him his daughter Zipporah for a wife. She bore for him a son, whom Moses named Gershom, meaning "stranger." In time she bore him another, whom they named Eliezer, "God is my help." Here Moses spent the second forty-year period of his life in the tranquility of a shepherd's task (Acts 7:30). In such an environment God could adequately prepare him for the difficult task ahead. Not only could he learn patience; he could become familiar with all sources of food and water and learn every valley and every crag of that lonely terrain. He would acquaint himself with the other tribes and peoples and learn the ones that were friendly and the ones unfriendly. The hand of God can be easily discerned in both these early periods of Moses' life.

5. The Burning Bush

As the first forty-year period ended in a dramatic experience, so did the second. While tending his flock Moses came to Mount Sinai, or Mount Horeb, as it was also called. "And the angel of Jehovah appeared unto him in a flame of fire out of the midst of a bush; and he looked, and behold, the bush burned with fire, and the bush was not consumed" (Ex. 3:2). As he endeavored to determine the cause of this mysterious happening, God spoke to him from the bush. "Moses, Moses." Moses answered; and God warned, "Draw not nigh hither: put off thy shoes from off thy feet, for the place whereon thou standest is holy ground" (Ex. 3:3–5).

God identified himself to Moses as the God who had spoken so many times to Abraham, Isaac, and Jacob. He had seen the affliction of his people, had heard their cry, had seen their sorrow, and was now coming down to deliver them to a good and large land, a land flowing with milk and honey. (Ex. 3:6–8). "Come now therefore, and I will send thee unto Pharaoh, that thou mayest bring forth my people the children of Israel out of Egypt" (Ex. 3:10).

Feeling very inadequate for such a gigantic task, Moses began to make excuses. (1) He said to God, "Who am I, that I should go unto Pharaoh, and that I should bring forth the children of Israel out of Egypt?" This is the excuse of being too insignificant a person, to which God said, "Certainly I will be with thee" (Ex. 3:11–12). (2) But who was this "I" that would go with him? When he told the Israelites that the God of his fathers sent him to deliver them, they would say, "What is his name?" To this feeble excuse of not knowing the name of God, God replied, "I AM THAT I AM. . . . Thus shalt thou say unto the children of Israel, I AM hath sent me unto you." Then God spoke to Moses with a reassuring note, telling him exactly what to do and what to say when he went back to his people and to appear before Pharaoh. He even announced that Pharaoh would refuse to let the people go and that he would therefore smite Egypt with his wonders, after which Pharaoh would let the people go. All this would bring favor to the Israelites in the eyes of the Egyptians (Ex. 3:13–22). (3) Still Moses was not satisfied and said to God, "But, behold, they will not believe me, nor hearken unto my voice; for they will say, Jehovah hath not appeared unto thee." To the excuse of lack of belief on the part of the Israelites God gave Moses outward signs to confirm his God-given authority. (a) The first sign was the changing of the rod into a snake, and then back into the rod. (b) The second was that Moses' hand became leprous and then clean again when alternately placed within and without his bosom. (c) The third sign was the changing of water from the river into blood when poured out upon dry land. (4) Moses' fourth excuse was lack of eloquence. "Oh, Lord, I am not eloquent, neither heretofore, nor since thou hast spoken unto thy servant; for I am slow of speech, and of a slow tongue." God replied that he would be with his mouth and teach him what he was to say. (5) Moses' fifth excuse was purely lack of faith in himself. "Oh, Lord, send, I pray thee, by the hand of him whom thou wilt send." Maybe there was someone else who could perform the task better. God became angry with this feeble remark and appointed Aaron to help Moses. "And he shall be thy spokesman unto the people; and it shall come to pass, that he shall be to thee a mouth, and thou shalt be to him as God" (Ex. 4:13–17).

6. Before Pharaoh

God told Aaron to go into the wilderness to meet Moses; when he did so, Moses related to him all that God had instructed him to do. Proceeding on to the land of Goshen they gathered together the elders of the people and informed them of God's plan, Aaron doing the speaking. When they performed the signs before the children of Israel, they believed; and when they realized that God had heard their cry, they bowed their heads and worshiped.

Surely Moses realized only too well the obstacles before him.

Not only must he secure Pharaoh's permission for the Israelites to depart—a task difficult enough in itself; he must also build up in the children of Israel a confidence sufficient for the hardships before them. Having been slaves for years, they were defeated and demoralized. The consciousness of their mission as a race called of God had become dim. To these two obstacles was added a third, that of planning all the details involved in moving a huge caravan of approximately 2,000,000 men, women, and children with all their possessions through desert areas infested by hostile tribes.

Moses and Aaron now appeared before Pharaoh himself in order to obtain his permission for the Hebrews to depart. This first appeal failed miserably. "Who is Jehovah, that I should hearken unto his voice to let Israel go? I know not Jehovah, and moreover I will not let Israel go" (Ex. 5:2). This reply denotes the idea of a national god so prevalent at that time, that a god of a nation had power only over that nation and that his authority extended to the borders of that nation alone. Here was the God of a slave nation requesting something of the monarch reigning over that nation, a God completely unknown to that monarch. Had not this God allowed his worshipers to endure a long and degrading bondage? Pharaoh not only refused to let the Hebrews go; he increased the severity of their task by requiring of them the same daily quota of bricks but not supplying them with straw. This they must gather themselves. Because it was almost impossible to obey such a tyrannical order, the Hebrew officers, who had been placed over the slaves by the Egyptian taskmasters, were beaten. Then the Hebrews rebuked Moses and Aaron and charged them with increasing the severity of their task (Ex. 5:1–21).

Reassured of the Lord with the ultimate success of their task, Moses and Aaron spoke to the Israelites all the renewed promises of Jehovah, which God had reviewed to them so clearly and forcefully. "But they hearkened not unto Moses for anguish of spirit, and for cruel bondage" (Ex. 6:9). Moses and Aaron again entered the royal palace to appear before Pharaoh and again stated their request, even though God had said, "And I will harden Pharaoh's heart, and multiply my signs and my wonders in the land of Egypt. But Pharaoh will not hearken unto you, and I will lay my hand upon Egypt, and bring forth my hosts, my people the children of Israel, out of the land of Egypt by great judgments. And the Egyptians shall know that I am Jehovah, when I stretch forth my hand upon Egypt, and bring out the children of Israel from among them" (Ex. 7:3–5). By all these miracles Egypt must realize that Jehovah is the one and only God, supreme over all nations.

Aaron threw down his rod before the king and the royal court, and it became a serpent. The Egyptian magicians also cast down their rods, and they became serpents; but Aaron's serpent swallowed up their serpents. And Pharaoh's heart was hardened (Ex. 7:8–13). The signs from that time on became plagues.

7. The Ten Plagues

Each succeeding plague brought on the Egyptians became more severe, reaching a climax in the tenth plague, the death of the first-born. Moses, or Aaron, was the agent in performing the first nine; the angel of death was the agent in the tenth. Also, these plagues affected only the Egyptians and were throughout all Egypt. But the Hebrews, mainly living in Goshen, were not subjected to them.

Many of these plagues had been known to Egypt over a small area and in a small way from time to time. But their intensity at this time, plus their swiftness in coming, added to the fact that they were called into being at the command of Moses, made them appear indeed miraculous. That the Hebrews were not affected puts the finishing touch on their miraculous element.

In every case an Egyptian god was insulted, for each plague showed that Jehovah was in complete control. The Nile was called "The Father of the Gods." Frogs were considered sacred, as were cattle. The national god idea must be revealed as false and Jehovah discerned as the one supreme God over all the earth. And this manifestation of the power of God was for the benefit of the Hebrews as well as for the consternation of Pharaoh. Jehovah, the God of the Hebrews, must be shown to be superior to every god of the Egyptians.

The plagues were ten in number.

(1) The Nile, the "Father of Life," the "Father of the Gods," as it was called by the Egyptians, was turned to blood. All the

water in all the streams and ponds in Egypt was turned to blood. The Egyptian magicians also succeeded in imitating this plague (Ex. 7:14–25).

(2) In seven days frogs came up over the whole land, entering into all the houses. Frogs were considered sacred by the Egyptians. The Egyptian magicians succeeded here also in their imitation (Ex. 8:1–15).

(3) The third plague was lice, or gnats, swarming over the whole land. Lice were considered unclean, quite humiliating to an Egyptian priest with his many rules for cleanliness. This plague the magicians of Egypt could not perform, so they confessed to Pharaoh, "This is the finger of God" (Ex. 8:16–19).

(4) The fourth plague consisted of flies, attacking both man and beast with fury. Pharaoh was willing to let the people sacrifice within the country, but not leave it. Moses would not accept this, so Pharaoh said they could go a little way into the wilderness. However, he revoked even this concession when the flies were gone (Ex. 8:20–32).

(5) The fifth calamity to strike the land was murrain among all the animals of Egypt. Even the sacred goats, calves, and bulls died. Not one animal of the Hebrews in Goshen was affected (Ex. 9:1–7).

(6) Moses and Aaron threw handfuls of ashes up toward heaven, and boils broke out upon man and beast. Even the magicians did not escape (Ex. 9:8–12).

(7) Hail constituted the seventh plague, hail accompanied by thunder and lightning. This plague was so destructive that Pharaoh asked Moses to intercede for him, admitting that he had sinned. But when the plague ended he again refused to abide by his word (Ex. 9:13–35).

(8) The eighth plague was that of locusts, eating up all that had escaped the fury of the storm of hail. Even the Egyptians, when Moses announced the coming of the plague, begged Pharaoh to let the Hebrews go. He did say he would allow the Hebrew men to go and serve their God, but the women and children must remain. So the plague was called forth upon the Egyptians (Ex. 10:1–20).

(9) Darkness came over the whole land of Egypt, except Goshen. The darkness, lasting three days, was so thick it could be felt. Ra, the sun god, was one of the main dieties of the Egyptians. At the end of the three days Pharaoh was willing to let the Hebrews go,

but their flocks and herds must remain. This Moses also rejected (Ex. 10:21–29).

(10) The tenth plague, the death of the firstborn throughout Egypt was administered by the angel of death (see Ex. 11:1 to 15:21). After every other plague it says that God hardened Pharaoh's heart, or that his heart was hardened. (The word "hardened" means "made strong.") But God promised Moses before this plague that it would result in their freedom. Human help would not be used, nor would the elements of nature be employed; God himself would execute this judgment upon Egypt. As in all the other plagues the Hebrew homes were not affected; no Hebrew lost his life.

8. The Passover

On the evening before the killing of the firstborn two important events happened for the Israelites. One, their calendar was changed. "And Jehovah spake unto Moses and Aaron in the land of Egypt, saying, This month shall be unto you the beginning of months: it shall be the first month of the year to you" (Ex. 12:1–2). It was the Hebrew month of Nisan, or Abib, "the month of green ears." From now on this was to be the first month of their sacred year; it corresponds roughly to our month of April. The first month of their civil year was still to be Tisri, corresponding to our month of October in the fall.

The second event was the celebration of the first Passover, the most important of all the Jewish festivals. The Israelites were told to kill a lamb and to put its blood upon the sideposts and upper doorpost of their houses. Then they were to roast the lamb whole and eat it that evening along with unleavened bread and bitter herbs, symbols of sorrow and of haste. Each household was to do this, clothed, with shoes on their feet, with staves in their hands, as though ready to leave hurriedly. Then at midnight, while they were eating the meal, God would pass through the land and kill all the firstborn, both man and beast, of all the houses of the Egyptians. "Against all the gods of Egypt I will execute judgments: I am Jehovah" (Ex. 12:12). God would pass over all the homes where he saw blood, so all the Hebrews would escape this calamity.

This feast, a memorial feast, was to be held each year from that time on. On the tenth day of Nisan they were to select the lamb; on the fourteenth day they were to prepare the lamb; on the fifteenth day (which began at six o'clock in the evening) they were to eat the lamb along with the bitter herbs and unleavened bread. They were told to eat unleavened bread, beginning with this day, for seven days, which is the reason the Feast of the Passover is also called the Feast of Unleavened Bread.

9. The Deliverance

It happened just as God said. While the Israelites were feasting at midnight a great cry was heard throughout Egypt, for there was not an Egyptian house in which there was not one dead—from the house of Pharaoh even down to the captives in the dungeon. All the cattle were also included. Pharaoh and the people urged the Hebrews to leave immediately. The people said, "We are all dead men." As Moses had directed, they asked the Egyptians for their jewels of silver and gold and also for clothing, which they gave them. Then they departed and went forth from Rameses. There were 600,000 fighting men, so the total number is estimated to have been about 2,000,000. "Now the time that the children of Israel dwelt in Egypt was four hundred and thirty years" (Ex. 12:40).

10. Crossing the Red Sea

They did not strike out toward Philistia, the shortest route to Canaan, for God had in store for them great experiences at Sinai. The first day they went from Rameses to Succoth, which was at the very edge of the land fit for cultivation. The next day they journeyed to Etham, "in the edge of the wilderness" (Ex. 13:20). From here on God was to employ a miracle for directing their path to the Land of Promise. There was to be a pillar of cloud by day and a pillar of fire by night, a miracle of nature sorely needed to bring faith on the part of the newly freed slaves. They were then led to Pihahiroth, between Migdol and the Red Sea, over against Baal-zephon. Here they looked up to discover a pursuing Egyptian army, chariots and all, sent out by Pharaoh; for God had hardened Pharaoh's heart, and he had changed his mind relative to the Hebrews. The Israelites cried out to Jehovah and complained to Moses.

Moses said, "Fear ye not, stand still, and see the salvation of Jehovah, which he will work for you today" (Ex. 14:13). God told Moses to lift up his rod and stretch forth his hand toward the sea and divide it. Then the angel of God and the pillar of fire went behind them, between them and the Egyptians. Moses stretched out his hand toward the sea, and a strong east wind, blowing all night, divided the water, so as to furnish dry ground with a wall of water on each side. The Hebrews started across, pursued by the Egyptian army. The Hebrews went across safely; but the Egyptian army was engulfed by the receding water, so that "there remained not so much as one of them" (Ex. 14:28). "And Israel saw the great work which Jehovah did upon the Egyptians, and the people feared Jehovah: and they believed in Jehovah, and in his servant Moses" (Ex. 14:31). The Song of Moses, in celebration of this great event, is found in Exodus 15:1–18.

Sinai and the Covenant
(Exodus 15—Leviticus 27; Deuteronomy)

1. Route of the Exodus

It is hard to determine the exact route that the Israelites took in their flight from bondage. Most scholars believe that the crossing took place at the modern Lake Timsah, or Crocodile Lake, a body of water through which the Suez Canal runs today. It is also located just east of ancient Pithom, one of the two treasure cities (along with Rameses) that the Israelites were forced to build for Pharaoh.

The shortest route to Canaan would have been a course straight eastward to the southern part of the land and then to the north. But God had great experiences in store for the Israelites at Sinai. When he spoke to Moses at the burning bush near Mount Sinai he said, "When thou hast brought forth the people out of Egypt, ye shall serve God upon this mountain" (Ex. 3:12).

As soon as the crossing of the sea occurred the once-degraded tribe, now independent, made its way along the eastern shore of the Red Sea, just at the western base of the high tableland that forms the northern part of the peninsula of Sinai. They traveled three days and found no water. When they did find water at Marah, it was bitter; hence it was named Marah, meaning "bitter." Moses sweetened it by cutting a tree and casting it into the water. Then they came to Elim, a veritable oasis, and camped by the water. When they left, they entered the wilderness of Sin, which was between Elim and Sinai, having been on the way a month and a half. They complained against Moses for bringing them there to die of hunger, for they had had their fill in Egypt, even though slaves. They charged Moses with the responsibility of getting them into their difficulties, the first of many rebellions against him and his leadership (Ex. 15:22 to 16:3).

2. Quail and Manna

God spoke to Moses about the murmuring of the people and

told him that he would supply them with flesh and with bread from heaven, "And ye shall know that I am Jehovah your God" (Ex. 16:12). That evening quail came up and covered the ground; and the next morning, when the dew was gone, there was spread over the ground a small round thing. When they saw it, they said, "What is it?" This phrase in Hebrew is *man hu*—hence the name "manna." They were told to gather just what they needed for that day, and no more. It was then miraculously supplied each day, and they were to gather that day's supply and not above that. If they did so and had some remaining, it would be foul the next day. But on the sixth day they were to gather a double supply, and it would not be foul on the seventh, the sabbath. They were to rest on the sabbath (Ex. 16:30). They named it manna, and it was white, like coriander seed; and it became their food for forty years. Aaron laid up some of it for a testimony and kept it.

3. Happenings at Rephidim

They journeyed from the wilderness of Sin and came to Rephidim, meaning "places of rest." For the second time there was no water, and as usual the people complained. God told Moses to use his rod and to strike "the rock in Horeb," and water would come forth. He did so, and there was water for every one (Ex. 17:1–7).

Here also they encountered the fierce and warlike Amalekites, people who were descendants of Esau and governed by a chief named Agag, meaning "burner," or "destroyer." They came upon the rear of the Hebrews and struck at the feeble ones when they were weary (Deut. 25:17–19). To direct a counterattack Moses commanded a young man, whose appearance in the biblical story is noted here for the first time, to draft able-bodied men and meet the sons of Amalek in the valley. This young man was Joshua, whose name means "God saves" and is the Hebrew equivalent to the New Testament name Jesus. Moses stood on the top of the hill and held out his rod. "And it came to pass, when Moses held up his hand, that Israel prevailed; and when he let down his hand, Amalek prevailed" (Ex. 17:11). Putting Moses on a stone for a seat, Aaron and Hur held up his arms till sunset, and Joshua won the battle.

Moses' father-in-law, Jethro, came to him at his encampment and brought Zipporah, his wife, and his two sons, Gershom and Eliezer; for he had kept the three while Moses was freeing the Hebrew people from Egypt. When Moses told him of all that God had done for them in Egypt and along the way, Jethro exclaimed, "Now I know that Jehovah is greater than all gods" (Ex. 18:11). After this he offered a burnt offering and sacrifice to God. When Jethro saw Moses judge the people personally from morning to evening, he made a very practical suggestion. Knowing that the settlement of these petty disputes for such a multitude of people would wear him out, he counseled Moses to appoint "able men, such as fear God" to be "rulers of thousands, rulers of hundreds, rulers of fifties, and rulers of tens," that they might judge the people, leaving the weightier matters for Moses himself. Moses adopted his advice and appointed the men (Ex. 18:13–27).

4. Sinai

In the third month after departing Egypt the Hebrew caravan entered the wilderness of Sinai (named after Sin, the moon-god of Babylonia). Here in these majestic mountains there are several peaks, any one of which may have been the scene of the experiences of Israel as related in Exodus. Each peak has been advanced by one or more scholars as Moses' mountain, but Jebel Mousa presents great evidence as being the most likely one.

They encamped before the mount, and Moses immediately ascended for God's message. Here God spoke to the great leader of the covenant that would make Israel his people, his own possession, chosen from among all people. "And ye shall be unto me a kingdom of priests, and a holy nation" (Ex. 19:6). When Moses later assembled the people they said, "All that Jehovah hath spoken we will do." When Moses informed Jehovah of the words of the people, he gave him directions for the meeting when he would "come down in the sight of all the people upon mount Sinai" (Ex. 19:11). They were to purify themselves, and on the third day they were to come to the mount. Bounds were to be set; if anyone touched the mount, he was to be stoned or shot through. At the sound of the trumpet they were to approach the mount. The purpose of

5. Mount Sinai

all this was the realization upon the part of the people of the holiness of God.

On the third day, after the period of sanctification, they drew near the mount. The sight, so fearful and appalling, made the people tremble. Thunder, lightning, a thick cloud, and smoke ascending like a furnace, added to the earth's quaking and the trumpet's getting louder and louder, struck fear in the hearts of the people. God again warned the people through Moses of the holiness of the mount and that bounds had been set about the base of it. God was preparing the people for the greatest event in their whole history.

5. The Covenant

A covenant is an agreement between two parties. God entered into a covenant with Israel whereby they became his special people. All the provisions of the covenant must be read in their hearing, and the covenant formally accepted by them. Then they would be his people, and he would be their God. This would be the great act whereby the promises made repeatedly to Abraham, Isaac, and Jacob would be fulfilled. Those were covenant promises; this was the covenant fulfilled. The event of this day was the most important in the history of the Hebrews, for it marked the birth date of their nation. The Hebrews were to be God's special witnesses and representatives to the other nations of the world. They were to be unto God "a kingdom of priests and a holy nation," a rare privilege indeed. The great act of God whereby they could become his people was his redeeming them from Egypt. "Ye have seen what I did unto the Egyptians, and how I bare you on eagles' wings, and brought you unto myself" (Gen. 19:4).

The basis of the covenant was the great act of deliverance; the condition of the covenant was obedience to its requirements. "Now therefore, if ye will obey my voice indeed, and keep my covenant, then ye shall be mine own possession from among all peoples" (Ex. 19:5). God redeemed; then God covenanted. God commanded; Israel accepted. The people were treated as a whole and responded to God as a whole, though individuals could give up their rights under the covenant by not obeying its provisions.

The formal act by which Israel entered into a covenant with God at Sinai is seen in three elements, found in three consecutive sections of the book of Exodus: the Decalogue, or the Ten Commandments (Ex. 20:3–17); the Book of the Covenant (Ex. 20:22 to 23:19); and the Ritual of Acceptance (Ex. 24:1–11).

6. The Ten Commandments

God spoke, and the Ten Commandments were proclaimed. He spoke face to face out of the midst of the fire, with Moses standing between him and the people (Deut. 5:4,5,22). These Commandments, also called the Decalogue, were the fundamentals of God's law for the Hebrew people. They were to conceive of these as the charter of their constitution and the stepping-stones to the covenant between God and Israel. This covenant, or agreement into which they entered with Jehovah, made them his special people; now that they were his peculiar people, these ten rules were what God required in ethical living.

The first four have to do with man's relation to God; the last six have to do with man's relation to man. The Decalogue takes the upward look, but it also takes the outward look.

The Ten Commandments are as follows:
   (1) Thou shalt have no other gods before me.
   (2) Thou shalt not make unto thee a graven image.
   (3) Thou shalt not take the name of Jehovah thy God in vain.
   (4) Remember the sabbath day, to keep it holy.
   (5) Honor thy father and thy mother.
   (6) Thou shalt not kill.
   (7) Thou shalt not commit adultery.
   (8) Thou shalt not steal.
   (9) Thou shalt not bear false witness against thy neighbor.
   (10) Thou shalt not covet.

It is readily seen that these Commandments are mainly prohibitions, containing a "Thou shalt not." The first nine are objective in nature and involve outward acts or deeds; the last is subjective in nature, taking place within the mind and not necessarily apparent to the bystander. They are found in two places in the Old Testament: Exodus 20:3–17 and Deuteronomy 5:7–21.

These Commandments, or the Decalogue (from two Greek words

meaning "ten words"), show that the God of the Hebrews was holy, righteous, and ethical; quite a contrast to the pagan gods the Hebrews had observed in Egypt and elsewhere. These deities were characters of the most degrading sort, many of them animals and inanimate objects of nature. Their rites of worship were base, immoral, and licentious. They were gods to be appeased, so that the crops and animals would bring forth plentifully. The God of the Hebrews was the one and only God, who wanted the complete love and loyalty of his people, and who wanted them to be holy because he was holy. The tragedy is that the observance of these "words" by the Hebrews was highly inadequate and weak all through their history, almost to the point of being inoperative.

So great was the terror of the Hebrews when God spoke to them from the mount that they fled and stood afar off. They implored Moses, "Speak thou with us, and we will hear; but let not God speak with us, lest we die" (Ex. 20:19). Moses became the mediator between God and the people, for it appears that he ascended the mount to converse with Jehovah several times. Each time he would descend and relay God's messages to the terrified ones below.

7. The Book of the Covenant

The second element having to do with the covenant between Jehovah and Israel was the Book of the Covenant, which was a code of laws very ethical in nature. Jehovah demanded moral living, and all his requirements could not be contained in ten pithy sayings. A fuller description was required, which is found in Exodus 20:22 to 23:19. These laws are a series of social, civil, and religious demands made by God upon Israel, with the Ten Commandments acting as foundation stones. They contain detailed requirements in man's relation to God and to his neighbor, especially for a people living an agricultural life rather than a nomadic life. The yearly sabbath and the weekly sabbath were set down, as well as the three yearly feasts: the Feast of Passover, the Feast of Pentecost, and the Feast of Tabernacles.

8. The Ritual of Acceptance

The ritual, or ceremony, by which Israel accepted the covenant is the third element and is found in Exodus 24:1–11. "And Moses came and told the people all the words of Jehovah, and all the ordinances: and all the people answered with one voice, and said, All the words which Jehovah hath spoken will we do." After this Moses built an altar and twelve pillars, one for each tribe. Then burnt offerings and peace offerings were made, with God being thought of as on one side of the altar and the people on the other side. The blood was drained into bowls and half of it sprinkled on the altar. "And he took the book of the covenant, and read in the audience of the people: and they said, All that Jehovah hath spoken will we do, and be obedient." After this formal acceptance of the covenant, Moses sprinkled the remaining half of the blood, called "the blood of the covenant," over the people. Moses, Aaron, Nadab, and Abihu, and seventy elders of Israel "beheld God, and did eat and drink." This very impressive ritual sealed the covenant between Jehovah and Israel. Israel was now God's distinctive nation, wholly dedicated to him.

9. The Three Feasts

There were three important feasts that God ordained for the Hebrews. "Three times thou shalt keep a feast unto me in the year" (Ex. 23:14). The Feast of Passover, or the Feast of Unleavened Bread, was a seven-day feast in the month of Abib, or Nisan, corresponding to our month of April. This was a Memorial Feast for their deliverance out of Egypt. The second was the Feast of Pentecost, also called Feast of First-fruits, Feast of Weeks, and Feast of Harvest. It occurred fifty days after the passover meal, hence the name "Pentecost" (from the Greek word "fifty"). It occurred the next day after seven weeks after the passover meal, hence the name "Weeks." This occurence was in our month of June, and in their month of Sivan. It was a one-day feast symbolizing gratitude for the winter harvest. The third feast was the Feast of Tabernacles, also called the Feast of Booths and the Feast of Ingathering. It symbolized two things: gratitude for the fruit harvest and a rememberance of living in booths during the wilderness wanderings. It occurred during our October, or their month of Tisri, and was a seven-day feast. It was the most joyous of the feasts.

10. Moses Again in the Mount

"And Jehovah said unto Moses, Come up to me into the mount, and be there: and I will give thee the tables of stone, and the law and the commandment, which I have written, that thou mayest teach them" (Ex. 24:12). After committing the people into the care of Aaron and Hur, Moses took Joshua and ascended the mount of God. The glory of God was in the mount, and the cloud covered it six days. On the seventh day God called Moses alone still higher up and into the midst of the cloud. Here he remained forty days and forty nights (Ex. 24:18), while God gave further revelations and conversed with him (Ex. 25—31).

God gave Moses complete directions for making the sanctuary, or tabernacle, which was to be the solemn place of meeting for him and the people (Ex. 25—27). He also gave him complete directions for making the ark of the covenant, the table of showbread, the seven-branched lampstand, the altar of incense, the altar of burnt-offering, the brazen laver, and many things relative to the sacrificial system. God also gave him directions for the order of services and the ritual (Ex. 29; 30), as well as appointing Bezalel and Oholiab for the important task of building the sanctuary, or tent of meeting, as it is called in the Scriptures (Ex. 31:1–11). Finally, God gave Moses two tables of stone on which were the Ten Commandments "written with the finger of God" (Ex. 31:18).

11. The Tabernacle

"To tabernacle" means to dwell; therefore the tabernacle was the dwelling of Jehovah. During the days of the patriarchs they erected altars wherever they went, such as at Shechem, Bethel, and Hebron, and offered sacrifices to Jehovah in a simple, rural setting. Immediately following the acceptance of the covenant God commanded Israel to build a tabernacle, so that he might "dwell among them" (Ex. 25:8). There was to be only one sanctuary for Israel, quite in contrast to the many temples and places of worship they had seen in Egypt. The people were to bring an offering of materials with which to build the tabernacle: gold, silver, linen, animal skins, acacia wood, oil, spices, incense, and precious stones.

The tabernacle was not to be a fixed, masonry structure, permanent in location. This would come later in the form of the temple built during the days of Solomon. The tabernacle was to be made of staves and stakes, with walls of cloth and animal skins, ready to be gathered up and moved to a new location as soon as the pillar of cloud or pillar of fire should remove itself. This tabernacle proper stood in the midst of a large open yard, or court, 150 feet by 75 feet, enclosed by a tent wall, 7½ feet high. The only entrance was at the east end.

The eastern half of this open court was for the Hebrew who came to worship, for here was the brazen altar for sacrifice, with horns on each corner. It was built of acacia wood covered with bronze and had staves and rings so that it could be carried. Beyond the altar stood the great laver, where the priests washed their feet before going to the altar.

In the western half of the open court stood the tabernacle itself, which was 45 feet long, 15 feet wide, and 15 feet high. It was divided into two parts: at the east and in front was the holy place, and in back of this was the holy of holies, or the holiest place. The holy place was exactly twice the size of the holy of holies and was separated from it by a curtain. The priests went into the holy place each day; but only the high priest went into the holy of holies, and that only once a year, on the Day of Atonement.

The tabernacle walls were made of acacia planks overlaid with gold. The ceiling was of fine twined linen, overlaid with a double covering of skins for protection. Two veils were used for entrances, one at the east end of the tabernacle and one between the holy place and the holy of holies.

There were three pieces of furniture in the holy place containing equipment tended by the priests daily. The table of showbread was on the north side, on which was placed twelve cakes of unleavened bread every Sabbath, the old cakes being eaten at that time by the priests. This bread was also called "bread of the face," since it looked into the face of God continually. The golden lampstand, on the south side, was of one piece of gold and contained seven branches. These lamps were fed with olive oil and cared for daily by the priests. They burnt continuously, day and night. The altar of incense, standing in front of the veil going into the holy of holies, was overlaid with gold. On it incense was kept burning continuously, so that the smoke would ascend perpetually before the Lord. The incense was to be lit only with fire from the brazen altar in the court.

In the holy of holies there was only one piece of equipment, but a very important one, the ark of the covenant. It was an oblong chest of acacia wood overlaid with gold within and without. It stood on four feet, provided with four rings through which staves were passed. These staves, also made of acacia wood and overlaid with gold, were never to be withdrawn once they were inserted in the rings. The ark was three feet, nine inches long and two feet, three inches wide and deep. On top of the ark and covering it completely was a solid sheet of pure gold called the mercy seat. "And there I will meet with thee, and I will commune with thee from above the mercy-seat, from between the two cherubim which are upon the ark of the testimony, of all things which I will give thee in commandment unto the children of Israel" (Ex. 25:22). The mercy seat, representing the presence of God, was the place where God and man met (Ex. 30:6) and where God spoke to man (Ex. 25:22).

Not only did the ark contain the tables with the Decalogue (Ex. 25:21), but also a pot of manna (Ex. 16:34) and Aaron's rod that budded (Num. 17:10). Surely the ark of the covenant was the most sacred object in the religion of the Hebrews. It remained in darkness continually; for the seven-branched lampstand lighted the holy place, but there was nothing to light the holy of holies.

12. The Law of Moses

The encampment of the Israelites at Mount Sinai lasted for about thirteen months (Num. 1:1), and God continued to reveal himself to the people. The Decalogue and the Book of the Covenant were expanded into what became known as the Mosaic Law, which is found in Exodus 20—40 and Leviticus 1—27. The book of Leviticus has to do with the various sacrifices, the duties of the priests, laws of purification, the Day of Atonement, laws of holiness, regulations concerning food and dress, requirements concerning feasts and seasons, regulations for everyday living, and conditions necessary for God's blessings. Simply to obey these laws would distinguish the Hebrews from all the people around them.

These laws were moral, civil, and ceremonial. The moral part may be seen in the Ten Commandments, which are as binding today for all people as they were to the Hebrews in that day. The ceremonial part pertained to the details of worship and concerned sacrifices, priesthood, and holy seasons. The civil part, or the judicial, regulated property rights, court procedure, marriage relations, criminal punishments, and administration of justice. Many of the ceremonial and civil laws were temporary, and much of the ceremonial has been fulfilled in Christ (Heb. 10:1–18).

13. The Offerings

The Hebrews sacrificed prior to the giving of God's new revelation at Sinai, which is seen in the stories of Cain, Abel, Noah, the patriarchs, and Moses. Now that Israel was in covenant with God, various sacrifices were demanded. These were five in number, four of them being blood sacrifices and one not of blood. (They are fully discussed in Lev. 1—7.) Animals that were acceptable for sacrifice were clean and tame, whose flesh could be eaten, such as sheep, goats, oxen, male or female, young or old. In case of poverty pigeons could be substituted.

(1) In the burnt offering the entire sacrifice was consumed on the altar, the idea being that the offerer's complete consecration to God was symbolized in the complete consumption of the animal (Lev. 1:3–17). Israel was commanded to maintain a continual day-and-night burnt offering on the brazen altar (Ex. 29:38–42).

(2) In the peace offering the animal was cooked and eaten, the main feature being the eating of this sacrificial meal (Lev. 3:1–17). Part of the sacrifice was dedicated to God and consumed on the altar; part was eaten by the priest; and the remaining part eaten by the offerer, his family, and his friends, with the joyous fellowship signifying the renewed relationship between God and man. This offering was entirely voluntary.

(3) In the sin offering the offerer was seeking atonement for sins of ignorance done unintentionally (Lev. 4:1–35). The main motive

here is the need for expiation, or atonement, in approaching God. The requirements for the sin offering differed, the higher the person offering the more precious the animal offered. Even wrongs done inadvertently must be atoned for, showing that God's righteousness cannot overlook any sin.

(4) In the trespass offering the legal rights of a person and his property were set forth (Lev. 5:14 to 6:7). Confession must be made to the person injured or wronged, and restoration or compensation made for that injury or wrong; then an offering must be made to God. As in the sin offering the main idea is guilt, in the trespass offering the main idea is injury done to God or man. The sin offering brings atonement, while the trespass offering brings satisfaction.

(5) In the grain offering we encounter the one nonbloody sacrifice (Lev. 2:1–16). The King James Version terms this sacrifice "meat offering", thus giving a false concept of it. There is no meat whatsoever connected with it. The American Standard Version terms it "meal-offering," and the Revised Standard Version terms it "cereal offering." Being made of fine flour, a product of the soil and not of the flock or herd, it suggested man's homage to God. It was considered a gift pleasing to God; in fact, the Hebrew word for this sacrifice means "gift." When an Israelite presented this offering, he was presenting the fruit of his labor, thus dedicating his gifts to God. The burnt offering and the peace offering were always accompanied by a meal offering.

One rule applied to all sacrifices: they were to be offered only on the brazen altar in the court of the tabernacle, never on the old Canaanite high places or on any spot selected at random by the worshiper.

14. The Golden Calf

While Moses and Joshua were up on Mount Sinai for forty days and forty nights the people became restless, saying to Aaron, "Up, make us gods, which shall go before us; for as for this Moses, the man that brought us up out of the land of Egypt, we know not what is become of him" (Ex. 32:1). So Aaron yielded to their plea and asked them to bring their golden earrings to him. With these he made a golden calf similar to those worshiped in Egypt, saying, "These are thy gods, O Israel, which brought thee up out of the land of Egypt" (Ex. 32:4). He even became so devout in his new service to the people that he built an altar and proclaimed "a feast to Jehovah," as represented by the molten calf. They immediately offered burnt offerings and peace offerings and were so joyous in their ritual that they "sat down to eat and to drink, and rose up to play." In a little over a month's time they had broken the Second Commandment and had violated the covenant they had made with God.

God told Moses to descend immediately, for the people had corrupted themselves, made a molten calf, and had even sacrificed to it. God suggested that he consume this people and start a new nation with Moses. "And Jehovah said unto Moses, I have seen this people, and, behold, it is a stiffnecked people: now therefore let me alone, that my wrath may wax hot against them, and that I may consume them: and I will make of thee a great nation" (Ex. 32:9–10). But Moses interceded for them, and God accepted his plea. As Moses and Joshua went down from the Mount, with Moses carrying the tables of stone containing the Decalogue, Joshua mistook the noise and the turmoil below to be war; but Moses corrected him. When the tumult finally burst upon his sight, "Moses' anger waxed hot, and he cast the tables out of his hands, and brake them beneath the mount. And he took the calf which they had made, and burnt it with fire, and ground it to powder, and strewed it upon the water, and made the children of Israel drink of it" (Ex. 32:19–20). After Aaron made a very feeble excuse for his part of the pagan scene, Moses sternly rebuked him. Then he challenged all who were faithful to Jehovah to come to his side, put on his sword, "and go to and fro from gate to gate throughout the camp, and slay every man his brother, and every man his companion, and every man his neighbor." The sons of Levi responded, and 3,000 of the people were destroyed that day because of their sin (Ex. 32:21–29).

15. Intercession for the People

Moses again ascended the mount to intercede for the people and to plead for their forgiveness on the part of God. As an example of the supreme character of Moses he offered to permit God to

blot him out of his book if the sin of the people was too great
to be remitted, to which God replied, "Whosoever hath sinned
against me, him will I blot out of my book" (Ex. 32:33). He then
instructed Moses to continue leading the people, that he would send
his angel before them; for he would not go up in the midst of them,
"for thou art a stiffnecked people; lest I consume thee in the way"
(Ex. 33:1–3). The people moaned at such news from God and stripped
themselves of their ornaments from Mount Sinai onwards.

Moses, having pitched his own tent without the camp, marched
out toward it with all the people watching at their tent doors. When
Moses entered the tent, the pillar of cloud descended and stood
at the door. "Jehovah spake unto Moses face to face, as a man
speaketh unto his friend" (Ex. 33:11). Moses again made entreaty
with God, both for himself and for the people; and his plea was
heard. God said to him, "My presence shall go with thee, and
I will give thee rest" (Ex. 33:14). Becoming bold at having prevailed
with God, Moses asked to see the glory of God. God answered,
"Thou canst not see my face; for man shall not see me and live."
He then promised to place Moses in a cleft of a rock and to cover
him with his hand until he had passed by. "I will take away my
hand, and thou shalt see my back, but my face shall not be seen"
(Ex. 33:17–23).

16. New Tables of Stone

Having been directed of God to cut two new stones like the ones
he had destroyed and to reascend the mount alone, Moses obeyed
and again met with Jehovah. "And Jehovah descended in the cloud,
and stood with him there, and proclaimed the name of Jehovah"
(Ex. 34:5). In very dramatic words God proclaimed to Moses that
he is a God of justice, mercy, love, and grace, after which Moses
bowed his head, worshiped, and prayed for himself and the people.
God heard his prayer and said, "Behold, I make a covenant: before
all thy people I will do marvels, such as have not been wrought
in all the earth, nor in any nation" (Ex. 34:10). Then God stated
all that he would do for them in their conquest of the Promised
Land and also what he would expect of them as his covenant people.
"And Jehovah said unto Moses, Write thou these words: for after

the tenor of these words I have made a covenant with thee and with Israel'' (Ex. 34:27). Moses was then alone with God forty days and forty nights neither eating nor drinking, and he wrote upon the tables the Ten Commandments.

When he descended from the mount with the two tables, his face shone by reason of his having been with God. Though this was unknown to Moses himself, the people were afraid to come near him. When he finally secured their confidence, he related to them all that God had said. ''And when Moses had done speaking with them, he put a veil on his face'' (Ex. 34:33).

Moses next gave the people complete directions for making the tabernacle and all the equipment needed within it. He commanded that the offerings be brought for its construction and announced that Bezalel and Oholiab would direct the work. It was duly finished and brought to Moses, complete in every detail. When it was erected and assembled, ''the cloud covered the tent of meeting, and the glory of Jehovah filled the tabernacle'' (Ex. 40:34).

The Wanderings and the Conquest of Eastern Palestine
(Numbers and Deuteronomy)*

1. Departure from Sinai

The Israelites had been at Sinai for more than a year, and it was now time for them to march toward Canaan. The Covenant had been contracted, the law had been given, the tabernacle had been erected, and the priests had been set apart. Since the occupation of this new land would necessitate a conquest, Jehovah directed that Moses and Aaron number all the males twenty years and older who were capable of fighting for Israel. The total number came to 603,550 men (Num. 1:46). The Levites were not numbered in this group since it was their duty to care for the tabernacle and to transport it from place to place. Aaron and his sons, also descendants of Levi, the third son of Jacob, were designated as priests.

Before leaving Sinai on their journey to Canaan the Israelites celebrated the first anniversary of the Passover. "And they kept the passover in the first month, on the fourteenth day of the month, at even, in the wilderness of Sinai" (Num. 9:5). Directing the group to leave Sinai and its surroundings, God gave to Moses and the people a means whereby they were to know when to start marching and when to stop. The very day the tabernacle was erected the cloud covered it; then this cloud appeared as fire by night. Whenever the cloud left the tabernacle they were to break camp and leave; whenever it stayed, they were to stop and make camp. "At the commandment of Jehovah they encamped, and at the commandment of Jehovah they journeyed" (Num. 9:23). God not only had a certain arrangement for the location of this tabernacle and the tribes in an encampment, with the tabernacle occupying the center; he also had a certain arrangement for the tribes as they marched (Num. 10:13–28), with the ark, borne by some of the Levites, leading the way.

Immediately before departing, Moses invited Hobab, his brother-in-law, to accompany them on the journey, stating that Jehovah would bless him. He refused, at which Moses urged him a second time to go with them, stating that he could aid them by being to them "instead of eyes." His answer is not given in this passage of Scripture (Num. 10:29–32); but he must have accepted, since he is mentioned later in Judges 1:16 and 4:11.

When the ark set forward on the march, Moses cried, "Rise up, O Jehovah, and let thine enemies be scattered; and let them that hate thee flee before thee." Whenever the ark rested, he said, "Return, O Jehovah, unto the ten thousands of the thousands of Israel" (Num. 10:35–36).

2. Events of the Journey

Three days' journey out the people started murmuring and complaining. They had done this repeatedly before reaching Sinai, but to do so after the marvelous experience at the mount, where they had become God's covenant people, made their sin doubly grievous. God sent fire among them as a punishment, which only ceased after Moses made a plea unto God for them. They named the place Taberah, which means "burning" (Num. 11:1–3).

Soon after this incident another spirit of discontent erupted, for the Israelites complained of having no "flesh to eat" but of having to be satisfied with manna continually. They bragged of having had fish, cucumbers, melons, leaks, onions, and garlic in Egypt, probably an exaggeration. Moses, pouring out his soul to God, begged for relief from the daily burden that had settled upon him. "I am not able to bear all this people alone, because it is too heavy for me. And if thou deal thus with me, kill me, I pray thee, out of hand, if I have found favor in thy sight; and let me not see my wretchedness" (Num. 11:14–15). In response to his plea God commanded him to appoint 70 elders to assist him, to whom God would grant a portion of his Spirit, the same Spirit that was upon Moses. This Moses did, and God fulfilled his promise. Two of the 70, Eldad and Medad, did not get to the appointed place with the others; but they also received the same Spirit as the remaining 68.

To satisfy the people God produced another miracle. "And there went forth a wind from Jehovah, and brought quails from the sea, and let them fall by the camp" (Num. 11:31). The people gathered quail for two days, as well as the night between, and began to indulge in a much-wanted feast. God's punishment for the unnecessary murmuring soon followed, for a plague was sent which took many lives. The place was named Kibroth-hattavah, "the graves of lust" (Num. 11:31–34).

From here they traveled to Hazeroth, where another event disappointing to Moses occurred, the rebellion of Miriam and Aaron. The jealousy seems to have arisen from two causes. First, Moses had married a Cushite woman, probably one of the "mixed multitude" (Num. 11:4) accompanying the Israelites. Second, they had a feeling that Moses did not have a monopoly on divine revelation. "Hath Jehovah indeed spoken only with Moses? hath he not spoken also with us?" (Num. 12:2). Was not Aaron a priest and Miriam a prophetess (Ex. 15:20)? God showed Moses to be more than a prophet, for he spoke to him "mouth to mouth" (Num. 12:6–8). As a punishment to Miriam she was turned leprous, and only at the intercession of Moses was she restored to her original condition. The whole procession was held up seven days while Miriam, sent outside the camp, became ceremonially pure (Num. 12:9–15).

3. Spies into Canaan

After leaving Hazeroth Moses and his group entered the wilderness of Paran and came to Kadesh-barnea, or simply Kadesh (Deut. 1:19; Num. 13:26), a place approximately 40 miles south and a little to the west of Beersheba. From here twelve men, one from every tribe, were sent into the land of Canaan to spy out the territory from the extreme south even to as far north as Hamath, a city in what is later to be Syria. At the end of forty days they returned, bringing not only a report of the land and of the people but also grapes, pomegranates, and figs from the valley of Eshcol ("cluster"). When the congregation was assembled, they heard the report of the spies, a unanimous one up to a certain point. All twelve agreed about the fertility of the land, even bringing proof of it in a cluster of grapes so big it had to be born on a staff carried by two men. They also agreed about the strong and fortified cities and the size of the inhabitants. "And all the people that we saw in it are men of great stature" (Num. 13:32). But when it came to the prospects of a conquest there was disagreement. Ten of the spies declared that occupation of the land would be impossible, but two—Joshua of the tribe of Ephraim and Caleb of the tribe of Judah—said that with the help of God conquest could be achieved. The people immediately sided with the ten men and against Joshua and Caleb, and a great rebellion against God took place. (In the listing of the twelve spies Joshua is called Hoshea, but Moses changed his name to Joshua, meaning "God saves," as is seen in Numbers 13:8, 16.)

4. Rebellion at Kadesh

The people cried and wept and murmured against Moses and Aaron. "Would that we had died in the land of Egypt! or would that we had died in this wilderness!" (Num. 14:2). They even suggested that they appoint a new leader to take them back to Egypt. Caleb had been the spokesman for the minority report earlier; at this time both Joshua and Caleb appealed to the people to have faith in Jehovah, that he would help them to possess it—a good land flowing with milk and honey. "Jehovah is with us: fear them not." When the congregation almost stoned them, the glory of Jehovah appeared at the tent of meeting (Num. 14:1–10).

In speaking to Moses God poured out his wrath and utter disgust upon a faithless people whose great sin was lack of faith in a God who had performed miracle after miracle in the journey thus far. The ten spies and the people saw the giants and forgot God. Caleb and Joshua saw God and forgot the giants. Caleb's words, "Let us go up at once, and possess it; for we are well able to overcome it" (Num. 13:30), demonstrated the faith that the whole group should have possessed. God offered to set them aside and make Moses a new nation greater than they; but Moses again interceded, using as his argument that if God were to wipe them out the other nations would say he did so because he was not able to bring them into the land he had promised them. "Pardon, I pray thee, the iniquity of this people according unto the greatness of thy lovingkindness, and according as thou hast forgiven this people, from Egypt even until now" (Num. 14:11–19).

So God pardoned them, but not without punishment. This faithless generation was to remain in the wilderness until all the people that were twenty years or older on leaving Egypt had died—with the exception of Caleb and Joshua. Then a new generation would go to possess the land that they had rejected. For every day the spies had been away in their venture the Israelites would wander in the wilderness; the forty days would become forty years. The ten men who brought the evil report were consumed with a plague for their special punishment (Num. 14:20–38).

When the people became stirred up by what happened to the ten and by what had been decreed for them, they mourned and confessed their sin. But evidently their repentance was insincere, since they determined to enter Canaan regardless of God's sentence of forty years of wandering. Even though warned by Moses that they would be defeated by the Amalekites and the Canaanites, they ventured forth and were beat down by these warlike tribes (Num. 14:39–45).

5. Rebellion of Korah, Dathan, and Abiram

The wilderness wanderings of 38 years begins in Judges 15:1 and goes through 19:22, for the two years leading up to the faithless demonstration at Kadesh were included in the forty years. The Scriptures do not reveal much of what happened during their wandering period, while the old generation was being replaced by the new. Just at what time the rebellion of Korah, Dathan, and Abiram took place in this period is not known, but it is another incident that added to the many anxieties of Moses (Num. 16:1–40).

Korah was of the tribe of Levi but not a descendant of Aaron; therefore he was a Levite and not a priest. It is assumed that he was jealous of the priestly line of Aaron. Dathan and Abiram were of the tribe of Reuben, the firstborn son of Jacob. Therefore it is assumed that their ill-feeling resulted from the taking of the right of the firstborn from their tribe and giving it to another. The mutiny, a cooperative effort of these two parties, was against the leadership of Moses and Aaron. They were even successful in winning over 250 princes of the people. The accusation was blunt: "Ye take too much upon you, seeing all the congregation are holy, every one of them, and Jehovah is among them: wherefore then lift ye up yourselves above the assembly of Jehovah?" (Num. 16:3). They believed that Moses and Aaron had assumed functions that should have been shared by the congregation at large.

Moses decided to let God settle the matter; so he called them all together on the morrow, including Aaron himself. The earth opened up to swallow Dathan, Abiram, and all their families; Korah also was swallowed up. Fire came forth and devoured the 250 princes. Even with all this the next day found the people murmuring against Moses and Aaron, saying, "Ye have killed the people of Jehovah" (Num. 16:41). A plague soon erupted and consumed 14,700 of the rebellious wanderers.

But God wished that the priesthood of Aaron be further vindicated, so he used a miraculous sign (Num. 17:1–11). Each tribe was to present an almond rod to Moses with the name of the tribe written on it. These were placed before the ark in the holy of holies. On the morrow it was discovered that Aaron's rod (of the tribe of Levi) had budded, bloomed, and brought forth almonds. This rod, along with the tablets of stone and the urn of manna, were placed inside the ark (Heb. 9:4). Thus Aaron's branch of the tribe of Levi was confirmed as to the priesthood, with the priests to be taken from the descendants of Aaron only. The Levites were to be servants of the priests and caretakers of the sanctuary. The Levites and the priests were not included in the allotment of land (except for certain cities); instead the Levites received the tithe given by the people and in turn gave a tithe of what they received to the priests (Num. 18:20–32).

6. Waters of Meribah

We do not know much concerning the other events of the wandering period, but Deuteronomy 8:2–6 gives a brief glimpse. When they returned to Kadesh, Moses was saddened by two incidents. Miriam died and was buried there (Num. 20:1). And again, as many times before, the people caused Moses grief. The water failed; so the people broke into murmurings as bad as their fathers had done years before at Rephidim. Moses was commanded of God to assemble the people before a rock and to speak to the rock, that it might bring forth water. He obeyed, saying, "Hear now, ye rebels; shall we bring you forth water out of this rock?" With this he struck the rock twice with his rod, and water came forth abundantly. This great error on Moses' part was threefold. First, he lost his self-control, calling the people rebels. Second, he gave himself and Aaron credit for the miracle by use of the word "we." Third, he struck the rock when he had been instructed to speak to it. For this sinful display of character God prohibited the two brothers from entering the Promised Land. They had not sanctified Jehovah in the eyes of the people. The waters were called Meribah, meaning "strife," because the people strove with Jehovah (Num. 20:2–13).

7. Death of Aaron

Moses' next move was an endeavor to secure from the Edomites (the descendants of Esau) the privilege of going through their country. This request was not only met with a direct refusal; the Edomites put a strong force guarding their country. Therefore it was necessary to strike south and then east around Edomite territory before going north into Canaan (Num. 20:14–21).

At Mount Hor, not far from Petra, the capital city of the Edomites, Aaron came to the end of his days. Moses, Aaron, and Eleazar, Aaron's son, ascended the mount, where the priestly garments were taken from Aaron and placed on Eleazar. There Aaron died and was buried, Eleazar then assuming the office of high priest. The people mourned for Aaron thirty days (Num. 20:22–29).

8. The Fiery Serpents

Even before they could leave Mount Hor the group was attacked by the Canaanite king of Arad, who took some of the Israelites captive; but God led his people to a complete victory over the Canaanites. The place was called Hormah, meaning "utter destruction" (Num. 21:1–3).

As they proceeded away from Mount Hor the Israelites again complained against God, against Moses, and against the tedious journey. Divine punishment came in the form of serpents. "And Jehovah sent fiery serpents among the people, and they bit the people; and much of Israel died" (Num. 21:6). When the people repented and came to Moses, Moses interceded with God in their behalf. God instructed him to make a serpent of brass and to place it upon

6. South end of Dead Sea near probable site of Sodom

a standard, so that all who looked upon it could be healed. If a man had been bitten by a fiery serpent, he merely looked upon the brazen serpent and lived (Num. 21:4–9).

Years later in the days of Hezekiah the brazen serpent had to be destroyed, for the people were burning incense to it. Hezekiah broke it into pieces, calling it Nehushtan, "piece of brass" (2 Kings 18:4). Jesus used this incident as a symbol of his death upon the cross (John 3:14–15).

The Israelites resumed their march, skirting Edom and traveling in a northerly direction till they encamped at the brook Zered, a stream running into the Dead Sea at its southeast corner. Then they proceeded on north till they came to the Arnon ("swift"), a rushing stream entering into the Dead Sea about halfway up the eastern side, the first river they had seen since they left the Nile. Between the Zered and the Arnon lived the Moabites, the people descendant from Lot. So the Israelites were encamped at the northern border of Moabite territory (Num. 21:10–20).

9. Defeat of the Amorites

The next two foes to be defeated were two Amorite kings: Sihon, king of Heshbon, and Og, king of Bashan. Sihon occupied all the land north of the Arnon and up to the Jabbok, a large river running into the Jordan fifteen miles north of the Dead Sea. (It was at the Jabbok that Jacob had had his memorable encounter with God and received his new name Israel.) At some previous time Sihon had defeated the Moabites, driving them all south of the Arnon. Living at his capital, Heshbon, Sihon denied the Israelites passage through his country, gathering his army instead. The battle took place at Jahaz, just south of Heshbon, where the Amorites went down in total defeat (Num. 21:21–31).

Another Amorite chief, Og, occupied all the territory north of the Jabbok, consisting of sixty cities and a rock stronghold called the Argob, "stony." Here was the capital city of Edrei, with the whole territory, from the Jabbok to the foot of Hermon, known as the land of Bashan. The Israelites attacked Og at Edrei, and he was utterly routed and his cities taken, including his capital. Then the Israelites retraced their steps and encamped in the plains

of Moab overlooking the Jordan. They were in control of vast territory with many, many cities, both fenced and unfenced, stretching
from the Arnon up to the foot of snowcapped Hermon (Num. 21:33
to 22:1).

10. Balaam and Balak

Though Israel had passed through their territory the Moabites
had remained unchanged by the Hebrew invasion. Yet they viewed
with alarm the sweeping success of the Israelites over the strong
and able kings Sihon and Og. The people of Moab said to the Midianite elders, "Now will this multitude lick up all that is round about
us, as the ox licketh up the grass of the field" (Num. 22:4). Balak,
king of Moab, in great fear sent messengers to the far north, to
Pethor by the Euphrates River, to a prophet named Balaam, that
he might come down and place a curse on the Hebrews, "for they
are too mighty for me" (Num. 22:6). Balaam was a prophet of
Jehovah, the same God the Israelites worshiped, one whose fame
had spread even to the land of Moab.

Elders of Moab and Midian went to Mesopotamia with rich gifts
in order to try to induce Balaam to do as Balak desired. Balak,
undecided as to the lawfulness of the venture, asked for a night
to determine the will of Jehovah. The answer the next day was
negative. "And God said unto Balaam, Thou shalt not go with
them; thou shalt not curse the people; for they are blessed" (Num.
22:12). When the embassy returned to Balak with this unfavorable
answer, Balak sent a second embassy to Balaam, one with more
noble princes. The prophet answered, "If Balak would give me
his house full of silver and gold, I cannot go beyond the word of
Jehovah my God, to do less or more" (Num. 22:18). Again he
asked for a night to determine Jehovah's will, and this time God
gave him permission to go but to speak only God's word (Num.
22:7–20).

On the way down to Moab a remarkable incident occurred. The
dumb beast on which Balaam was riding saw the angel of the Lord
standing in the way; and the prophet, claiming to be a powerful
seer of God, did not. Twice the beast endeavored to avoid the
angel and was twice struck by Balaam. When the beast spoke in

the accents of a man, Balaam's eyes were opened; and, being rebuked
by the angel of the Lord for his wilfulness, he proposed that he
turn back rather than displease God. But again he was permitted
to go and again was warned to speak only what God allowed (Num.
22:21–35).

Down in Moab he faithfully declared God's message four times.
On three different occasions on three different mountains Balak
and his princes prepared sacrifices of burnt offerings, each time
on seven altars. Though the Moabite king endeavored each time
to prepare an atmosphere for cursing, Balaam each time spoke words
of blessing for God's people. Balak said to Balaam, "I called thee
to curse mine enemies, and, behold, thou hast altogether blessed
them these three times. Therefore now flee to thy place: I thought
to promote thee unto great honor; but, lo, Jehovah hath kept thee
back from honor" (Num. 24:10–11). Balaam, dismissed without a
reward, uttered a fourth prophecy, pointing out Israel's future victories over Moab, Edom, and the Amalekites (Num. 22:36 to 24:25).

11. War with the Midianites

But Balaam did not return to Mesopotamia; instead he lingered
among the neighboring Midianites and counseled them to join with
the Moabites in inviting the Israelites to indulge in the festival of
Beth-Peor. This was a very degrading feast, a heathen orgy, and
participation in its hideous rites would defile the Israelites before
the Lord and bring on them a curse worse than any Balaam himself
might have effected. The Israelites fell into the snare and, coming
to the festival, defiled themselves. God, being angry, commanded
Moses that the chiefs of the people be hanged. There was also
a plague that was not stayed until 24,000 of the people had died
(Num. 25:1–9).

After a second numbering of the people by Moses and Eleazar
(Num. 26:1–51) war was declared against the Midianites. "And
Jehovah spoke unto Moses, saying, Avenge the children of Israel
of the Midianites: afterward shalt thou be gathered unto thy people"
(Num. 31:1–2). A thousand warriors from each tribe comprised the
army, led not by Joshua but by Phinehas, son of Eleazar. The
Midianites were utterly routed, and five of their chiefs, as well as

7. North end of Dead Sea with Canaan to the west from Mount Nebo

all of their mules, were slain. The cities were burnt, the women and children taken captive, and even Balaam died by the sword (Num. 31:1–12).

12. Request of Reuben and Gad

The country east of the Jordan, recently taken from Sihon and Og, was a long tableland famed for its rich pasturage. The tribes of Reuben and Gad, noted for their multitudes of cattle, requested that they be allowed to settle down there permanently. Moses suspected that the motive behind their request was to avoid fighting for the possession of Canaan. Therefore he promised them the land they requested on the condition that their armed men should cross the Jordan with the other tribes and help subdue the Canaanites west of the river; then they might return and occupy their rich pasture land. "And the children of Gad and the children of Reuben answered, saying, As Jehovah hath said unto thy servants, so will we do" (Num. 32:31). So Moses gave to Gad, and Reuben, and half the tribe of Manasseh the land formerly belonging to Sihon and Og. They settled their families in the fortified cities and then prepared to fight with the other nine and a half tribes (Num. 32:1–42)

13. Addresses of Moses

Moses was well aware of the fact that his ministry was almost complete and that he was not going to be permitted to enter the Promised Land. As their faithful leader he delivered several addresses to his people in which he admonished them to be true to the God who had delivered them out of bondage. The whole book of Deuteronomy (meaning "second law"), consisting primarily of these discourses, starts out, "These are the words which Moses spake unto all Israel beyond the Jordan in the wilderness" (1:1). Here he gave the people final and specific instructions relative to the future government of their nation. His dramatic review of the past forty years depicted to them the reasons Jehovah had not wiped them out in wrath. He reminded them that through unbelief and rebellion their fathers were denied entrance into the Promised Land and had died in the wilderness. He also reminded them of their recent victories over the Amorites and of the allotment of land to some tribes who pledged to support the rest in their future conquest. He assured them that God would grant them victory under Joshua and warned them to avoid the mistakes of their fathers (Deut. 1:6 to 4:40).

Moses' second speech was a review of the law and its significance for the people. The covenant relation was reviewed, and the Decalogue was restated. There were laws concerned with living in Canaan, and the blessings and curses of obedience and disobedience were clearly stated (Deut. 4:44 to 28:68).

Moses' third speech had to do with the final preparation of the people and his own farewell (Deut. 29:1 to 33:29). He admonished them, "Be strong and of good courage, fear not, nor be affrighted at them: for Jehovah thy God, he it is that doth go with thee; he will not fail thee, nor forsake thee" (Deut. 31:6). He then very dramatically commissioned Joshua to lead the people in the conquest of Canaan, stating that Jehovah would go before him and be with him. Chapter 32 contains what is termed the "Song of Moses," while chapter 33 contains the "Blessing of Moses." The latter contains pictures of war and victory, where Ephraim and Manasseh seem to stand in the forefront.

14. Death of Moses

Before his death, Moses was privileged to view the Promised Land from Mount Nebo, up above the plains of Moab. "And Jehovah said unto him, This is the land which I sware unto Abraham, unto Isaac, and unto Jacob, saying, I will give it unto thy seed" (Deut. 34:4). There Moses died at the age of 120, and God buried him in the valley in the land of Moab. And they wept for him thirty days. "And there hath not arisen a prophet since in Israel like unto Moses, whom Jehovah knew face to face" (Deut. 34:10).

There was never to be a man more revered in all Hebrew history than Moses. His patience, his persistence, and his unyielding confidence in Jehovah had enabled him to deal with a childlike people, a mass of freed slaves, so as to bring them to the brink of the Promised Land. His meek and unselfish giving of himself to the good of his people, even though he himself suffered thereby, enabled him stubbornly to overcome all obstacles and to open the doors of the inheritance God promised the Hebrews. His endurance and resourcefulness seem almost incredible; only a man of his greatness could have undertaken the supreme task of rescuing his people from the bondage of an Egyptian Pharaoh. His personal influence infiltrated every phase of Hebrew life, leaving an indelible stamp upon Israel's culture and spiritual fiber.

Joshua and the Conquest of Western Palestine
(Joshua)

1. Preparation for the Jordan Passage

Joshua, the son of Nun of the tribe of Ephraim, was selected by the command of Jehovah to replace Moses as the leader of Israel. Moses designated him as such before he died, at which time there was a formal "laying on of hands" by Moses in the presence of all the people and of Eleazar the priest (Num. 27:18–23). Joshua's name had already entered the picture several times during the exodus wanderings. It was he who led the Hebrew forces against the Amalekites immediately after their departure from Egypt; it was he who attended Moses during one of his ascents of the mount; it was he who was given the general oversight of the tent of meeting; and it was also he, along with the faithful Caleb, who gave the true and courageous minority report after spying out the Promised Land. Moses changed his name from Hoshea to Joshua (Num. 13:8,16).

Just as there had been thirty days of mourning when Aaron died, so there were thirty days of mourning when Moses died, after which Joshua was encouraged of God to undertake the conquest. "There shall not any man be able to stand before thee all the days of thy life: as I was with Moses, so I will be with thee; I will not fail thee, nor forsake thee. Be strong and of good courage; for thou shalt cause this people to inherit the land which I sware unto their fathers to give them" (Josh. 1:5–6). Joshua commanded a three days' preparation of food and reminded the tribes of Reuben and Gad and the half tribe of Manasseh of their promise to aid in the conquest beyond Jordan and to share in the hardships of the campaign (Josh. 1:10–18).

The first step necessary to conquering the country beyond Jordan was to capture Jericho, for this important walled city commanded the two most important passes into the central mountains beyond. Therefore Joshua sent two men to spy out the city and surrounding country. From the meadows of Acacia where the Hebrews were encamped the two men crossed the river and entered the house of a woman named Rahab, only to have their arrival there observed and reported to the king of the city. When the king immediately sent to Rahab's house and demanded their surrender, she stated that the men had escaped. Truthfully she had hid them under the stalks of flax laid out on the roof. Then she assisted the men to escape by descending the outside of the wall by a cord, for her house was built on the wall. As a reward for her kindness she was to tie a scarlet cord in the window so that the Hebrews might remember and spare her family in the impending destruction of the city. The men escaped to the mountains to hide for three days, after which they recrossed the river and announced to Joshua the utter fright of the inhabitants of Jericho. This city had heard of the victories east of the Jordan and trembled at what they knew soon would happen to them (Num. 2:1–24). After three days of ceremonial purification the Israelites were ready for the crossing.

2. Over the Jordan

It was the time of harvest, which comes about three weeks earlier in the Jordan at the plain of Jericho than in other parts of the country. The Jordan was wide, for the latter rains had just ceased. It was the tenth day of Nisan (a month corresponding to our month of April) and four days before Passover. The priests descended into the water first, bearing the ark of the covenant. Immediately the waters were cut off from about fifteen miles upstream to about five miles downstream, or to the Dead Sea. When all the Israelites had finally passed on dry ground, the priests were given the signal by Joshua to come out of the riverbed also. They obeyed and were preceded out by twelve chiefs from the twelve tribes carrying twelve stones from the bed of the Jordan. No sooner had they reached the other side than the waters rushed to their accustomed channel, and the river flowed on as before (Josh. 4:8–18). Just as God had opened the Red Sea forty years before that the Hebrews might be delivered from Egyptian bondage, at this time he pushed back the mighty Jordan that they might gain entrance into a new homeland.

On reaching the west bank of the river several significant events took place: (1) They set up the twelve huge stones brought out of the midst of the Jordan on the upper bank of the river at Gilgal as a memorial to future generations of the miraculous crossing, "that all the peoples of the earth may know the hand of Jehovah, that it is mighty; that ye may fear Jehovah your God for ever" (Josh. 4:19–24). In fact, it appears that two memorials were set up, for we read, "And Joshua set up twelve stones in the midst of the Jordan, in the place where the feet of the priests that bare the ark of the covenant stood: and they are there unto this day" (Josh. 4:9). This memorial in the bed of the river would be in addition to the one described in verses 19–24 set up at Gilgal to be used as a reminder to future generations of God's parting of the waters. (2) The rite of circumcision, long neglected during the wilderness wanderings, was performed. This was necessitated due to the dying out of all the older generation and the emergence of a new one in the desert. When this was done, God said, "This day have I rolled away the reproach of Egypt from off you" (Josh. 5:9). (3) The Passover was celebrated on the evening of the fourteenth day of Nisan there on the plains of Jericho. (4) The manna ceased on the next day just as miraculously as it had begun forty years prior to that. After they ate of the produce of the land raised by the Canaanites the heaven-sent food ceased to appear. "Neither had the children of Israel manna any more; but they did eat of the fruit of the land of Canaan that year" (Josh. 5:12). The exodus had ended.

3. The Capture of Jericho

Joshua was prepared for the conquest of the land of Canaan by an experience similar to that of Moses when God called him at the burning bush (Ex. 3). A man with a drawn sword in his hand suddenly appeared to him and declared himself to be "prince of the host of Jehovah." He said, "Put off thy shoe from off thy foot; for the place whereon thou standest is holy" (Josh. 5:13–15).

God explained to Joshua in detail how he was to capture the strategic city of Jericho, for it was not to be attacked in regular military manner. Once a day for six days the Israelites were to march around the city. On the seventh day they were to go around seven times, preceded by seven priests with the ark, each priest

8. Ruins of Jericho; excavation revealed occupation dating to about 8000 B.C.

carrying a ram's horn trumpet. When the seventh round was complete, they were to sound a blast on the trumpets and the people were to shout. When they did so, the walls came down, walls tremendously thick and very high; "so that the people went up into the city, every man straight before him, and they took the city" (Josh. 6:1–21).

The people were told to consider everything in the city as "devoted" to Jehovah. All the people and all the animals in the city were to be killed and the city burnt with fire. But Rahab and her family were to be spared, for Rahab had befriended the two spies sent out by Joshua. Also the vessels of gold and silver and of brass and iron were to be saved and consecrated to the service of Jehovah. Thus was the "City of Palmtrees" reduced to rubble and destruction. Joshua placed upon anyone attempting to rebuild the city a curse; if he set up the foundation his firstborn son would die, and if he set up the gates his youngest son would die (Josh. 6:22–26) This is exactly what happened in the time of Ahab, for a man named Hiel from the city of Bethel attempted to rebuild it. Joshua's curse was fulfilled with Hiel (1 Kings 16:34), for both Abiram, his oldest son, and Segub, his youngest son, died in the manner predicted.

4. The Fall of Ai

With Jericho out of the way the next objective of the Israelites was Ai, a city in the central highlands not far from ancient Bethel. They marched against this city of 12,000 people with an army of 3,000 men, only to suffer a severe defeat. The man of Ai chased them down the descent and slew about 36 men. This humiliation brought Joshua and the elders of Israel to their knees in utter grief and fear, but God immediately revealed the cause of the surprising defeat. "Israel hath sinned; yea, they have even transgressed my covenant which I commanded them: yea, they have even taken of the devoted thing, and have also stolen, and dissembled also; and they have even put it among their own stuff" (Josh. 7:11). It was necessary to take away the accursed thing from among them before they would be able to stand before their enemies. They had been told that none of the people were to be saved, except the family of Rahab, and that none of the valuables were to be taken by the Israelites. But a portion of the spoil had been taken and concealed (Josh. 7:2–15).

When all Israel was assembled by tribes, it was revealed that Achan of the tribe of Judah was the transgressor. He confessed that he had stolen a Babylonish robe, 200 shekels of silver, and a bar of gold weighing 50 shekels, and that it was all buried beneath his tent. A search party verified his statement. So he, his family, and all their possessions were brought to the valley of Achor and destroyed by stoning and by burning. A heap of stones was raised over the remains. Achor very appropriately means "troubling" (Josh. 7:1,16–26).

Ai was again attacked, this time more successfully. Joshua selected 30,000 men and set out from Gilgal by night. He placed about 5,000 men in ambush behind the city, between Ai and Bethel. The following morning Joshua and the remaining men marched toward the city from the north as though to attack it. When the men of Ai came out to move against them, they fled in retreat, with the enemy pursuing after them and leaving their city unprotected. Then the 5,000 men in ambush entered the city, set it afire, and started after the army of Ai. The army, thus caught between the forces of the Hebrews, was utterly annihilated. Ai was completely sacked and burned and all the 12,000 inhabitants destroyed. "So Joshua burnt Ai, and made it a heap for ever, even a desolation, unto this day" (Josh. 8:28). It appears that Bethel was also taken, and that without a fight (Josh. 8:17).

5. Ratification of the Law

The next event in Israel's history occurred between Mount Ebal and Mount Gerizim, the twin peaks of central Palestine. Ebal, about twenty miles north of Ai, was the place where the Israelites erected an altar of unhewn stones and sacrificed burnt offerings and peace offerings to Jehovah. After the sacrifice the stones were then plastered with lime and a copy of the law of Moses inscribed thereon (Josh. 8:32). By "law of Moses" the Scriptures probably mean either the Ten Commandments (Deut. 5:6–21) or the blessings and cursings (Deut. 27:15–26; 28:3–14). Joshua assembled half of the people in front of Mount Gerizim (mount of blessings) and half in front of Ebal (mount of curses), with the priests, the Levites, the ark, the elders, the officers, the judges, and Joshua himself in the valley between. When Joshua read one of the curses, the six tribes in front of Mount Ebal shouted "Amen," and when he read one of the blessings the six tribes in front of Mount Gerizim shouted "Amen" (Josh. 8:33–35).

All this took place at Shechem; for Shechem, meaning "ridge," was situated on the shoulder between Mount Ebal and Mount Gerizim, peaks about ten miles apart. Moses had commanded this verbal acceptance of the covenant before they had crossed the Jordan, giving detailed directions for all that Joshua did at Mount Ebal and Mount Gerizim (Deut. 27:1–14). The generation that accepted the covenant at Sinai had died out; it was necessary that the new generation be forcefully reminded of the covenant between God and his special people by a ceremony in which they too verbally accepted the terms of the covenant.

It was probably on this occasion that the coffin containing the embalmed body of Joseph was buried. The bodies of Jacob and Joseph were both embalmed according to the Egyptian method used for nobility. Jacob was brought home from Egypt and buried in the cave of Machpelah near Hebron immediately after his death, but Joseph was embalmed and kept in Egypt in a coffin for 400 years and carried out in the exodus under Moses. Here at Shechem was the parcel of ground that Jacob gave to Joseph (John 4:5). Before he died in Egypt Joseph made them promise to carry his bones out of Egypt. "So Joseph died, . . . : and they embalmed him, and he was put in a coffin in Egypt" (Gen. 50:25–26). And he was buried at Shechem (Josh. 24:32).

6. Deceit of Gibeon

When the news of the Israelite conquest of Jericho and Ai spread throughout Canaan, the kings of the highlands and the lowlands began to unite in order to resist them (Josh. 9:1–2). But the people of Gibeon, not wishing to join in the undertaking, decided to resort to deceit. The inhabitants of this city, located eight miles north of Jerusalem, dressed in worn-out clothing and carried dry and moldy bread as they approached Joshua, thus presenting the appearance that they had traveled for miles. They expressed their fear of Israel's God and offered to be servants, if Joshua would only enter into a covenant with them. "And Joshua made peace with them, and made a covenant with them, to let them live: and the princes of the congregation sware unto them" (Josh. 9:15). Because Israel's leaders failed to seek divine guidance they fell for the deception of their tattered visitors from the city just to the south. Three days later the Israelites, discovering they had been tricked, made the Gibeonites "hewers of wood and drawers of water unto all the congregation" (Josh. 9:21). Then another great city of Canaan came under the power of Israel, along with three other cities in league with it (Josh. 9:1–27).

7. Victory in the South

When Adonizedek, king of Jebus, heard of the destruction of Ai and the surrender of the great city of Gibeon, he immediately appealed to the kings of four other southern cities to enter into a confederacy with him to go against Gibeon. These cities were Hebron, Jarmuth, Lachish, and Eglon, all ruled by Amorite kings (Josh. 10:1–5). Since Gibeon had already made an alliance with the Israelites the men of that city appealed to Joshua for help, and that quickly. Again Joshua went up by night, having been given confidence by the Lord, and unexpectedly appeared at Gibeon. Defeating the confederate kings there he then chased them through the pass of Beth-horon (also known as the valley of Aijalon) into the foothills below. Jehovah cast down hailstones upon them, so that "they were more who died with the hailstones than they whom the children of Israel slew with the sword" (Josh. 10:11). But Joshua evidently needed more time to pursue the enemy, so he cried out in the sight of all Israel,

Sun, stand thou still upon Gibeon;
And thou, Moon, in the valley of Aijalon.
And the sun stood still, and the moon stayed,
Until the nation had avenged themselves of their enemies.

The Scriptures say that the sun "hasted not to go down about a whole day" (Josh. 10:12–13). In the lengthened afternoon the pur-

9. South end of Sea of Galilee

suit of the enemy continued without a pause.

When the escaping five Amorite kings of the five-city confederacy arrived at Makkedah, they hid themselves in a well-known cave. Learning of their whereabouts during the tide of battle, Joshua had great stones rolled to the mouth of the cave and set men to guard it. After the battle was over and Joshua and the men could return to the cave the five kings were dragged forth, killed, and hanged upon five trees until evening. The bodies were then taken down, thrown back into the cave, and sealed up for good by stones at the opening (Josh. 10:16–27). Thus ended the great battle of Beth-horon, which sealed the fate of all the other southern cities. One by one they were conquered—Makkedah, Libnah, Lachish, Eglon, Hebron, and Debir. All the territory was taken from Kadesh-barnea in the south to the plain of Esdraelon in the central section (Josh. 10:28–43).

8. Victory in the North

Jabin (the "wise") was the most powerful chief in northern Canaan, and his capital Hazor was the principal fortress in that part of the country. Hearing of Joshua's victories in the south he determined to make a last effort stand against the Israelites and gathered together into a confederacy many cities in and around that territory. Hazor was located near the waters of Merom about ten miles north of the lake of Galilee; it was near Merom that the battle took place, a complete victory for Joshua and the Israelites. The army gathered together by Jabin was characterized by an unusually large number of horses and chariots, but Joshua "hocked their horses, and burnt their chariots with fire." He destroyed all the inhabitants of Hazor, burnt the city, and took command of the cities of the remaining kings of the confederacy (Josh. 11:1–15). Israel now occupied all the country west of the Jordan from Kadesh-barnea in the south to the valley of Lebanon below Mount Hermon. The Scriptures list thirty-one kings as having been defeated by Joshua, city-kings ruling over city-states. Among these were the Hittites, the Amorites, the Canaanites, the Perizzites, the Hivites, and the Jebusites—a mixture of peoples who had migrated into this territory at some time or other in the preceding centuries. However, even though the kings were defeated, not all of the cities were captured and occupied. Joshua merely subdued the inhabitants of the land to the extent that the Hebrews could settle down in their Promised Land. Joshua 11:16 to 12:24 gives a running account of Israel's conquest of the entire land of Canaan.

9. The Allotment of Canaan

Jehovah said to Joshua concerning the territory west of the Jordan, "Now therefore divide this land for an inheritance unto the nine tribes, and the half tribe of Manasseh" (Josh. 13:7). Reuben, Gad, and the other half of Manasseh had received their portion of the land east of the Jordan under Moses and Eleazar (Josh. 13:8–33; Num. 32). Joshua and Eleazar, the high priest, made assignments of most of the territory, but to some extent strong leaders obtained certain portions for themselves. Caleb reminded Joshua that Moses had promised him the portion around Hebron; so he took a fighting force and obtained it from the Anakim. But the casting of lots was the means generally used for determining what each tribe received. Judah, the strongest tribe of all, received the south-central portion extending from the Dead Sea to the land of the Philistines. Simeon was situated southwest of Judah. Dan was northwest of Judah by the sea. Benjamin was given the territory directly north of Judah in the western highlands, but a portion smaller than Judah's. Ephraim was north of Benjamin, and half of Manasseh was in turn north of Ephraim. Issachar got the fertile plain of Esdraelon, between Galilee and Samaria. Zebulon, Asher and Naphtali were located in the far northern section, later known as Galilee. It will be noticed that Joseph's name is not mentioned; his two sons, Ephraim and Manasseh, represent him. Also, Levi's name is not mentioned; this priestly tribe was to be supported by the tithes of cattle and agricultural products of the remaining tribes. In addition, each tribe was to furnish four cities for the tribe of Levi, making forty-eight cities in all. Thirteen of these cities were for the priests; for the priests were the descendants of Aaron, who in turn was a descendant of Levi. "So they made an end of dividing the land" (Josh. 19:51).

10. A Misunderstanding

After the allocation of the newly-conquered territory the people of Reuben, Gad, and half of the tribe of Manasseh were given permission by Joshua to retrace their steps across the Jordan to their previously designated portion of the land. When they came to the river, they set up an altar, "a great altar to look upon," which was to be a perpetual witness that they were not divided in purpose and origin from their brothers west of the river. This would mark their common loyalty to the God of their nation that had delivered them from Egypt. As soon as the tribes west of the Jordan heard of the altar they misunderstood the motive of its construction, thinking it was for the purpose of sacrificing to foreign gods. So they immediately assembled themselves at Shiloh and declared war upon their eastern brothers. But they very wisely sent an embassy, composed of Phinehas (son of Eleazar) and ten princes, to Reuben, Gad, and half-tribe of Manasseh to search out their motive in the building. When the two and a half tribes heard of this accusation they were startled, maintaining their innocence in the matter and declaring that the altar was not built for sacrificing but for a memorial of their common interest and purpose. The explanation was willingly accepted, after which the two and a half tribes named the altar Ed, meaning "witness" (Josh. 22:1–24).

It is not known how long Joshua lived after the campaign to conquer the land. Joshua 14:6–12 leads one to believe that the conquest of Canaan was accomplished in about seven years. How much later his farewell address took place is unknown; but at that time he gathered all the tribes together at Shechem, the place of Joseph's burial and the ratification of the covenant. After a review of all the mighty acts of God that had made them a great nation he advised them to put away all the gods their forefathers had served beyond the Euphrates and in Egypt and to serve Jehovah. He sternly advised them to choose that day whom they would serve, "but as for me and my house, we will serve Jehovah" (Josh. 24:15). Therefore the people solemnly renewed the covenant they had previously made at that same spot, and Joshua set up a stone pillar as a memorial of their promise and wrote out the words of the covenant "in the book of the law of God." Joshua died at the age of 110 and was buried in Timnath-serah, the place he had inherited in the territory by Ephraim (Josh. 24:29–30).

The Judges and Spiritual Decline
(Judges and Ruth)

1. Dark Ages of Hebrew History

The nation that had been given the oracles of God now possessed the Promised Land. Joshua did not appoint a successor, as Moses had appointed him. Yet even during the days of Joshua much of the government was carried on by the chiefs of the tribes and by the heads of families, clans, and houses. God was their king; he manifested himself at the Tabernacle at Shiloh and revealed his will through the high priest.

Yet with all this privilege Israel was surrounded by dangers and trials. There were Midianites and Amalekites to the south and southeast. There were Canaanites in all the lowlands. The Philistines were in the southwest on the Maritime Plain. The Phoenicians were also on the Maritime Plain but to the northwest. Remnants of Jabin's confederacy still existed. The Moabites and the Ammonites were across the Jordan; and the Amorites still were to be feared, as well as the Edomites below the Dead Sea.

The few years that followed the death of Joshua might be termed "the days of the elders," a period relatively good in God's sight. "And the people served Jehovah all the days of Joshua, and all the days of the elders that outlived Joshua, who had seen all the great work of Jehovah that he had wrought for Israel" (Judg. 2:7). A later verse gives the keynote for the decline that is found in the entire period of the judges. "And also all that generation were gathered unto their fathers: and there arose another generation after them, that knew not Jehovah, nor yet the work which he had wrought for Israel" (Judg. 2:10). The period of the judges has been called the "dark ages" of Hebrew history. Since the Canaanites and all their pagan neighbors had not been fully dislodged the occupation of the land was not complete. Not only was there a constant effort for the native people to reoccupy their lost territory; there was also a constant temptation for the Israelites to appropriate the pagan gods of the land and leave the worship of Jehovah. It was a time of compromise, as well as a period of spiritual and moral decline. There is a biblical phrase that constantly recurs: "And the children of Israel did that which was evil in the sight of Jehovah." There were no great scriptural writings produced in this era, so far as we know. No great leader emerged throughout the entire period until the very end, and that one was Samuel; and he formed the transition between the period of the judges and the kingdom. Decline, disorder, and demoralization were the order of the day. The quotation "Every man did that which was right in his own eyes" (Judg. 21:25) describes the terrifying condition that existed. Even the judges themselves were not men of ideal character (except Samuel), for their many weaknesses are plainly told in the Bible.

2. Five Perils of the Period

There were five dangers confronting the Israelites at this time. The first was a military one, since all the inhabitants were not wiped out and the land completely subjugated. There was a temptation to compromise with the enemy and relax too early, rather than to conquer him.

The second danger was a social one. There was the temptation to make friends with their neighbors, then to trade with them, then to intermarry and thus lose their social identity. This would tend to reduce their feeling of a special mission to the world.

The third danger was religious in nature. The fertility cults of the Canaanites were alluring enough to ensnare the Hebrews and lead them away from a strict worship of Jehovah and an adherence to the law of Moses.

The fourth danger was a vocational one, for the switch from the nomadic life of a shepherd to that of a settled agricultural one would require adjustment in a large segment of their living.

The fifth danger was civil in nature, for some plan of governing themselves was absolutely essential. This would require experimentation in government that would of necessity involve mistakes.

3. A Recurring Scene

The book of Judges deals with certain characters that are more "deliverers" than they are "judges," for they must deliver the people from an oppressing nation before they can judge them. These judges were not successive in "ruling," as kings were; two or more may have "judged" at the same time. Also, they were provincial and not national in authority, each judge holding sway over a small territory and not over the whole land of Canaan.

A repeating sequence, or cycle, is discerned in the book of Judges, one having five phases. The story of each judge follows the same pattern. (1) The people of God do that which is evil, such as going after false gods. (2) Jehovah sends an oppressing nation to persecute and enslave them, forcing them to pay tribute. (3) The people cry out in distress and pray for deliverance. (4) God raises up a deliverer to defeat the enemy and cast off the yoke. (5) The deliverer judges the people so many years. However, it must be admitted that this sequence does not hold true for some of the judges, for whom only a verse or two is allotted in the Scriptures. Tola and Jair are in this category.

4. List of the Judges

If Ruth is not counted as a judge, there are fifteen in all: Othniel, Ehud, Shamgar, Deborah, Gideon (Jerubbaal), Abimelech, Tola, Jair, Jephthah, Ibzan, Elon, Abdon, Samson, Eli, and Samuel. Eli is also a priest as well as a judge, and Samuel is both prophet and priest as well as a judge—the greatest of them all. Even though Eli and Samuel are not mentioned in the book of Judges, but are considered in 1 Samuel 1:1 to 8:22, they are judges nevertheless. Theirs was a time of transition from the period of the judges to the kingdom.

5. Othniel and the Mesopotamians

Othniel came as the first deliverer, serving not long after the death of Joshua. This man, the nephew of Caleb, led the people to throw off the eight-year bondage to Cushan-rishathaim, a Mesopotamian king. When the people could stand the oppression no longer, they cried unto Jehovah, who put his Spirit upon Othniel. This capable man soon routed the Mesopotamians and gave peace to the land for forty years (Judg. 3:17–11).

6. Ehud and the Moabites

Moab was the next invader to cause trouble for Israel. Eglon, king of this pagan nation east of the Jordan, with the help of the Ammonites and the Amalekites was successful in capturing Jericho. For eighteen years he exacted tribute from his foothold in Israelite territory. When the people cried unto Jehovah he called Ehud, a left-handed warrier from the tribute of Benjamin, to deliver them. By delivering the tribute money himself he was successful in getting a private meeting with the Moabite king. "And Ehud said, I have a message from God unto thee. And he arose out of his seat. And Ehud put forth his left hand, and took the sword from his right thigh, and thrust it into his body: and the haft also went in after the blade; and the fat closed upon the blade, for he drew not the sword out of his body; and it came out behind" (Judg. 3:20–22). Running from the room he locked the door and crossed the Jordan, going on to the hill country of Ephraim. Here he gathered an army, went down to the Jordan, and utterly defeated the Moabites, killing 10,000 men. The land had rest for eighty years due to the work of this second judge.

7. Shamgar and the Philistines

There is only one verse about Shamgar. "And after him was Shamgar the son of Anath, who smote of the Philistines six hundred men with an ox-goad: and he also saved Israel" (Judg. 3:31). He was the third judge.

8. Deborah and the Canaanites

Jabin, the Canaanite king living at Hazor in the northern part of Canaan, with the help of Sisera, captain of his army, oppressed the children of Israel twenty years. During this time Deborah gained recognition as a prophetess in the territory of Ephraim near the cities of Ramah and Bethel. She persuaded Barak to raise an army from the tribes of Zebulun and Naphtali, which he did, with the understanding that she would go with him to war against Jabin's army led by Sisera. He collected an army of 10,000 men and took them up to Mount Tabor overlooking the valley of Esdraelon.

Sisera's army contained 900 chariots of iron. "And Deborah said unto Barak, Up; for this is the day in which Jehovah hath delivered Sisera into thy hand; is not Jehovah gone out before thee?" (Judg. 4:14). Barak descended the mount with his army, meeting Sisera on the banks of the Kishon River in Esdraelon.

The Canaanite forces were routed. The Bible seems to indicate that there was a great storm with much water in the Kishon valley, thus making the chariots of the Canaanites useless in the mud (Judg. 5:4,15,20–21). Sisera fled in confusion and was killed very dramatically by Jael, the wife of Heber the Kenite. When he fled to Kadesh in Naphtali, he was given shelter in the tent of Jael. After she fed him and he had fallen asleep she drove a pin through his head and pinned him to the ground. This is all recorded in Judges 5, a long poem called the Song of Deborah. In this song depicting the battle and giving glory to Jael, Deborah also displayed her anger at the tribes that did not come to assist her and Barak fight the Canaanites. After a continued warfare against Jabin, the land had rest forty years (Judg. 4:24; 5:31). Deborah was the fourth judge.

9. Gideon and the Midianites

"And the children of Israel did that which was evil in the sight of Jehovah: and Jehovah delivered them into the hand of Midian seven years" (Judg. 6:1). The Israelites had to flee to caves and dens in order to find shelter and escape the invaders. Not only that, the crops and the flocks and herds of the Israelites were destroyed by the ever-increasing number of Midianites, Amalekites, and "children of the east." "They came in as locusts for multitude; both they and their camels were without number: and they came into the land to destroy it" (Judg. 6:5).

When the Israelites cried unto the Lord, he sent a deliverer named Gideon, or Jerubbaal, from the tribe of Manasseh. The day God called him he was threshing wheat for his father, not on a threshing floor high on a hill, but low, in a winepress, to hide from the Midianites. The angel said to him, "Jehovah is with thee, thou mighty man of valor" (Judg. 6:12), and with this gave him a commission to deliver the Israelites from the hand of the Midianites. Upon receiv-

ing the assignment he asked from the angel a sign to verify it, whereupon the sacrifice he prepared was miraculously consumed by "fire
out of the rock" (Judg. 6:19–21). Later the Lord commanded him
to destroy the altar of Baal on his father's estate and to erect an
altar to Jehovah in its place. When the villagers became angry at
the destruction of their altar Gideon's father, Joash, defended him
and changed his name to Jerubbaal, meaning "tryer of Baal" (Judg.
6:25–32).

The Midianites were encamped in the valley of Jezreel, along
with their allies the Amalekites and the "children of the east."
Gideon assembled his army from the tribes of Asher, Zebulon,
Naphtali, and Manasseh. Asking God for a further sign of his leadership he put out a fleece of wool on the threshing floor. The next
morning the fleece was extremely wet with dew and the ground
dry. Repeating his act the following night he found later at daylight
that the fleece was dry and the ground wet (Judg. 6:33–40).

He was told by the Lord that his army of 32,000 was too large,
so he proposed to the men that all who were fearful should leave.
Twenty-two thousand accepted his offer and departed. When told
that his army was still too large, he devised another scheme to
reduce the number. The men were taken to the source of water
to drink. Three hundred took water in their hands up to their mouth,
while the rest got down on their knees to drink; Gideon took the
300 as his select group, sending the others away (Judg. 7:2–8).

As a further confirmation that he was with Gideon, God directed
him to take his servant Purah with him and descend to the camp
of the Midianites. There he overheard a Midianite relate to his fellow
a dream he had had: a cake of barley bread rolled into the camp
of Midian, hitting a tent and making it fall flat. His friend interpreted
the dream to mean nothing else than the sword of Gideon and the
defeat of their own hosts (Judg. 7:9–14).

Returning to his camp Gideon divided the 300 men into three
companies and gave to each man a horn, an earthen pitcher, and
a torch (or firebrand), with the torches under the pitchers so as
to keep down the light. Then Gideon and the 300 men crept under
cover of night down toward the enemy. At a given signal from
Gideon they blew the trumpets and broke the pitchers, thus allowing

the torches to blaze, and shouted, "The sword of Jehovah and of Gideon." The Midianites, thinking them a much larger force, ran away in confusion down toward the Jordan and crossed it into the lands beyond. Two Midianite princes were slain before they crossed the Jordan, Oreb and Zeeb, and also two kings beyond Jordan, Zebah and Zalmunna (Judg. 7:15–25).

When the men of Israel offered to make Gideon king, he refused. "And Gideon said unto them, I will not rule over you, neither shall my son rule over you: Jehovah shall rule over you" (Judg. 8:22–23). But he did make a request that they bring him the golden earrings, crescents, pendants, and such taken as spoil; and from these he made an ephod and put it in his native city of Ophrah, where "it became a snare unto Gideon, and to his house" (Judg. 8:24–27). Gideon, the fifth judge, who had many wives and 70 sons was successful in giving Israel rest for 40 years (Judg. 8:28–32).

10. Abimelech, the "Bramble King"

Soon after Gideon's death the people returned to the worship of Baal, forgetting the God who had miraculously delivered them. Gideon's son, Abimelech, by a woman of Shechem, appealed to the Shechemites with his claim as successor to his father and secured from them a political fund of 70 pieces of silver. With these he hired a band of vain men to go with him to Ophrah, where he slew all but one of his half-brothers on one stone; Jotham, the youngest, hid himself and escaped the assassin's axe. After this violent incident the men of Shechem assembled themselves and made Abimelech king (Judg. 9:1–6).

When Jotham heard the news, he spoke unto the men of Shechem the earliest parable recorded in the Bible, the parable of the "bramble king." When the trees of the forest desired one to rule over them, they approached the olive tree, the fig tree, and the vine. All were too busy. But the bramble tree would be glad to be their ruler; so the Shechemites had a "bramble king" over them. Jotham invoked God's curse upon the Shechemites for their mistreatment of Gideon's family (Judg. 9:7–21).

"And Abimelech was prince over Israel three years" (Judg. 9:22). Revolt broke out and the Shechemites rebelled; Abimelech destroyed Shechem and sowed the ruins of the city with salt (Judg. 9:23–45). When he was approaching a fortified tower within the city of Thebez, he was struck on the head by a millstone thrown from a window by a woman. Not wanting to die at the hands of a woman he asked his armor bearer to run him through with a sword, and the youth obeyed (Judg. 9:50–54). He was the sixth judge.

11. Tola and Jair

Little is said in the Scriptures concerning these two. No feats of battle are mentioned. Tola, from the tribe of Issachar, judged twenty-three years. Jair, from Gilead, judged twenty-two years. They are the seventh and eighth judges (Judg. 10:1–5).

12. Jephthah and the Ammonites

For eighteen years the Ammonites oppressed Israel, for the people served many foreign gods; "they forsook Jehovah, and served him not" (Judg. 10:6). The oppression not only was felt by the two and a half tribes east of the Jordan but was carried over into the territory of Judah, Benjamin, and Ephraim. When the Hebrews repented and put away the false gods, God was grieved for their misery (Judg. 10:6–16).

Jephthah, illegitimate son of Gilead, driven from home by his half-brothers, became a leader of outlaw forces in the land of Tob. The Israelite chiefs in Gilead requested that he lead them in driving out the Ammonites, which he agreed to do on one condition: being their head if successful in the campaign (Judg. 11:1–11).

His first step was to send an embassy to the Ammonites to discuss the matter. The Ammonites claimed the land as theirs originally, with the Israelite messengers likewise claiming it as belonging to Israel. The embassy's being unable to influence the Ammonites necessitated Jephthah to prepare for open battle; but before he embarked on his military venture he vowed a rash vow. "And Jephthah vowed a vow unto Jehovah, and said, If thou wilt indeed deliver the children of Ammon into my hand, then it shall be, that whatsoever cometh forth from the doors of my house to meet me, when I return in peace from the children of Ammon, it shall be

Jehovah's, and I will offer it up for a burnt-offering" (Judg. 11:30–31). Jephthah was so successful in battle that he conquered 20 cities with great slaughter of the inhabitants. When Jephthah returned to his home in Mizpeh, the first to walk out of his house was an only child, a daughter. Now in Israel when a person made a vow he was under obligation to keep it (Num. 6:1–21). The implication in the Scriptures is that Jephthah fulfilled his vow and sacrificed his daughter (Judg. 11:39), and this without adherence to the strict commands of the law on the subject of child sacrifice (Lev. 18:21; Deut. 12:31). Jephthah judged Israel six years and was the ninth judge.

13. Ibzan, Elon, and Abdon

Very little is said about the tenth, eleventh, and twelfth judges. The first judged Israel seven years, the second ten years, and the third eight years (Judg. 12:8–15).

14. Samson and the Philistines

The Philistines were "strangers" who had made at least three immigrations into the low country, or Shephelah, of southern Palestine. They were sea pirates establishing themselves along the Mediterranean and becoming a snare to the Hebrews even down through the reigns of Saul and David. The power of Philistia was concentrated in five cities, each set on a slight hill and each having its own king, or prince. These cities, replacing the old capital of Gerar, were united in a confederacy; they were Gaza, Ashdod, Ashkelon, Gath, and Ekron.

The oppression of the Philistines extended north to the little tribe of Dan, from which God was to send a deliverer, Samson. An angel appeared to the wife of a man named Manoah, of the town of Zorah, telling her she was to be the mother of a son. The angel, who was none other than the angel of Jehovah, even appeared to her a second time. When she called her husband, the angel gave to them a greater confirmation that God was in it all, for as Manoah's sacrifice was consumed the angel ascended toward heaven in the flames (Judg. 13:2–20). When the child was born, he was named Samson, which means either "the sunlight" or "the strong." Even before his birth his mother was informed that he was to be a Nazirite, one who should avoid certain foods and drinks and never cut his hair. (For the full requirements of being a Nazirite the reader should see Num. 6:1–21.)

The story of Samson differs from those of the other judges in that there were no princes, no battles, no tribal uprisings involved. Instead there is merely a collection of weird hero-tales having to do with Samson's dealings with the Philistines. Though his freakish acts may be somewhat inspiring to a small boy, they appear as the effects of an immature mind to the older reader. Samson is a strange and disappointing character whose exploits finally resulted in his death. In all his experiences one sees no sign of piety. He never seemed to understand the possibilities of using his great strength to become a mighty deliverer of his people.

Down in Timnah he saw a Philistine girl that he desired for a wife. Even though his parents protested such a marriage, Samson persisted in his request till they agreed; so they all went down to Timnah to arrange for the marriage. In the vineyards of Timnah Samson killed a young lion with his bare hands, but he did not inform his parents of his supernatural act. On a second trip to Timnah to claim his bride Samson saw that the bees had swarmed in the carcass of the lion; so he ate some honey and gave some later to his parents to eat (Judg. 14:1–9).

The wedding festival was to last several days, on the first day of which he put forth a riddle to his 30 Philistine "companions." Being unable to guess the riddle the 30 Philistines, by means of threat, secured the answer from Samson's wife on the seventh day. Mad at this, Samson went to Ashkelon, killed 30 Philistines, and returned with spoil with which to fulfill his vow due to the riddle (Judg. 14:10–20).

Samson returned in anger to his house in Zorah, but when wheat-harvest time came he decided to take a present and return to his wife. When he arrived, he found that his father-in-law had given her to another man and requested that Samson take her prettier younger sister instead. Again being angry Samson caught 300 foxes, tied their tails together, two by two, and with a torch between each pair sent them into the standing grain fields of the Philistines. The angry Philistines burnt Samson's father-in-law and his daughter, to which Samson retaliated by killing the Philistines with a great slaughter. Then he fled to the cliff of Etam, near Bethlehem (Judg. 15:1–8).

The Philistines asked the men of Judah to help in the capture of Samson; so 3,000 men of Judah, with Samson's permission, brought him bound with two new ropes to the enemy at Lehi. When the Philistines began to celebrate, Samson broke the ropes and killed 1,000 Philistines with a "jawbone of an ass" (Judg. 15:9–15).

Later, when at Gaza, the Philistines tried to capture Samson by locking the gate of the city, thinking to kill him in the morning. When he later found the gate closed, he uprooted gate, posts, and all and carried them to the hill outside Hebron many miles away.

Samson loved a woman of the valley of Sorek whose name was Delilah. To this woman the five lords of the five great Philistine cities offered a sizable reward if she would only discover for them the secret of Samson's strength. She begged him to reveal the mystery, but he put her off with trickery. Green withes, new ropes, the binding of his seven locks of hair to the web—all were powerless to hold him a prisoner. Finally, after three unsuccessful attempts, she found the secret of his great physical strength. "And he told her all his heart, and said unto her, There hath not come a razor upon my head; for I have been a Nazirite unto God from my mother's womb: if I be shaven, then my strength will go from me, and I shall become weak, and be like any other man" (Judg. 16:17). When she was successful in getting him asleep, she called for a man to shave his head, after which his strength left him. "And she said, The Philistines are upon thee, Samson" (Judg. 16:20). They captured him, put out his eyes, took him to Gaza, and made him grind grain in the prison house. "Howbeit the hair of his head began to grow again after he was shaven" (Judg. 16:22).

A day was fixed to honor Dagon, a Philistine god that was half man and half fish, to whom they gave the credit for the capture of Samson. In the midst of the feast Samson was brought in to make sport for the large throng gathered in the temple. There were even 3,000 clustered on the roof! Samson called unto Jehovah and prayed for a return of his strength. Taking hold of the two main pillars, he bowed himself with all his might, praying, "Let me die with the Philistines." The temple walls fell in, crushing all the assembled crowd. Samson's body, pulled from the wreckage and brought home by his family, was buried in the burial place of his father (Judg. 16:23–31). God had said that Samson would "begin" the work of delivering Israel from the Philistines, and this he did. Samson was the thirteenth judge.

15. Spiritual and Moral Degeneracy

The last five chapters of the book of Judges contain two stories that reveal to us how low the actual living conditions descended during the period of the judges. "In those days there was no king in Israel: every man did that which was right in his own eyes" (Judg. 21:25). Chapters 17 and 18 tell the story of Micah, his idols, his Levite priest, and the migration of the Danites to capture the city of Laish and rename it Dan. It is a story showing just how depraved the Hebrews became spiritually, while all the time their loyalty should have been directed to the God who had delivered them out of Egypt and placed them in a new land.

The second story, found in Judges 19—21, is that of the Levite and the crime at Gibeah. It reveals to us how low the Hebrews descended morally and ethically, being influenced by the low standards of the people with whom they were associated. Both of these accounts must be read in the Bible for a full understanding of the degrading condition of that era.

16. Ruth the Moabitess

There is a third story which has its setting in "the days when the judges judged" (Ruth 1:1) that gives a brighter glimpse; it shows that everything was not all crime, carnality, idolatry, and bloodshed. Even though it is found in a separate book of the Bible, it still has its roots in the same period as Gideon, Jephthah, and Samson. The story has been likened to an oasis in the wide stretch of moral desert we find in the period of the judges.

Due to a famine in Judah an Israelite family migrated to Moab east of the Dead Sea. There were Elimelech, Naomi, and their two sons, Mahlon and Chilion. Soon after the death of Elimelech the two sons married Moabite girls, Orpah and Ruth. After about ten years the two sons died, leaving no children; so Naomi decided to return to Judah. When the two daughters-in-law expressed a desire to accompany her home, she tried to persuade them to remain in Moab. In this she was successful with Orpah, but not Ruth; so Ruth returned with her to Bethlehem (Ruth 1:1–22).

There was in Bethlehem a man named Boaz, kinsman of Elimelech, the former husband of Naomi. Ruth requested of Naomi that she might go to the fields to glean, a privilege granted unto the poor by the Mosaic law to stave off starvation. Leviticus 19:9–10 states that the reapers of a harvest were not to "wholly reap" the corners of the field, nor "gather the gleanings" of the harvest. This was to allow the poor and the foreign to enter and to gather up the remaining bits of grain. So Ruth gleaned in the field of Boaz and secured his attention, thus bringing to her special privileges; she was to share in the provisions brought to his own laborers. Being instructed of Naomi, Ruth claimed kinship with the wealthy Boaz; nor did he seem displeased at such a thought.

According to Mosaic law if a man died childless his brother was to take his widow for a wife, and the first child born to this marriage was to be the child of the dead brother. Such an arrangement would prevent the name of the dead man from being "blotted out of Israel." This is known as the Levirate law of marriage (Deut. 25:5–6). If a man did not wish to marry under such a circumstance, he could refuse, but certain conditions were required of him (Deut. 25:7–10).

Boaz desired to marry Ruth. But not only was he not the brother of Mahlon, Ruth's deceased husband; he was not even the next of kin. That place belonged to another man. This man, refusing to redeem the land of Elimelech, and Mahlon, and Chilion, and refusing to marry Ruth, opened the way for Boaz to claim her. "So Boaz took Ruth, and she became his wife" (Ruth 4:13). The son born to them was Obed, the father of Jesse, who was the father of David the king.

Samuel and Saul
(1 Samuel 1—15)

1. Times of Transition

The times of Eli and Samuel mark an era of change from the spasmodic and interrupted leadership of the judges to the rise of a kingdom, an Israelite monarchy. Eli and Samuel, even though not mentioned in the book of Judges, are still considered as judges, although Eli is also priest, and Samuel is also both prophet and priest. The story of these two is found in 1 Samuel 1—8. (The two books of Samuel were originally one, as were also the two books of Kings. They were first divided into two in the Latin Vulgate of Jerome.)

2. Philistine Power

The Hebrew tribes were scattered and unorganized, with little connection one with another. The Philistines had not been checked by Samson's sporadic personal attacks but had pushed their boundaries and outposts up into the hill country and had made the Hebrews pay tribute. The five Philistine strongholds (Ashkelon, Ashdod, Ekron, Gaza, and Gath) were independent in themselves, but the five "lords" banded together for political and military purposes. The Philistines held the edge over Israel in that they had the secret of smelting iron, the first people to use the process in Palestine. "Now there was no smith found throughout all the land of Israel: . . . but all the Israelites went down to the Philistines, to sharpen every man his share, and his coulter, and his axe, and his mattock" (1 Sam. 13:19-20). Saul was able somewhat to check the advance of Philistia, but it was not until the time of David that they were really subdued. By conquering Edom to the south of Palestine David not only learned the secrets of using iron but secured access to the sources of iron ore in the Sinaitic peninsula. Then he gained military supremacy.

3. Eli and the Boy Samuel

Eli the priest, the fourteenth judge, was judging Israel at Shiloh, near the center of Palestine. Here was located the tabernacle containing the ark of the covenant. It was Eli's duty to oversee the sacrifices and offerings and to counsel with those who came to worship. Near the doorpost of the tabernacle he had a "seat" where he used to view the people entering to worship; especially was he there on the high days of the annual feasts. Among the worshipers were Elkanah and Hannah, the parents of Samuel, the boy who was an answer to prayer. Elkanah was a Levite from Ramathaim-zophim who had two wives: Peninnah and Hannah. This was quite unusual for a man from the ranks of the common people, for generally only kings and those of great wealth could afford more than one wife. Polygamy was not for the poor. Peninnah, who had several children while Hannah had none, taunted her rival about being childless. At the close of one of the feasts Hannah remained long in prayer, her lips moving but no sound coming forth. Weeping and praying at the same time she implored Jehovah to give to her a man-child, promising to return him to God "all the days of his life." Her further vow was that a razor should not touch his head, meaning that he, like Samson, would be a Nazirite (1 Sam. 1:9–11).

Eli, observing her and thinking her to be drunken, commanded her to put away her wine. But she immediately defended her integrity and made him realize his grave mistake, for her motive was an extremely noble one indeed. Then he answered her, "Go in peace; and the God of Israel grant thy petition that thou hast asked of him." Hannah had supreme faith that God would grant her request, for "her countenance was no more sad" (1 Sam. 1:12–18); and within a year she gave birth to a son, naming him Samuel, "asked of God." When she had weaned the boy, she brought him to Shiloh to present him, along with an appropriate sacrifice, to Jehovah. Hannah's song of thanksgiving, a very beautiful hymn, is found in 1 Samuel 2:1–10. Here in Shiloh at the tabernacle Samuel began his training under the aged Eli. "Moreover his mother made him a little robe, and brought it to him from year to year, when she came up with her husband to offer the yearly sacrifice" (1 Sam. 2:19). After this Han-

10. Ruins of Shiloh

nah gave birth to other children also.

The aged Eli had two sons, Hophni and Phinehas, men who had become so evil and so carnal that the Israelite people disliked to come to Shiloh to worship. Even when Eli charged the boys with their lustful conduct they would not change (1 Sam. 2:12–17,22–26). It was a dark day in Israel, with religion at an all-time low, for Eli's sons "knew not Jehovah." In fact they made Shiloh resemble a place of Canaanite worship, with all its baseness and degeneracy. Yet Samuel, growing up in such an environment, seems not to have been influenced by Eli's sons.

4. God's Warnings to Eli

Eli was sternly warned of God twice, first by an unnamed prophet and second by little Samuel himself. A man of God rebuked Eli for honoring his sons more than Jehovah; therefore his sons would lose their lives and another, a faithful priest, would serve in their stead. The sign unto Eli that would take place was that Hophni and Phinehas would die on the same day (1 Sam. 2:27–36).

"And the word of Jehovah was precious in those days; there was no frequent vision" (1 Sam. 3:1). But God spoke to little Samuel, giving him a message that he was reluctant to take to old Eli; this was the second warning of coming doom. One night, before it was yet light, God called Samuel. The young boy said, "Here am I," and ran to Eli, thinking him to be the one who called. But Eli advised him to go back and to lie down again. This happened two more times, but by the third time Eli realized God had a message for the boy. So he said to the youth, "Go, lie down: and it shall be, if he call thee, that thou shalt say, Speak, Jehovah; for thy servant heareth" (1 Sam. 3:9). God revealed to Samuel that he was going to perform against the house of Eli that which he said he would do, bring judgment upon the house because Eli knew the iniquity of his sons and did nothing to restrain them. The next morning Samuel was afraid to relate to Eli the vision; but Eli, surmising that God had spoken with Samuel, demanded to know all. "And Samuel told him every whit, and hid nothing from him. And he said, It is Jehovah: let him do what seemeth him good" (1 Sam. 3:18). Samuel grew; and all Israel knew that he was the prophet of God, for God spoke with him. His influence was so great that he might even be considered the leader of a religious reformation. But the influence of Eli, already weakened, became even feebler.

5. The Philistine Encounter

At this time there was an upsurge of Philistine might, as they advanced to Aphek, not far from the fortress of Jebus (later to be made into Jerusalem) and attacked the Israelites, killing 4,000 of their men. Alarmed at such a defeat, the Israelites decided to obtain the ark at Shiloh and take it into battle, accompanied of course by Hophni and Phinehas. Even though extreme fear came upon the Philistines because of the sacred object of the Hebrews, the Philistines were again victorious, this time killing 30,000 footmen of their enemy. But this was not all that put dismay into the hearts of God's people; the ark was captured and Hophni and Phinehas were killed! (1 Sam. 4:1–11).

Old Eli was sitting on his elevated "seat" awaiting news of the battle, his heart filled with anxiety because of the absence of the ark. When a runner came with the dread news of the battle, Eli fell backward from the seat, broke his neck, and died. He had judged Israel forty years. When the wife of Phinehas heard of the awful news, including the death of Phinehas and the death of Eli, she gave birth to a son and called his name Ichabod, meaning "no glory" (1 Sam. 4:12–22). Although the Bible does not mention the destruction of Shiloh, it is believed that the Philistines destroyed it at this time. Other evidence in the Scriptures point in the same direction. (See Jer. 7:12–14, as he talks four generations later.)

6. The Philistines and the Ark

The Philistines took the ark to their city of Ashdod and presented it to their chief god, Dagon. The next morning Dagon had fallen from his pedestal on his face before the ark. They replaced him in position, only to find something worse the following morning. He had fallen on his face again and his head and his hands had broken off. The men of Ashdod were also plagued with an epidemic of boils, or tumors. So they sent the ark to the city of Gath, only to have the same plague break out there. When they sent it to the city of Ekron, the people there said, "They have brought about the ark of the God of Israel to us, to slay us and our people" (1 Sam. 5:10).

Therefore the Philistines decided to return the ark to Israel. "And the ark of Jehovah was in the country of the Philistines seven months" (1 Sam. 6:1); this was time enough for suffering and death! On the advice of the priests and diviners it was sent back to Israel in a new cart drawn by two milk cows that had never been yoked, along with appropriate trespass offerings for the God of Israel that the plague might cease. The ark was taken to Beth-shemesh, meaning "house of the sun," just inside the territory of Dan. Offering the two cows as a burnt offering to Jehovah the people of Beth-shemesh rejoiced at the return of the sacred symbol. But their joy was mixed with calamity; for when some of the people profaned the ark by looking within it, they were struck dead—50,070 men in all. So they asked the people of the city of Kiriath-jearim to come and get the ark, which they did. Here it remained in the house of Abinadab until the days of David (1 Sam. 7:1-2). It would appear that it was not in public use during this time.

7. Samuel as Leader

When Eli died, the people turned to Samuel for leadership. Escaping from Shiloh, this man of God made his home at Ramah. Even though he erected here an altar to God, there is no indication that Ramah became a new religious center of the nation. The tabernacle is never mentioned in connection with Samuel. Psalm 78:60 says that God "forsook the tabernacle of Shiloh."

Samuel urged the people to renounce their devotion to the foreign gods and return to Jehovah. He called an assembly at Mizpeh, where the people said, "We have sinned against Jehovah" (1 Sam. 7:6). When the Philistines gathered their forces and marched toward Mizpeh, the people became afraid; so Samuel offered a young lamb as a burnt offering to God. "And Samuel cried unto Jehovah for Israel; and Jehovah answered him" (1 Sam. 7:9). When the Philistines drew near for an attack, God sent a thunderstorm and routed them, making the Israelites easily victorious. Samuel set up a stone to commemorate his very significant triumph and called it Ebenezer, "the stone of help" (1 Sam. 7:12). There was no trouble from the Philistines from this time throughout the remaining days of Samuel's leadership. In fact, not only did the Philistines restore many cities that they had captured from Israel; there was also peace between Israel and the Amorites. Samuel's one military conquest brought good results and distinguished his judgeship.

Samuel made a circuit as he judged Israel from year to year, doing so at Bethel, Gilgal, and Mizpeh; but the circuit always brought him home to Ramah, another place for judging. Here was his altar for the worship of Jehovah (1 Sam. 7:15–17). As Samuel began to grow old he gave to his sons, Joel and Abijah, the right of judging also, setting them up in Beersheba far to the south. But as the two sons of Eli were unlike their father, so the two sons of Samuel were the reverse of their father. They accepted bribes, judged evilly, and were held in extreme disfavor by the people.

8. The Demand for a King

As Samuel grew older and his sons became even more wicked there arose a new notion among the people. They clamored for a king, which was expressed by a delegation of the people assembled at Samuel's home in Ramah. "Behold, thou art old, and thy sons walk not in thy ways: now make us a king to judge us like all the nations" (1 Sam. 8:5). Back of the request was a fear of Philistine aggression on the part of the tribal leaders of Israel; nor could they rid their minds of the might of the Ammonites east of the Jordan. A strong king to lead their forces into battle might help tremendously.

Such a demand shocked Samuel, displeasing him greatly. He knew the dangers that would be involved in a monarchy, but he did not ignore their petition. When Samuel prayed to God, his answer was that he should listen to the people; for they had not rejected Samuel but had rejected God from being king over them (1 Sam. 8:7). God granted their request, but required that Samuel "show them the manner of the king that shall reign over them." This Samuel obeyed in a very dramatic and forceful way, for he pictured to them in concrete fashion the despotic king that would rule over them (1 Sam. 8:10–18). By the end of Solomon's reign the vivid picture Samuel presented had come to pass. In spite of Samuel's vivid portrayal the people were unchanged, so God said to the prophet, "Hearken unto their voice, and make them a king" (1 Sam. 8:22).

9. Samuel Anoints Saul

A man of the tribe of Benjamin named Kish had a son Saul, who was from his shoulders up higher than any of the people. "And the asses of Kish, Saul's father, were lost;" so he sent Saul, along with one of the servants, to find them. Finally arriving in their search at the village of Ramah, they decided to call upon "the man of God" for advice regarding their journey. Receiving directions from some young girls, they arrived at Samuel's home.

Samuel, having been foretold of God that a man from the land of Benjamin would come who would be king over Israel, welcomed Saul. He informed him that his straying animals were found but puzzled him with his further remarks. "And for whom is all that is desirable in Israel? Is it not for thee, and for all thy father's house? (1 Sam. 9:20).

Samuel prepared for Saul a sacrificial feast on the high place, with Saul in the position of honor among the thirty guests. Returning to Samuel's home the two talked, retired for the night, and arose early. Accompanying the two for a short time on their return trip home, Samuel asked that the servant be sent on ahead. Then he anointed Saul with a vial of oil as "prince" over Israel, "Jehovah's inheritance," signifying that his kingship was to be a sacred trust. He told Saul of three things that would happen to him on his way home, all three of which did occur (1 Sam. 10:2–7) and which were signs that God would be with him. With this he sent the newly-anointed young man on his way home. "And it was so, that, when he had turned his back to go from Samuel, God gave him another heart" (1 Sam. 10:9). This was Saul's first anointing as king, a private one at Samuel's home.

10. Saul Anointed a Second Time

Samuel called the people together at Mizpeh for a public confirmation of Saul's kingship; and here Saul was selected by lot from all the tribes, clans, families, and individuals gathered there. Very modestly he had hidden himself during the casting of lots but was brought out of his hiding and proclaimed king. His stature struck the people with admiration, and there was a shout of "Long live the king" that signified his acceptance by the people (1 Sam. 10:17–24). Since Israel had no capital, Saul returned to his home in Gibeah. But all was not completely serene; for we read, "But certain worthless fellows said, How shall this man save us? And they despised him, and brought him no present. But he held his peace" (1 Sam. 10:27). Saul's physical appearance, his modesty, and his self-control—at least so far evident—constitute good kingly characteristics.

11. Saul's Testing Campaign

The Ammonites, arising again from their defeat under Jephthah, furnished Saul an opportunity to vindicate his selection as king. These people, under the leadership of Nahash, had laid siege to Jabesh-gilead, a city east of the Jordan. The only condition upon which Nahash would make a covenant with the people of that city would be that the right eye of every man be put out. The inhabitants immediately appealed to Saul, who in turn appealed to all the tribes to rally to his aid; for "the Spirit of God came mightily upon Saul" when he heard of the plight of the people of the city. The tribes rallied "as one man," Israel furnishing 300,000 men and Judah furnishing 30,000, all gathered together at Bezek, not far from Jabesh-gilead. Dividing his forces into three companies, Saul made a swift night march and surprised the Ammonites in the morning hours, completely overwhelming them (1 Sam. 11:1–11).

12. Saul Made King a Third Time

Saul's victory was so great that some proposed that the few who had not acknowledged him as king at Mizpeh be put to death; but Saul refused to do so, stating that Jehovah had brought salvation to Israel that day. Samuel suggested that the people go to Gilgal, "and there they made Saul king before Jehovah in Gilgal" (1 Sam. 11:15). There were peace offerings and great rejoicings.

Samuel used this opportunity to make a farewell speech to the people he had guided so wisely (1 Sam. 12), challenging them to state any way or manner in which he had dealt with them unfairly or unjustly. With one voice they bore witness to the integrity of his public life. He then exhorted them to remain faithful to Jehovah in the years ahead. As a sign from God that they had acted wickedly in asking for a king Samuel called upon Jehovah to let it rain, and this at wheat harvest when thunder and rain seldom or never occurred in Palestine. Rain between May 15 and June 15 would truly be miraculous. At Samuel's word the sky became black, the thunder rolled, and the rain came. Again Samuel pled with them to remain faithful to Jehovah. "Moreover as for me, far be it from me that I should sin against Jehovah in ceasing to pray for you" (1 Sam. 12:23).

13. Dark Days in Israel

Saul's overwhelming popularity at the beginning of his reign seemed to indicate success, but this opportunity was soon ruined by disobedience, suspicion, and hatred. Recovering from their defeat at Ebenezer, the Philistines had penetrated to the mountains in the territory of Benjamin. Saul resolved to throw off this yoke, so he gathered an army of 3,000 men, placing 1,000 under Jonathan, his son, at Gibeah and 2,000 under himself at Michmash. With youthful ardor Jonathan attacked the Philistine garrison at Geba and put it to flight. At this the Philistines swarmed through the passes of Benjamin and put Saul to flight, who in turn retreated to Gilgal and summoned a general assembly of the nation. The Philistines meanwhile assembled their army at Michmash, quite a large one compared to the 600 men that Saul had remaining. So the Hebrews panicked, hiding themselves in caves, in thickets, in rocks, in coverts, and in pits. Some even fled across the Jordan to the land of Gilead (1 Sam. 13:1–7,15). This left the Philistines in possession of central Palestine.

There was another condition that made the situation even worse. "Now there was no smith found throughout all the land of Israel; for the Philistines said, Lest the Hebrews make them swords or spears. . . . So it came to pass in the day of battle, that there was neither sword nor spear found in the hand of any of the people that were with Saul and Jonathan: but with Saul and with Jonathan his son there was found" (1 Sam. 13:19–22). Not only did the Hebrews not have arms for war, they had even to go to the Philistines to get their agricultural tools sharpened.

It was a crisis indeed, a crisis made even worse when Samuel did not arrive at Gilgal within the appointed time, seven days. Saul, in desperation due to his scattered following and the mounting number of Philistines at Michmash, needed Samuel greatly to offer a sacrifice to God and, possibly, to obtain the divine will. When Samuel failed to arrive, Saul offered the sacrifice himself, only to have Samuel appear on the scene soon afterward with words of strong disapproval. "Thou hast done foolishly; thou hast not kept the commandment of Jehovah thy God, which he commanded thee: for now would Jehovah have established thy kingdom upon Israel for ever. But now thy kingdom shall not continue: Jehovah hath sought him a man after his own heart, and Jehovah hath appointed him to be prince over his people, because thou has not kept that which Jehovah commanded thee" (1 Sam. 13:13–14). This was Saul's first great sin, the sin that took the kingly line away from his family and placed it upon David and his descendants.

14. The Battle of Michmash

Jonathan decided to strike another blow, so he and his armor bearer descended into the ravine and climbed on hands and knees up the opposite side toward the encamped enemy lines. Rushing upon the Philistines they killed 20 men, causing fear and trembling throughout the camp. An earthquake added even more anxiety on the part of the enemy, to the point that Saul and his garrison of 600 at Gibeah noticed the confusion and the tumult and that the Philistines "melted away." Saul also discovered that Jonathan and his armor bearer were missing. Putting himself at the head of his men he led a general attack. Even the Israelites that had gone over with the Philistines and those that had hid themselves joined in the battle. Saul made a rash vow, placing a curse on anyone who stopped to eat anything that day till the enemy be conquered.

Jonathan, not knowing of his father's rash statement, ate some honey to strengthen himself. When he was advised later of what his father had done, he merely stated his regret and went on chasing the enemy. When the day was far advanced, the people took sheep and oxen as spoil from the Philistines and hurriedly ate them without draining the blood from the carcasses. This was completely against the Mosaic law, so Saul reproved them for it. When Jonathan later confessed that he had eaten honey, Saul was going to kill him; but the people rescued him, stating, "There shall not one hair of his head fall to the ground; for he hath wrought with God this day" (1 Sam. 14:45). The Philistines returned to their lowlands, but there was war between Israel and Philistia all the days of Saul.

15. Saul and the Amalekites

Saul carried out successful campaigns also against the Moabites, the Ammonites, the Edomites, the Amalekites, and the kings of Zobah. But Saul's second great sin came in connection with the Amalekites. Samuel brought him a command from Jehovah: "Now go and smite Amalek, and utterly destroy all that they have, and spare them not; but slay both man and woman, infant and suckling, ox and sheep, camel and ass" (1 Sam. 15:3). Saul gathered a force of 210,000 men and obeyed the order, except that he brought back Agag the king of the Amalekites as a trophy and also the best of the sheep and oxen, and fatlings and lambs. On his way home he erected a memorial to his victory at Carmel. When Samuel met him at Gilgal, Saul said to him, "Blessed be thou of Jehovah: I have performed the commandment of Jehovah" (1 Sam. 15:13). Samuel, with keen sarcasm about the bleating of the sheep and the lowing of the cattle, received from Saul his weak excuse, that "the people spared the best of the sheep and of the oxen, to sacrifice unto Jehovah thy God." Then Samuel angrily denounced him for his lack of obedience, saying, "Hath Jehovah as great delight in burnt-offerings and sacrifices, as in obeying the voice of Jehovah? Behold, to obey is better than sacrifice, and to hearken than the fat of rams. For rebellion is as the sin of witchcraft, and stubborness is as idolatry and teraphim." Then he announced that God had rejected him from being king over Israel (1 Sam. 15:17–23).

Saul repented and confessed his sin; and as Samuel turned to go away the king caught hold of his robe and tore it, which brought from Samuel the added remark, "Jehovah hath rent the kingdom of Israel from thee this day, and hath given it to a neighbor of

thine, that is better than thou'' (1 Sam. 15:28). Then Samuel ordered
Agag brought forth, whom he immediately slew with a sword. Samuel
left for Ramah, seeing Saul no more till the day of his death. "And
Jehovah repented that he had made Saul king over Israel'' (1 Sam.
15:35). Samuel grieved for Saul, but God gave him the honor of
being the one to anoint Saul's successor.

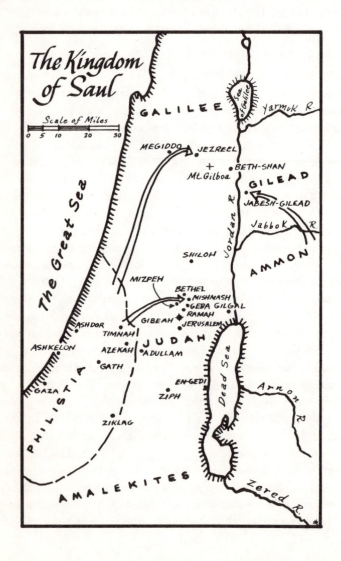

David and the Empire
(1 Samuel 16—2 Samuel 24)

1. Samuel Anoints David

David is introduced to the reader in 1 Samuel 16, and after this his life is closely interwoven with Saul's until the death of Saul on Mount Gilboa. Being told of God to take a vial of oil and go to Bethlehem to anoint another king from among the sons of Jesse, Samuel feared a reprisal from Saul. God told him to take a heifer to sacrifice, that this might be the apparent reason for his visit.

As seven of the sons of Jesse were brought before him, beginning from the eldest on down, God revealed to him that the king was to come from none of these, "for man looketh on the outward appearance, but Jehovah looketh on the heart" (1 Sam. 16:7). When Samuel asked if there were any others, he was told that the youngest was looking after the sheep. So Jesse sent and brought him in. "Now he was ruddy, and withal of a beautiful countenance, and goodly to look upon. And Jehovah said, Arise, anoint him; for this is he." Samuel did so, " . . . and the Spirit of Jehovah came mightily upon David from that day forward." And Samuel returned to Ramah (1 Sam. 16:6–13). This private anointing, all unknown to Saul, was to be followed by two public anointings later at Hebron. Jesse was the son of Obed, who was the son of Boaz and Ruth the Moabitess; so David came from a leading family of the tribe of Judah and might be called "the Benjamin of Jesse's house." His name means "beloved."

2. David at Saul's Court

Saul's rejection proved a great blow to the king; and even though allowed to rule his people till his death, his last years were tragic indeed. Immediately after learning of his rejection there is a significant verse. "Now the Spirit of Jehovah departed from Saul, and an evil spirit from Jehovah troubled him" (1 Sam. 16:14). He became moody, being affected by some sort of madness and subject to fits of frenzy. His servants advised that one skillful on the harp be procured to play for him at such times, and the suggestion pleased Saul. David was the one selected and was sent immediately by Jesse to Saul. "And David came to Saul, and stood before him: and he loved him greatly, and he became his armorbearer." The whole venture worked; "so Saul was refreshed, and was well, and the evil spirit departed from him" (1 Sam. 16:14–23). It seems that Saul was not aware that this lad had already been anointed to succeed him.

3. Goliath and the Philistines

Apparently David returned home to his old occupation of sheep-tending, and it could be that it was during this span of his life that he slew the bear and the lion (1 Sam. 17:34–36). At any rate, God prepared him on the bleak hills of Bethlehem for the trying years ahead when he would be ruling over the Hebrew nation. A very dramatic incident occurred that brought David back into the limelight and that caused Saul to change his attitude toward him. Again the Philistines gathered their forces for war against the Israelites, the armies set in battle array over against each other. The champion of the Philistines was Goliath of Gath, a man of enormous height and size and clad in complete armor of great weight. "The staff of his spear was like a weaver's beam." This man openly defied any one man of the Hebrew army to personal mortal combat, with the outcome to determine which people would be supreme. Even Saul was afraid to accept the challenge, and the challenge had continued for forty days.

This was the situation one morning when David, now grown older, entered the camp of the Israelites, having been sent by Jesse to take grain and loaves to his three oldest brothers in Saul's army. He heard the entire story, including Goliath's challenge and Saul's promised reward to the Israelite subduing him. David's offer to fight the giant finally reached Saul's ears, and he was brought into the king's presence. Saul made David try on his own armor; but he put each piece off, for he said he had "not proved them." Instead he selected five smooth stones from the brook and approached Goliath. The Philistine heaped upon young David both cursing and sarcasm, but David declared that he came to him "in the name of Jehovah of hosts, the God of the armies of Israel, whom thou hast defied. This day will Jehovah deliver thee into my hand; and I will smite thee, and take thy head from off thee; and I will give the dead bodies of the host of the Philistines this day unto the birds of the heavens, and to the wild beasts of the earth; that all the earth may know that there is a God in Israel" (1 Sam. 17:45–46). With this David ran to meet the giant, and using only a stone and a sling he sank the stone deep in the forehead of his defiant enemy. Running to Goliath he drew Goliath's huge sword and cut off his head. This put the Philistines to flight, to be utterly defeated by the Israelites. If the Philistines were defeated at Michmash because of Jonathan, they were defeated here because of David.

Strange as it may seem, Saul did not recognize David, and even Abner his general did not know him. David revealed to Saul his identity, and Saul put him in a place of responsibility in his army. The women of Israel sang a disturbing song:

> Saul hath slain his thousands,
> And David his ten thousands.

With this Saul's anger and jealousy mounted, and he eyed David in a different light "from that day and forward" (1 Sam. 18:1–9).

4. David's Relation to Saul

Saul's jealousy increased, as did his attempts to either kill David or have him killed. The very day after the lilting song of the women Saul threw a spear at David, but David escaped. Saul also sent David upon a raid among the Philistines. "Now Saul thought to make David fall by the hand of the Philistines" (1 Sam. 18:25). Saul even commanded Jonathan and all his servants to slay David (1 Sam. 19:1). And David could have easily slain Saul twice in the years that he was forced to flee from the king, but he refused to do so.

As the rift between Saul and David became deeper, the bond between Jonathan and David became firmer. They made a covenant between them, a vow of undying friendship, for "Jonathan loved him as his own soul" (1 Sam. 18:1,3). Saul promised David his daughter Merab for a wife, but when the time came for marriage he gave her to another. Then he offered David Michal, his second daughter, whom David married. "And Michal, Saul's daughter, loved him" (1 Sam. 18:27). And the love of Jonathan and Michal for David was matched by the people, for "all Israel and Judah loved David; for he went out and came in before them" (1 Sam. 18:16). Due to Jonathan there was a partial reconciliation between Saul and David, and David returned to Saul's presence. But it was not for long, for again Saul threw a spear at David, only to have David again escape. The next day Michal helped David escape from Saul's messengers (1 Sam. 19:7–17), and David fled to Samuel to confer with the prophet. David and Samuel went to Naioth and dwelt there for a while, along with Samuel's school of the prophets.

5. David's Outlaw Life

When one refers to this period of David's life when he was fleeing from Saul as his "outlaw" life, it must be remembered that he was fleeing not from justice but from injustice. Saul's jealousy increased in scope to the point that it would engulf David.

David and Jonathan met again and renewed their covenant but decided it would be best for David to stay out of Saul's reach, so he fled to Nob, to Abimelech the priest, who befriended him. Then he fled to Achish, king of Gath, of the city of Goliath whom he had slain. From here he escaped by acting as though he were mad. Then he took refuge in the cave of Adullam in the hills of Judah, where his brothers and all his father's house joined him. Here he amassed a following of 400 men. Then David went to Mizpeh of Moab; but, being advised by the prophet Gad to get back into the land of Judah, he returned to the forest of Hereth (1 Sam. 20:1 to 22:5).

When Saul heard that Abimelech the priest had befriended David at Nob by furnishing him food and the sword of Goliath, he had Abimelech and all the priests of Nob killed—eighty-five in all. Then he had all the other inhabitants of the city killed also (1 Sam. 22:6–19). Hearing that the Philistines were raiding Keilah on the border, David and his men charged against them and defeated them, rescuing the men of Keilah. When Saul endeavored to capture David within this walled city, Gad warned David, so that he and his 600 men escaped to the wilderness of Ziph. Here Jonathan visited David, so that they were able to renew their brotherly covenant (1 Sam. 23:1–18). The Ziphites, volunteering to help Saul capture David, pursued him to the wilderness of Maon; but Saul, having David just about surrounded, received a call to return and ward off a raid of the Philistines. This gave David a chance to escape to Engedi, a small oasis on the western shore of the Dead Sea. In a large cave at Engedi David could have easily killed Saul, but he refused to do so; for Saul had taken refuge in the same cave as that sheltering David and his men (1 Sam. 23:19 to 24:7). The next morning David revealed to Saul that he could have taken his life, whereupon Saul was penitent and deeply affected and acknowledged that David would be his successor. He also made David promise not to destroy his name out of his father's house (1 Sam. 24:8–22).

About this time the aged prophet Samuel died, was lamented by all Israel, and was buried in his house at Ramah (1 Sam. 25:1). Thus passed on a great man, one who was judge, priest, and prophet at one and the same time. He had anointed the first two kings of Israel and thus had seen the passing of the period of the judges and the beginning of the monarchy. He also saw the passing away of Shiloh as the place of worship and the start of a new order of priests located at various cities throughout the land. His schools of the prophets brought a new day to prophecy in Israel.

David married Abigail of Carmel, widow of a sheep-master named Nabul, meaning "fool." Nabul lived up to his name; for David tried to befriend him, expecting only some wool for guarding his sheep and goats. But Nabul insulted David's messengers sent at sheep-shearing time, and only Abigail with her fine diplomacy saved the day for Nabul. When Nabul died ten days after he had suffered a stroke, David took her for his wife. David also married a woman named Ahinoam; but he no longer had Michal, for Saul had given her to another man (1 Sam. 25:2–44).

David next went to the hill of Hachilah, where he had another chance to kill Saul but refrained from doing so. When Abishai, David's nephew, wanted to run a spear through the sleeping Saul, David said, "Destroy him not; for who can put forth his hand against

Jehovah's anointed, and be guiltless?'' (1 Sam. 26:9). Saul later acknowledged his guilt and blessed David.

6. David Among the Philistines

In desperation to escape the jealousy of Saul, David even resorted to living in the land of the Philistines. Achish, king of Gath, gave him and his 600 men the border city of Ziklag. Living here for a year and four months, David and his men made raids on the people to the south who roamed the desert plateau. Achish, thinking these raids were upon southern Judah, was convinced of David's loyalty to the point that he made him captain of his bodyguard (1 Sam. 27:1–12).

During this time the Philistines again gathered their forces to fight against Israel, and Achish started out with his army toward Aphek in the valley of Jezreel, which is the same as the plain of Esdraelon. David consented to take his 600 men and accompany him, but along the way the Philistine chiefs suspected David's loyalty and convinced Achish to send him back to Ziklag. When David arrived home he found that the Amalekites had raided and burnt Ziklag, had taken their wives and their children, and had escaped to the south. Receiving divine approval to pursue them, David and his men headed south, overtook the raiders, and utterly defeated them. ''And David recovered all that the Amalekites had taken; and David rescued his two wives,'' as well as the wives and children of his men and all the spoil that had been taken. Arriving back at the former site of Ziklag he proceeded to send throughout all the cities of Judah portions of the spoil he had collected from the defeated Amalekites—''a present for you of the spoil of the enemies of Jehovah'' (1 Sam. 30:1–31). Thus David was able to repay the kindness of many of his own tribe, those who had befriended and protected him during the long period of his wanderings.

7. Saul and the Witch of Endor

Saul's unhappy situation grew worse, climaxing with his tragic death on Mount Gilboa. Instead of constructive planning for his kingdom and the constant pursuit of his enemies he was more interested in endeavoring to capture David. Added to this was the gradual transfer of the national sympathy for Saul to young David.

The Philistines amassed their army, chariots and all, at Shunem in the plain of Esdraelon, while Saul amassed his army on the opposite heights of Mount Gilboa. Discouraged by the immense size of the Philistine host compared to his own pitiful following, he inquired of Jehovah what to do; but "Jehovah answered him not, neither by dreams, nor by Urim, nor by prophets" (1 Sam. 28:6). As a final resort he made a visit, accompanied by two of his men, seven or eight miles across enemy lines to the witch of Endor, a woman with "a familiar spirit." Since Saul had endeavored to run such out of his kingdom it was necessary that he disguise himself for his visit.

The thing that happened at Endor was very strange, for the woman said, "Whom shall I bring up unto thee? And he said, Bring me up Samuel. And when the woman saw Samuel, she cried with a loud voice; and the woman spake to Saul, saying, Why hast thou deceived me? for thou art Saul" (1 Sam. 28:11–12). Saul, assuring her of no harm, proceeded to converse with Samuel. Here he learned from the old prophet that the next day was to be for him one of doom; for Samuel informed him, "Jehovah will deliver Israel also with thee into the hand of the Philistines; and tomorrow shalt thou and thy sons be with me" (1 Sam. 28:19). This crushing news made Saul fall full length upon the earth, with no strength left in him. Though he had not eaten for a day and a night they had to persuade him to eat the meal the woman prepared for him. All three ate and returned to their camp on that dismal night.

8. The Death of Saul

The battle, taking place the following day on Mount Gilboa, was a victorious one for the Philistines. Three sons of Saul, including Jonathan, were slain, and Saul "was greatly distressed by reason of the archers." Asking his armor bearer to thrust him through with his sword, he was refused; so he fell upon his own sword and died, with the young man doing likewise. The rout of the Israelites was complete, even to the point that the Philistines crossed the Jordan, occupying cities on both sides of the river (1 Sam. 31:1–7).

When the Philistines discovered the bodies of Saul and his sons, they cut off Saul's head and sent his armor back to their temple of Ashtaroth as a trophy. They took the bodies of the four men and fastened them to the wall of the Canaanite city of Beth-shan just west of the Jordan. On the opposite side of the river was the city of Jabesh-gilead, the very city that Saul had rescued from the Amalekites early in his kingly career. The men of this city crossed the Jordan in the darkness of the night, got the bodies, and returned home. There they burnt the bodies and buried the bones under a terebinth in their native town (1 Sam. 31:8–13).

This was the news David received at the ruins of Ziklag from a young Amalekite who had been present at the battle. Bringing Saul's crown and bracelet, he pretended to have slain Saul at Saul's request. David ordered his immediate execution for killing "Jehovah's anointed." Then he expressed his grief by composing an elegy in honor of Saul and Jonathan (2 Sam. 1:1–27).

9. David Anointed at Hebron

Although Saul was God-chosen and anointed by Samuel, the prophet and spokesman of God, he never quite realized the importance of obedience in the sacred trust given him by God as the ruler over his people. With the start of David's reign and continuing through that of Solomon the golden age of Israel's history stood out, an age never duplicated at any later time. In fact, later prophets looked back on the Davidic kingdom as the ideal period of Hebrew history and looked forward to its glorious return with the future coming of the Messiah.

David, beginning his reign with the small kingdom of Judah, had previously been anointed by Samuel at Jesse's home in Bethlehem. Now seeking and receiving God's will, David went up to Hebron, accompanied by his men and their households and by his two wives, Ahinoam and Abigail. "And the men of Judah came, and there they anointed David king over the house of Judah" (2 Sam. 2:1–4). This public anointing was David's second time to be declared king. "And the time that David was king in Hebron over the house of Judah was seven years and six months" (2 Sam. 2:11).

Of the family of the late king Saul, son of Kish, there remained only two people: Ishbosheth, his youngest son, and Mephibosheth, his grandson, lame son of Jonathan who was five years old. Ishbosheth took the throne of Israel in place of his father and established his capital at Mahanaim, meaning "two hosts," a city east of the Jordan. Supported by Abner, Saul's general, he ruled over Israel two years, beginning at the age of forty years (2 Sam. 2:10).

10. Strife Between Israel and Judah

The first battle between the armies of the two kings took place at Gibeon in the territory of Benjamin, with Abner the general for Israel and Joab the general for Judah. With Joab were his two brothers, Abishai and Asahel, all three of them nephews of David the king by his sister. The battle was opened by a duel between twelve select men from each side, all of which were killed. Then the troops of Abner were routed and defeated by Joab's army, with Asahel being slain during the course of the fighting by Abner himself. When Asahel was pursuing Abner, the latter begged him to cease; but he would not do so. So Abner killed him, thus bringing upon himself the anger of both Joab and Abishai. The men of Benjamin rallied around Abner and saved him, thus freeing him to return to Mahanaim the capital.

The strife between the two kingdoms continued, "and David waxed stronger and stronger, but the house of Saul waxed weaker and weaker" (2 Sam. 3:1). Abner was definitely the dominant man in Israel, though Ishbosheth ("man of shame") was king; and Ishbosheth turned against the very man he needed most. Abner took Rizpah, former concubine of Saul, which, according to the view of the people of the Near East of that day, almost amounted to treason. Angrily Ishbosheth rebuked Abner; so the latter threatened "to transfer the kingdom from the house of Saul, and to set up the throne of David over Israel and over Judah, from Dan even to Beersheba" (2 Sam. 3:10). Abner sent messengers to David, asking that they make an agreement whereby Abner would help David bring all Israel under his rule. David agreed to it on one condition, that Abner return to him Michal, the daughter of Saul who had been given by her father to another even though married to David. Michal was returned to David, so Abner proceeded to put his plan in effect by rallying the elders of Israel and by going

to visit David at Hebron, taking 20 men with him. David made
for them a feast, and after Abner had agreed to swing Israel over
to David's side, the men departed for home. When Joab returned
to Hebron and learned that Abner had been there to see David
and had departed, he called him back and murdered him in the
gate of the city, holding Abner responsible for the death of his
brother Asahel. For this treacherous act David rebuked Joab and
put a curse on his descendants. He said unto his servants, "Know
ye not that there is a prince and a great man fallen this day in
Israel?" (2 Sam. 3:38).

Not long after this incident Ishbosheth was murdered in bed by
two of his captains, Baanah and Rechab, who ran to Hebron hoping
to be rewarded by David for removing his rival at Mahanaim. Instead
David rebuked them and had them executed immediately (2 Sam.
4:1–12).

11. King Over Judah and Israel

After ruling at Hebron for seven and a half years over Judah
alone, David was anointed at Hebron again (his third anointing)
and began his reign over both Israel and Judah. A group from all
the tribes of Israel came to Hebron and offered him the crown,
so the third anointing for David took place with much rejoicing.
His band of 600 loyal men grew into an army, for he received 300,000
fighting men from Israel. There was a three-day festival celebrating
his coronation (2 Sam. 5:1–5).

12. Jerusalem, the New Capital

David needed a better site for a capital, since Hebron was not
easily fortified and was not centrally located. Jebus, the city of
the Jebusites, was ideal for a controlling city, as well as being on
the border of his own tribe Judah and that of Benjamin. David
declared that the man who led in its capture would be his commander-
in-chief. "And Joab the son of Zeruiah went up first and was made
chief" (1 Chron. 11:6). So David captured the citadel, built on a
rocky mass, with the Kidron, Hinnom, and Tyropoen valleys on
three sides, and saved all the inhabitants. It became known as Zion,
or the city of David, or Jerusalem. The city grew to the north and

west, but the southeast corner was the old fortress. It then became David's capital, where he ruled for thirty-two and a half years and became greater and greater (2 Sam. 5:6–10). This city was destined to play from this moment on an important part in the history of the Hebrew nation and to be enshrined in the hearts of thousands of people who have never seen it, even down to the present day. It became known as the "Holy City."

13. The Ark to Jerusalem

David realized that the only way his nation could endure would be to have a strong center for the worship of their God, Jehovah. The ark, which symbolized the presence of Jehovah, had been located for twenty years at Kiriath-jearim in Judah at the home of Abinadab (1 Sam. 7:1–2). David went to get the ark to bring it up to Jerusalem, having it placed on a new cart drawn by oxen and driven by Uzzah and Ahio, sons of Abinadab. The ark was not carried by the Levites with long staves through the rings of the ark, as required by the Mosaic law.

Great rejoicing accompanied the moving of the ark to Jerusalem till one tragic moment. The oxen stumbled; and when Uzzah put forth his hand to steady it, he fell dead. David became afraid and said, "How shall the ark of Jehovah come unto me?" (2 Sam. 6:9). The Mosaic law, however, said that the Kohaths that bore the ark should not touch it; "but they shall not touch the sanctuary, lest they die" (Num. 4:15). Resolving to take the ark no further at that time, David had it carried aside to the house of Obed-edom, where it remained three months. At the end of this time David, the Levites, and Zadok and Abiathar, priests of the Aaronic family, went to get it and bring it to Jerusalem to place it in a new tabernacle that David had built. The procession was led by David himself, with singing and dancing. This time the ark was being carried by the Levites by the staves in the sides. When it was placed in the new tabernacle, sacrifices were made and the people dismissed to their homes. When David had passed by the apartment of Michal, she deemed his dancing undignified, "and she despised him in her heart." When he returned to meet her, she taunted him; so he placed on her the curse of childlessness. "And Michal the daughter of Saul

11. **Excavating lower walls of old city of Jerusalem**

had no child unto the day of her death" (2 Sam. 6:1–23).

14. A Refusal and a Promise

It was David's desire to build a great temple for the worship of Jehovah, saying to Nathan the prophet, "See now, I dwell in a house of cedar, but the ark of God dwelleth within curtains" (2 Sam. 7:2). As soon as David had become well established in Jerusalem Hiram, king of Tyre, sent to him workmen and materials, including cedar, for constructing a palace (2 Sam. 5:11). Now he wanted God's house to be more ample and permanent. This desire received God's approval, and David even made ready for the building; but God would not let him build it, reserving this work for his son Solomon. "But God said unto me, Thou shalt not build a house for my name, because thou art a man of war, and hast shed blood" (1 Chron. 28:3). Solomon was to have this privilege instead.

But this refusal, making David's heart heavy, was accompanied by a promise that should have brought him joy. God announced through Nathan that his dynasty would be permanent, that the mercy of Jehovah would not be taken from him as it had been from Saul. A son would carry on his work. "He shall build a house for my name, and I will establish the throne of his kingdom for ever." David's line would not cease, for God promised him, "Thy throne shall be established for ever" (2 Sam. 7:1–17).

Immediately after this David uttered a long and humble prayer to God, one filled with thanksgiving and praise and magnifying the names of God. A reading of this remarkable prayer gives insight into the real character of Israel's king (2 Sam. 7:18–29).

15. David's Foreign Conquests

David began a series of campaigns aimed at the conquest of surrounding nations. (1) On the southwest he attacked and conquered the Philistines, even capturing the city of Gath. (2) Then he conquered Moab east of the Jordan and put many to death. (3) Next he went to the northeast and conquered Hadadezer of Zobah, defeating him severely. (4) When the Syrians to the north came to the aid of Hadadezer, David defeated them also, they too losing

many men. (5) On the south were the Edomites, where David placed
garrisons and became master of the eastern arm of the Red Sea.
(6) The Ammonites were east of the Jordan and north of Moab.
Nahash, king of the Ammonites, had befriended David. At his
death David endeavored to have the same good relationship with
Hanun, the new king. Instead David's ambassadors were ill treated;
whereupon David sent Joab to attack the sons of Ammon. The
Ammonites secured Syrians as mercenaries; so Joab sent his brother
Abishai to confront the Ammonites while he himself confronted
the Syrians. The brothers were successful, David himself getting
into the fray before it was over. The next year Joab again started
out against the Ammonites, accompanied by the ark and its Levitical
guard. Driving the Ammonites into their citadel and capital, Rabbah,
he laid siege to it, continuing in this endeavor for almost two years.
Finally the citadel was taken, David himself also assisting, after
which the inhabitants were cruelly killed. (All these conquests are
recorded in 2 Sam. 8:1–14; 10:1–19; and 12:26–31.) With these many
wars complete David was master of all the territory from the
Euphrates River on the north to Egypt on the south, and from the
Mediterranean on the west to the desert on the east—a kingdom
of some 50,000 square miles. The international respect that David
established for Israel went unchallenged by other powers till near
the end of Solomon's reign, the next king.

16. David's Grievous Sin

At one time during the siege of Rabbah, capital of the Ammonites,
David tarried behind at Jerusalem and here committed his double
sin of adultery and murder. David found the enemies within himself
even harder to overcome than those on the battlefield. Arising from
his bed one evening and walking upon his roof he observed a woman
very beautiful to look upon. He inquired of her and found that
she was the wife of Uriah the Hittite, who was fighting with Joab
at Rabbah. Sending for the woman, he committed adultery with
her, learning before very long that by that very act she had become
pregnant. Trying a scheme whereby Uriah would think the child
was his and having his attempt at deceit to fail, David resorted
to a more drastic measure. He sent a note to Joab by Uriah himself

saying, "Set ye Uriah in the forefront of the hottest battle, and retire ye from him, that he may be smitten, and die" (2 Sam. 11:15). Joab obeyed, and Uriah was consequently killed, not knowing of his wife's dishonor. After Joab sent word to David that the act was complete, David took Bathsheba as one of his wives. In an ordinary Oriental court such a thing would not be unusual; here in Jerusalem, the center of Jehovah worship, it was entirely a different matter, for "the thing that David had done displeased Jehovah" (2 Sam. 11:1–27).

God's reply to David was through a parable voiced by Nathan the prophet, the one who had proclaimed to him that his house would continue forever. It was the parable of the rich man and the poor man's little ewe lamb. David's wrath burnt deeply; he decreed the death penalty for the rich man and the fourfold replacement of the poor man's property. "And Nathan said to David, Thou art the man" (2 Sam. 12:7). This stinging remark was followed by a sermon just as sharp in which David learned that evil was to rise up against him from within his own house and that the sword should never depart from his house. He also was told that he himself would not die but that the child born to Bathsheba would die (2 Sam. 12:7–15). David confessed his sin, saying "I have sinned against Jehovah" (2 Sam. 12:13). It is believed that he wrote Psalm 51 on this occasion, which is the classic expression of the guilty sinner pleading for forgiveness. Some think that he wrote Psalm 32, a marvelous statement about the blessing of having been forgiven, after God forgave him.

The child born to Bathsheba became ill, lingered for awhile, and then died on the seventh day. David was so grieved for the child while it was sick that the men of the court feared to tell him of its death. David, however, accepted the death graciously, saying, "Can I bring him back again? I shall go to him, but he will not return to me" (2 Sam. 12:15–23). Later his wife Bathsheba gave him a second son, whom David named Solomon, "peaceful one."

In the meantime Joab, commanding David's army, succeeded in utterly defeating the Ammonites and capturing the lower town of Rabbah. David later came to his aid, helping him to capture the fortress itself. This made David's conquests complete and thereby raised his empire to the highest point of expansion yet attained; it now reached the limits foretold to the patriarch Abraham.

17. Domestic Trouble

According to the Old Testament David had nine wives and eighteen children. Since some of these wives were foreigners and since there were many half brothers and sisters, there was a great occasion for family feuds and factions. David's own example of lack of restraint did not help to bring moral stability to his large family.

David's son Amnon became infatuated with his half sister Tamar, whom he forced into the sin of fornication. Amnon, feigning to be sick, asked that Tamar be allowed to come and prepare his food. The request was granted, and Tamar was dishonored by her brother. Then Amnon hated her as much as he had previously loved her. Absalom, another of David's sons and full brother to Tamar, later had Amnon murdered at a sheepshearing festival. David first heard that Absalom had "slain all the king's sons," and there was "not one of them left" (2 Sam. 13:30), but he was later informed otherwise. Absalom fled to the court of Talmai, his grandfather, king of Geshur, where he remained three years.

David grieved for Absalom and longed to go to him, even though his crime deserved punishment. Joab finally succeeded in getting the king's permission for Absalom to return to Jerusalem; but even then David refused to see him, and it was not until two years later that he was permitted to come into the king's presence. This too was effected by Joab (2 Sam. 13:1 to 14:24).

18. Absalom's Rebellion

No sooner was Absalom ("father of peace") restored to the king's favor than he began to plot against his father. His two years of being practically exiled in Jerusalem had produced a growing resentment against David. He was not only young and handsome beyond compare in Israel; he was the next legal heir to the throne. He prepared a chariot and horses and fifty men to run before him, as well as setting up his stand by "the way of the gate." Here he dealt with people coming from the tribes of Israel for advice and for justice. Before long "Absalom stole the hearts of the men of Israel" (2 Sam. 15:6); within two years he perceived that the time for the revolt was at hand.

With the pretence of going to Hebron to worship he secured from David permission to leave and go to this old capital of his father, accompanied by 200 men of Jerusalem who knew nothing of Absalom's scheme. Here he called to his side Ahithophel, David's counselor. "And the conspiracy was strong; for the people increased continually with Absalom" (2 Sam. 15:12). Absalom even sent spies throughout the land to proclaim that he would be made king at the sound of the trumpet blast. The rebellion was a complete surprise to David, who, being unprepared to resist, marched out of Jerusalem with a great following and passed over the brook Kidron toward the city of Mahanaim beyond the Jordan. Not only did he send Zadok and Abiathar, the priests, back to Jerusalem with the ark; he also asked Hushai, a friend and counselor, to remain in Jerusalem and counteract the counsel Ahithophel might give to Absalom. When Absalom entered Jerusalem, Ahithophel advised him to pursue after David immediately, while he was weak and unprepared. Hushai was asked of Absalom to give his advice, which was that the new "king" prepare himself more adequately to attack David, that David and his men were mighty warriors. The scheme worked, and Hushai's advice was accepted, thus giving David more time to gather his forces. Ahithophel, embarrassed over having his counsel turned aside, hanged himself (2 Sam. 17:1–23).

19. Absalom's Defeat and Death

David led his following to the city of Mahanaim, where he set up his headquarters. Here Joab mustered an army and prepared to meet the advancing forces of Absalom. Absalom made Amasa, a nephew of David's, his commander in chief. The aged David wanted to lead the army himself, but Joab persuaded him otherwise. The forces of Absalom, no match for Joab and his men, were soon put to flight, with Absalom himself fleeing on a mule. Riding under a great oak, he caught his hair in the branches, and the mule went out from under him. Though David had requested that none touch Absalom, Joab threw three darts through his heart as he was hanging in the tree. Joab's ten armor bearers finished the killing, after which they threw Absalom's body in a pit and raised over it a mass of stones (2 Sam. 18:1–18).

David, rather senile by now, mourned the death of Absalom more than he celebrated the victory. When news came to him of Absalom's death, he wept, crying out, "O my son Absalom, my son, my son Absalom! would I had died for thee, O Absalom, my son, my son!" (2 Sam. 18:33). David was a king, but he was also a father. Joab promptly reproved the king, reminding him that the people had risked their lives in loyal support of him and his cause and requesting that he arise and meet the people in the gate. David immediately obeyed the blunt and colorful Joab (2 Sam. 19:1–8).

David seems to have pardoned the rebels. Not being able to forget Joab's deathblow to Absalom, and probably wishing to reconcile the tribe of Judah who had given its support to Absalom, David transferred the leadership of the army from Joab to Amasa. David then returned to the Jordan, where he was met by Gilgal by the Judeans as he proceeded in triumph to Jerusalem (2 Sam. 19:11–15).

20. Sheba's Rebellion

Soon another revolt occurred, this one led by Sheba, a man of the tribe of Benjamin. The northern tribes, grieved over the fact that they had not been properly recognized in welcoming David back to Jerusalem, rebuked Judah with strong words. When Israel rallied around Sheba, David ordered Amasa to gather the troops of Judah within three days. This he failed to do, so David sent out Abishai with the "Mighty Men" to stop the insurrection. Joab, also going along, murdered Amasa, his cousin, with a sword concealed in his clothing. Grabbing him by the beard, as though to kiss him, he treacherously ran him through. Abner, Absalom, and next Amasa—all cut down by the unscrupulous nephew of the king. Leaving the body of Amasa in the road, Joab pursued after Sheba, calling the people to his aid as he passed through the various tribes. Sheba and the rebels took refuge in the city of Abel-beth-maacah, a city located in the north near the waters of Merom. Laying siege to the city and partially destroying the wall, Joab promised to turn back if Sheba were killed. Soon the head of the revolter was thrown

over the wall; whereupon Joab and his army returned to Jerusalem
(2 Sam. 20:1-22).

21. A Famine and a Plague

Disaster after disaster seemed to trouble David during the last
years of his reign. Amnon's immorality was followed by the two
rebellions, and these were immediately succeeded by two other
devastating events. There was a three-year drought with its con-
sequent famine that sent David to inquire of Jehovah. It was discovered that this was a punishment for an act of faithlessness on the
part of Saul, for he had violated a covenant made by Joshua
with the people of Gibeon (Josh. 9:3-27) by slaying some of them
(2 Sam. 21:1-2). The Gibeonites were satisfied only when David
granted to them the lives of seven descendants of Saul, Mephibosheth
being spared only due to David's own oath. After this the drought
was stayed and the rains came (2 Sam. 21:1-14).

The other disastrous event was a plague, the result of a census
enacted by David. "And again the anger of Jehovah was kindled
against Israel, and he moved David against them, saying, Go,
number Israel and Judah" (2 Sam. 24:1). Even though Joab and
the captains protested, David numbered the people from Dan to
Beersheba. After nine months and twenty days the census was complete: 800,000 warriors in Israel and 500,000 warriors in Judah (2
Sam. 24:9). Afterwards David felt the guilt of sin and confessed
to Jehovah, "I have sinned greatly in that which I have done: but
now, O Jehovah, put away, I beseech thee, the iniquity of thy servant; for I have done very foolishly" (2 Sam. 24:10). It has been
suggested that the essence of David's sin was the desire to show
off his military strength. The prophet Gad sent to David to give
him a choice of three penalties to be visited upon Israel because
of his evil action: seven years of famine, three months of defeat
before his enemies, or three days of pestilence. David chose the
last of these; the plague fell and 70,000 men lost their lives. Just
as the angel of death stretched out his hand toward Jerusalem the
plague was stayed. David purchased the threshing floor of Ornan,
or Araunah, a wealthy Jebusite, and there he built an altar and

sacrificed to Jehovah (2 Sam. 24:1–25). This threshing floor later
became the site upon which Solomon built the temple and may
well have been the Mount Moriah where Abraham many years before
had been willing to offer up his only son Isaac. Even though Mount
Moriah was outside the city of Zion (Jerusalem) in David's time,
Solomon later included it in the capital bounds.

22. Preparation for a Temple

David had brought the ark to Jerusalem and housed it in a tent.
He had wanted to build a temple and had made great preparations,
gathering together stone, iron, brass, and cedar trees. "So David
prepared abundantly before his death" (1 Chron. 22:5). But God
would not permit him to build it, for he had shed much blood.
Instead his son would build it, for there would be peace in his
days. (Solomon means "peaceful.") David even commanded all
the princes of Israel to help Solomon build the house of God
(1 Chron. 22:2–19).

Solomon and the Temple
(1 Kings 1—11)

1. The Golden Era

David, through a brilliant military career and an innate aptitude for governmental organization, accomplished for Israel what no other leader did. By sheer diplomacy he succeeded in winning over Judah and also in bringing Israel into the fold. Consolidating the loosely organized tribes and locating the capital in Jerusalem, he marched forth in great military strides to conquer a vast territory extending almost to the Euphrates in the north and to the river of Egypt and the Gulf of Akabah in the south and southwest respectively. He truly founded a vast Hebrew monarchy with its Oriental grandeur. It will be recalled that Samuel painted in very vivid words the type of king that would rule over Israel, an Oriental despot of formidable and absolute ruling tactics (1 Sam. 8:11–18). David did not reach the sketch drawn by Samuel, that equal to the Egyptian, Babylonian, and Aramaean kings of 1000 B.C., when all the subjects were considered merely servants of the crown and all property available for the king's use. But his progress in that direction was very marked. However, Samuel's picture is complete and true by the end of Solomon's reign, the third and last king of the undivided monarchy.

Peace and prosperity characterized the reign of Solomon, the son of David and Bathsheba; this young king reaped the benefits of his father's wars and labors. As one reads the biblical account of Solomon he notices that the building and dedication of the Temple is the focal point, receiving more consideration than any other aspect of Solomon's reign. His other building projects, trade and commerce, and the wise administration of his kingdom are but briefly mentioned.

2. Plots for the Succession

Toward the close of David's reign his three oldest sons were dead—Amnon, Chileab, and Absalom. Adonijah, the eldest living son, surrounded himself with chariots and horsemen and began drawing people to his side. He succeeded in getting the support of the priest Abiathar and David's commander in chief, Joab, and then proclaimed a great sacrificial feast at the stone of Zoheleth, at En-rogel south of Jerusalem. To this festival he invited all the royal princes, except Solomon, and many of the captains of the army (1 Kings 1:5-10).

In the meantime, Nathan the prophet and Bathsheba the queen decided to inform David of Adonijah's activities. The king, though old and feeble, solemnly assured Bathsheba of his determination that Solomon, her son, would succeed him on the throne. Then he called Zadok the priest and Benaiah and commanded them, together with Nathan, to anoint Solomon as king at Gihon. These three, along with the royal guards, escorted Solomon, riding on the royal mule, down to Gihon in the valley of Kidron and there anointed him as king with a horn of oil from the sacred tent. Then there was a blast of trumpets and the shouts of the people, "Long live king Solomon," after which the procession filed back to the city, where Solomon sat upon the throne in David's stead.

Jonathan, son of Abiathar, burst into Adonijah's coronation feast and informed all present of Solomon's recent anointing. As would be expected, the guests departed, each slipping out before anything worse could happen. Adonijah sought refuge by going to the horns of the altar to await Solomon's mercy. Solomon said, "If he shall show himself a worthy man, there shall not a hair of him fall to the earth; but if wickedness be found in him, he shall die." Adonijah, after making obeisance to Solomon, departed to his home (1 Kings 1:41-53).

3. David's Last Days

Just before his death David, before a solemn assembly of the chiefs and elders of the peoples, the royal princes, the captains of the army, and his public officers, made a final charge to Solomon, exhorting him to fidelity in the service of Jehovah. He delegated to him the task that had been the desire of his own life, that of erecting the temple of Jehovah, and committed to him the vast materials that he had gathered for that purpose, as well as the patterns for the building. Then he thanked God for all his goodness, praying that he would bestow upon Solomon "a perfect heart," enabling him to keep his commandments and statutes and to build the temple. Solomon was then anointed king a second time, being accepted by all the people (1 Kings 2:1–9; 1 Chron. 28:1 to 29:25).

David, the son of Jesse, ruled as king forty years, seven and a half years at Hebron and thirty-two and a half years at Jerusalem. When he died he was buried in Jerusalem, the city that had once been the fortress of the Jebusites but was then known as the "city of David." "And Solomon sat upon the throne of David his father; and his kingdom was established greatly" (1 Kings 2:10–12).

4. Added Intrigue

Solomon had barely begun to reign when he was called upon to repress another situation that could have spelled danger. Adonijah, forgiven by Solomon, might have lived the rest of his days in peace, had he not made one fatal request; he asked Bathsheba that she in turn ask Solomon that he might have Abishag, the beautiful Shunamite nurse who took care of David during his last days (1 Kings 1:1–4), for a wife. But in an Oriental court the harem of a king always passed to his successor on the throne. Therefore, Solomon had a deep suspicion about Adonijah's request; for he interpreted it as a mark of treason. Accordingly, he sent Benaiah with orders to slay Adonijah. He also banished Abiathar to the little town of Anathoth, north of Jerusalem, as one worthy to die; but he spared his life only because he had helped to care for the ark during the days of his father. Joab, also coming under the wrath of the young king, fled to the refuge of the horns of the altar in the tent of Jehovah. Refusing to leave there, Solomon ordered Benaiah to execute him on the spot. The fourth man to feel the effect of Solomon's anger was Shimei, a man of the house of Saul who had cursed David and his followers on their way to Mahanaim while fleeing from Absalom. Forgiven by David at that time, he was warned by Solomon not to step outside the bounds of Jerusalem on penalty of death. Neglectful of the threat, he had gone after two runaway slaves; so Solomon sent Benaiah with orders to execute him also. With these four out of the way Solomon's crown could rest more easily. Solomon made Benaiah general over his army and Zadok high priest in place of Abiathar (1 Kings 2:13–46).

5. A Wise Choice

Solomon was young, probably between twenty and thirty years of age, when he began to reign. Sensing the need for divine wisdom he assembled a large gathering of the people at Gibeon, six miles northwest of Jerusalem, where, according to Chronicles, there was some sort of a high place. There he sacrificed a thousand burnt offerings to Jehovah. That night the Lord appeared to Solomon in a vision as he slept, requesting him to submit any request he desired. God said, "Ask what I shall give thee." Solomon modestly recognized all that God had done for David, and that he had chosen him to follow his great father, and that he knew not how to "go out or come in" before so great a people. "Give thy servant therefore an understanding heart to judge thy people, that I may discern between good and evil; for who is able to judge this thy great people?" This pleased God immensely; for he had not asked for long life, or riches, or the life of his enemies. Therefore God would not only grant his request but would give him riches and honor as well; and, if he walked in his ways and kept his commandments, he would give him a long life also. When Solomon awoke, he realized that it had been a dream. Coming to Jerusalem he offered up burnt offerings and peace offerings and made a feast for all his servants (1 Kings 3:4–15).

6. Solomon's Wisdom, Wealth, and Fame

It is traditional to think of Solomon as being very wise. Not only did he have a great knowledge of the natural world; he had great insight into human nature as well. His famous decision in the case of the two mother's claiming the same child illustrates this (1 Kings 3:16–28). Two women, living in the same house, each had a small baby. One lay upon hers one night, killing it. Arising, she placed the dead baby in the arms of the other woman, taking her live baby for her own. In the morning the other woman recognized that the dead baby in her arms was not hers. They took the dispute to Solomon, who immediately ordered the baby divided into two, so that each woman could have a half. The real mother cried out for the baby's life to be spared, while the pretending mother was cruelly agreeable to the demand. "And all Israel heard of the judgment which the king had judged; and they feared the king: for they saw that the wisdom of God was in him, to do justice" (1 Kings 3:28).

Solomon's wisdom was so great that it "excelled the wisdom of all the children of the east, and all the wisdom of Egypt. For he was wiser than all men." He is credited with 3,000 proverbs and 1,005 songs. People from all kingdoms came to hear of his wisdom (1 Kings 4:29–34).

His fame was known also due to the magnificence and splendor of his buildings, as well as by his vast wealth and the extravagance of his court life. The weight of gold that came to him each year was 666 talents, besides that which the traders, merchants, kings, and governors brought in. His throne was made of ivory overlaid with gold, with rampant lions on the steps leading up to it. His ships took three years for a round trip, bringing back gold, silver, ivory, apes, and peacocks. "So king Solomon exceeded all the kings of the earth in riches and in wisdom. And all the earth sought the presence of Solomon, to hear his wisdom, which God had put in his heart" (1 Kings 10:14–25).

When the queen of Sheba heard of the fame, wisdom, and wealth of Solomon she would not believe the report, so she came to make a personal observation. She came "to prove him with hard questions," but Solomon "told her all her questions." She admitted to him, "It was a true report that I heard in mine own land of thine acts, and of thy wisdom. Howbeit I believed not the words, until I came, and mine eyes had seen it: and, behold, the half was not told me; thy wisdom and prosperity exceed the fame which I heard." After placing her blessing on Jehovah, the God of Solomon, she presented to the king presents of gold, spices, and precious stones and then returned home (1 Kings 10:1–13).

7. Building the Temple

One of Solomon's first big undertakings during his 40 years' reign was to build the temple planned previously by David. It was to be built on the site of the threshing floor of Araunah (or Ornan) the Jebusite, where the tent of meeting was standing. God had refused

to permit David to erect it, since he had been "a man of war."
Since Shiloh's destruction by the Philistines the ark had dwelt in
several temporary structures; it was retained by the Philistines themselves seven months, and then was in the houses of Abinadab and
Obed-edom until David brought it to Jerusalem. To make room
for the foundation of the temple the platform of the hill was extended
270 feet over arches. This terrace is said to have had hidden reservoirs
of water.

The size of the temple was twice that of the tabernacle used
in the wilderness wanderings; as the tabernacle was merely a tent
that could be moved from place to place, the temple was a permanent
structure, elaborate and spacious, with a much larger surrounding
court. From the various statements given in the Scriptures it is
difficult to determine exactly the detailed plans of this magnificent
building. Therefore scholars differ as to the exact measurements
and arrangements. However, some idea of the plan can be easily
derived.

There was a large quadrangle surrounded by a wall forming an
open court, later known as the court of the Gentiles. Within this,
surrounded by a wall and on a higher level, was another wall enclosing
another court; this was the court of the Israelites. Within this, and
again on a higher level, was another court, the court of the priests;
here was the temple proper, consisting of the porch, the holy place,
and the holy of holies. The porch was 15 feet deep, 30 feet wide,
and 45 feet high. On either side were two pillars made of brass,
one called Jachin (durability) and the other Boaz (strength), highly
decorated. The holy place was 30 feet wide, 60 feet long, and 45
feet high and was made of hewn stone, paneled with cedar overlaid
with gold. As in the tabernacle the holy place contained the golden
altar of incense, the table of showbread, and the golden lampstands,
five on the right and five on the left. The holy of holies was 30 feet
by 30 feet by 30 feet, a perfect cube, and separated from the holy
place by a rich veil of blue, purple, and crimson. Here was placed
the ark, with two large cherubim, made of olive wood overlaid with
gold, at either end; the cherubim were 15 feet high, and at each
end of the ark facing each other, with wide extended wings. The
priests went into the holy place each day to tend the various things

located there, but only the high priest entered the holy of holies, and he only once a year on the Day of Atonement. On this day he entered to make atonement for the sins of himself and the priest, then for the people.

Outside the holy place but within the court of the priests stood the great altar of burnt sacrifice with a base 30 feet square and 15 feet high; it was made of brass and rested on the exact site of the threshing floor of Araunah. Here also was the molten sea, made of brass and supported by 12 oxen. It was a huge laver, providing water for the priests and Levites in their temple service. There were also 10 smaller lavers made of brass, five on each side.

The temple faced the east. All the vessels in the temple proper were gold, while the metal used outside in the courts was brass. Solomon secured the service of a man from Tyre named Hiram, a craftsman in brass, to fashion all the brazen articles. This man's mother was a Hebrew of the tribe of Naphtali and his father a Phoenician (1 Kings 7:14). Solomon also secured the aid of Hiram, king of Tyre, a wealthy and powerful ruler of that day. The treaty made between those two kings was that Hiram supply architects and craftsmen and cedar logs, while Solomon was to repay in grain, oil, and wine (1 Kings 5:1–12). The Israelites furnished the many laborers for this extensive building project. "And the house, when it was in building, was built of stone made ready at the quarry; and there was neither hammer nor axe nor any tool of iron heard in the house, while it was in building" (1 Kings 6:7). Every beam and every stone had to be cut accurately and then later be silently laid in place. The entire building required seven years to construct.

8. Dedicating the Temple

At the completion of this gigantic task Solomon invited the chiefs of the various tribes and all the notables of his realm, as well as all the priests and the Levites, to Jerusalem for the solemn dedication service. It was the greatest religious event in the history of the Hebrew people since the events at Sinai, for the erection of the temple confirmed the establishment of the Davidic throne in Israel. It also confirmed the establishment of the kingdom anticipated by Moses (Deut. 17:14–20).

Solomon, the key person in the dedication, was seated on a raised throne of brass. There was a solemn procession in which the ark of the covenant was brought from the tent where David had placed it and carried by the priests through the holy place and into the holy of holies, its resting place. The choir, trumpets, cymbals, and instruments of music were heard, all in praising and thanking Jehovah; and a great cloud filled the house, "for the glory of Jehovah filled the house of God" (2 Chron. 5:1–14).

Then Solomon gave a short dedicatory address in which he recited to the assembly the history of the building of the Temple (2 Chron. 6:4–11) and also a long dedicatory prayer, one of the greatest found in all literature (2 Chron. 6:14–42). This prayer reveals the extreme spirit of devotion toward God that this great king, whose name symbolizes wisdom, possessed. As Solomon concluded his prayer fire came down from heaven and consumed the burnt offerings and the sacrifices, "and the glory of Jehovah filled the house." Then many thousands of oxen and sheep were sacrificed. "So the king and all the people dedicated the house of God" (2 Chron. 7:1–5). The ceremony of dedication lasted seven days and was followed by the Feast of Tabernacles, which lasted two weeks, or twice the usual time.

9. Building Programs

Solomon spent seven years building the Temple and then spent thirteen years constructing his own palace. It was surrounded by beautiful gardens and stood opposite the Temple (1 Kings 7:1). This "palace complex" consisted of several sections. There was the "house of the forest of Lebanon," the anteroom to the throne hall, the throne room itself, his own house, and a special apartment for Pharaoh's daughter, one of his many wives.

To maintain Solomon's large standing army a vast network of buildings across the nation would be required. First Kings 9:15–22 gives an impressive list of cities, many of them store cities, that Solomon constructed. There were 550 chief officers over all the work.

10. Trade, Commerce, and Revenue

Ezion-geber, on the Gulf of Akabah, became the center of Solomon's fleet of merchant ships. The Phoenicians, with their ports of Tyre and Sidon, had controlled the eastern end of the Mediterranean for years as far as ships of commerce were concerned. So Solomon located his port to the south of Edom on the gulf opening into the Indian Ocean. He secured from Hiram, king of Tyre, experienced men to build and sail his ships, sending them as far as Ophir, wherever that was. Three years were required for the round trip; the ships returned laden with gold, silver, precious stones, ivory, apes, and peacock (1 Kings 9:26–28; 10:22).

To operate as lavish and stupendous a kingdom as Solomon's required a gigantic income. This was secured not only from the fleet of ships just mentioned but also from tolls exacted from the many caravans crossing his realm and tribute of the kings of the conquered and subdued nations. Also, archaeological evidence shows that at Ezion-geber there was located in the days of Solomon one of the largest smelting refineries in the Near East; the mining of iron and copper in Sinai and Edom was at a great height. Archaeologists have been seeking the location of Solomon's gold mines for years, for this was a tremendous source of income for the famous king. Solomon's international recognition was so great that there were gifts from far and near. The gifts of the Queen of Sheba serve as an example of what probably happened frequently.

11. Weaknesses in the Foundation

There was a certain sense in which all the luxuries and magnificence of Solomon's court was merely on the surface, for there were rumblings beneath that gave a portent of trouble. First, much of the massing of gold and silver was brought about by a process of severe taxation, added to the fact that most of the revenue from the commercial endeavors flowed into the royal treasury, not out to the people themselves. Second, Solomon surrounded himself with a huge harem—700 wives and 300 concubines (1 Kings 11:1–3). Besides the daughter of Pharaoh there were women from Moab, Ammon, Edom, Sidon, and the Hittites. "For it came to pass, when Solomon was old, that his wives turned away his heart after other gods; and his heart was not perfect with Jehovah his God, as was the heart of David his father" (1 Kings 11:4). The worship of

Ashtoreth, Milcom, Molech, and Chemosh was introduced into Jerusalem. In fact, Jehovah appeared unto him twice, commanding him not to divert to these gods; but he obeyed not (1 Kings 11:9–10). When he appeared to him the third time, it was to announce that he would rend the kingdom from him, giving it to his servant. Yet this would not be in his day, for the sake of David his father, but in his son's day. And even then, God would not rend it all away, but would keep one tribe for his son (1 Kings 11:11–13).

So the final chapter in Solomon's life was a tragic one indeed! How could one starting out so wisely and discreetly, and reaching such an apex of wisdom, wealth, and renown, end his career in such disrepute and disfavor with God? Solomon personally repeated what Israel previously had done in the wilderness. Shortly after Israel had entered into a marvelous covenant relationship with God at Mount Sinai, whereby they became his special people dedicated to obeying and serving him, they entered into apostasy and disgraced themselves by worshiping a golden calf in pagan revelry. Solomon, after building a magnificent Temple to Jehovah and dedicating it by means of such a comprehensive and devout prayer, sank to the low ebb of worshiping at degrading and abominable pagan altars. His allowing idol worship to enter Jerusalem led to his breaking of the First Commandment with all its consequences.

12. Three Troublemakers

Solomon had to reckon with three opponents, all of whom spelled trouble and brought ripples on the water. One of these was Hadad, the Edomite. When Joab, David's general, invaded that country, he remained there six months and massacred a large number of the male population. Hadad, a little child of royal blood, was carried off to Egypt, being hospitably received by Pharaoh. During the reign of Solomon, and being grown, he returned to Edom and organized a revolt against Solomon, threatening his communications with his port at Ezion-geber. The Scriptures say, "And Jehovah raised up an adversary unto Solomon, Hadad the Edomite" (1 Kings 11:14–22).

"And God raised up another adversary unto him, Rezon the son of Eliada." This opponent, from Damascus, was probably a greater threat to Solomon. Fleeing when David defeated Hadadezer of Zobah, he came back later with a following and seized Damascus. "And he abhorred Israel, and reigned over Syria" (1 Kings 11:23–25).

A third opponent was Jeroboam, the son of Nebat, an Ephraimite, a very capable man who was a labor leader in the construction of the fortress Millo. Solomon made him collector of the taxes from his native tribe of Ephraim, probably the strongest of the northern tribes. Ahijah, a prophet, met Jeroboam one day and, taking off his new outer robe, tore it into twelve parts. Giving Jeroboam ten of the parts, he assured him that he would rule over ten tribes of Israel. He also gave him the reasons that such a split would come in Solomon's realm. Evidently Solomon heard of the meeting of the two, for he "sought therefore to kill Jeroboam." But Jeroboam fled to Egypt to Shishak the king and remained there till Solomon's death (1 Kings 11:26–40).

After reigning 40 years Solomon died and was buried in Jerusalem. Rehoboam his son was crowned king in his stead.

Israel, Jeroboam to Jehu's Revolution
(1 Kings 12—2 Kings 8)

1. Rival Kingdoms

The books of Kings and the books of Chronicles present the story of the period following Solomon's reign; for the split of the kingdom that prevailed after the era of Saul, David and Solomon left two rival thrones holding sway over two rival territories: Israel in the north and Judah in the south. These two small domains were couched down in the midst of world powers, each of which dreamed of world conquest. Armies sauntered forth either to grasp new territory or to hold that already gained, while the Hebrews struggled valiantly to survive in this age of shifting national powers. Syria, Assyria, Babylonia, and Egypt were all involved in the destiny of the Israelite nation.

For about 200 years the dual monarchies of Israel and Judah existed side by side, with Judah continuing for about a century and a third after the fall of its northern rival. For approximately the first 60 years there was strife between the two neighboring nations. This was followed by a peaceful era of about 30 years, which was in turn succeeded by a second era of strife down to the fall of Israel well over a century later. The peaceful span of three decades was due much to a series of royal intermarriages, but Jehu's revolution soon ended the tranquility.

2. Comparison of the Two Realms

In size Israel was three or four times as large as Judah, with the additional advantage of being superior economically. There was not only a better trade location; the area was better for both agriculture and the raising of flocks and herds. But there were ways that Judah had the hand over Israel. Jerusalem, the historic capital, was there, with all its prestige and sacred tradition. Magnificent buildings, one of which was the Temple, adorned its site. And Judah also had a oneness of government not found in Israel, for there were strong ties of unity and national ideals that probably stemmed from Jerusalem's historic aspect.

Israel had nineteen kings and Judah nineteen kings, but all the kings of Israel could be termed "evil" kings in the sense that they did not endeavor to lead their people in the ways and commandments of Jehovah their God. The line of the kings of Judah was characterized by the fact that some were "evil" and some were "good." The writer of Kings uses one phrase to describe each of Israel's kings: "and did that which was evil in the sight of Jehovah." Due to the sins of its kings Israel was carried into captivity by Assyria in 722–721 B.C., and for the sins of Judah the Southern Kingdom also suffered the same disgrace by the Babylonians in 587–586 B.C. Israel had nine dynasties in its career, while Judah had only one dynasty, the house of David.

Israel had three capitals during its history of two and a third centuries. The first was at Shechem, which was replaced by Tirzah. This in time was replaced by Samaria, which was the capital when the final days came in 722–721. Judah had only one capital, Jerusalem, during its entire existence.

3. Revolt of the Ten Tribes

Rehoboam, son and successor of Solomon, was forty-one years of age when he fell heir to the throne of his father. He knew he had the loyalty of Jerusalem and all its environs; so he marched north to gain the confidence of the tribes there, especially those descending from the houses of Joseph, Benjamin, and Ephraim. "And Rehoboam went to Shechem: for all Israel were come to Shechem to make him king" (1 Kings 12:1).

A man named Jeroboam had been employed by Solomon as a tax gatherer in his native tribe of Ephraim, a job that he seems to have fulfilled quite well. Sometime before Solomon's death a prophet named Ahijah appeared to Jeroboam and acted strangely. Taking off his robe, he tore it into twelve pieces and gave ten of them to Jeroboam as a sign of his future rule over ten of the tribes. He said to Jeroboam, "Take thee ten pieces; for thus saith Jehovah, the God of Israel, Behold, I will rend the kingdom out of the hand of Solomon, and will give ten tribes to thee" (1 Kings 11:31). Evidently Solomon heard of this strange event, for he tried to kill Jeroboam; so the latter fled to Egypt where he became a friend of Shishak, king of Egypt, and where he remained until the death of Solomon (1 Kings 11:40).

As soon as Rehoboam arrived in Shechem for the ratification of his kingship by the northern tribes, the men of that region sent for Jeroboam to return from Egypt, which he immediately did. There was a historically significant encounter as these two men came face to face. Jeroboam and the assembly requested that the grievous taxes and other heavy burdens that had been imposed upon the northern tribes be reduced, after which they would be glad to serve Rehoboam. The son of Solomon requested three days for deliberation, during which he sought the advice both of the peers of his father and then those of his own age. The elder men, who had been the advisers of his father, unanimously agreed that he should accede to their demands and mitigate the burden; but the younger men of rank, companions of the king, advised him to deal with a high hand and a firm denial. His reply to the northern delegation was insolent. "My father made your yoke heavy, but I will add to your yoke: my father chastised you with whips, but I will chastise you with scorpions" (1 Kings 12:14). The writer of Kings interprets his answer as "a thing brought about of Jehovah," that Ahijah's prophecy might come true. Jeroboam and his delegation reacted with immediate decisiveness. "What portion have we in David? neither have we inheritance in the son of Jesse: to your tents, O Israel: now see to thine own house, David" (1 Kings 12:16). When Rehoboam unwisely sent his taskmaster, Adoram, who had been the chief receiver of tribute under his father and grandfather, to levy the usual dues, the people stoned him to death. Rehoboam fled to Jerusalem, while Jeroboam was made king over Israel. "There was none that followed the house of David, but the tribe of Judah only" (1 Kings 12:20).

Rehoboam's first impulse was to punish the northern rebellious tribes; so he gathered an army of 180,000 men from Judah and Benjamin with the express purpose of marching north in a civil war, but he was restrained in doing so by the action of Shemaiah, a man of God. This one interpreted the whole matter of the rending of the kingdom to be an act of God; therefore Rehoboam was forbidden to drive north to fulfill his revenge. The split was at last complete.

The immediate cause, or surface reason, for the breach was the impudent and rude answer of Rehoboam to the sincere request of the northern neighbors. Evidently the older and wiser men in Rehoboam's realm saw the impending peril and advised a cautious handling of the matter. This the younger men did not discern. But back of the direct cause was an indirect, or hidden one; the tribal jealousies between Judah in the south and the tribes in the north, especially Ephraim, had sustained a chasm that seemed incapable of healing. The animosity between the kingdom of Saul and that of David opened a rift between north and south during the first few years of David's reign, as was seen when he ruled over Judah alone; for the ten tribes held out under Saul's son, Ishbosheth, not forgetting their identity. Also, Solomon's grievous burden of forced labor and mounting taxes to support his monstrous harem and lavish living was beyond endurance. On top of all this was Ahijah's prophecy sent from Jehovah that Jeroboam the Ephraimite would rule over ten of the tribes.

4. Into Idolatry

Jeroboam, newly anointed as king of Israel, selected Shechem as his capital. Though not surrounded with the tradition and aura of sanctity that Jerusalem possessed, Shechem had figured prominently in Hebrew history for centuries. However, the deeply entrenched practice of all the people in going south to Jerusalem for the religious ceremonies presented an impending danger. So long as thousands of his subjects made their annual pilgrimages to the capital of another country, his power would be curtailed. Some of the Levites and priests even began to move to Judah. Jeroboam had no temple, no ark of the covenant, and no priesthood. Resolving to establish religious shrines in his own country he selected two cities, Dan and Bethel, for seats of national worship. The former was the most northern and the latter the most southern of the cities in his realm. His thinking was extremely selfish. "Now will the kingdom return to the house of David: if this people go up to offer sacrifices in the house of Jehovah at Jerusalem, then will the heart of this people turn again unto their lord, even unto Rehoboam king of Judah; and they will kill me, and return to Rehoboam king of Judah" (1 Kings 12:26–27). Making two golden calves, he set one at Dan and one at Bethel; and with words reminiscent of those used by Aaron when he made a similar golden calf years before at Mount Sinai (Ex. 32:4), he issued an invitation for worship. "It is too much for you to go up to Jerusalem: behold thy gods, O Israel, which brought thee up out of the land of Egypt" (1 Kings 12:28). The writer of Kings expresses his disgust by saying, "And this thing became a sin." Not only did he produce the golden calves; he made "houses of high places," pagan shrines of worship patterned after the Canaanites. He made priests from among the people and not from the tribe of Levi, besides ordaining his own festival of dedication during our month of November, the time of ripe grapes in the north.

Jeroboam's tragic mistake was in the nature of the worship he had established; it was not of Jehovah but was highly pagan in nature. He would rather lead his people into idolatry and heathen rites than run the risk of losing his newly-acquired throne. In doing so he set a fatal policy for his government; for each succeeding king of Israel followed the idolatrous pattern he established, which culminated at last in the downfall of the nation. Added later on to the worship of the golden calves was the worship of Baal, for in Israel this horrible practice found a congenial climate for growth. Jeroboam proved to be an able ruler, as far as organization and leadership go; his great sin was his promotion of idolatry. As the writer of Kings recounts the lives of the succeeding rulers in Israel he constantly talks about "the sins of Jeroboam the son of Nebat, wherewith he made Israel to sin." No king was strong enough to pull away from them and lead his country back to Jehovah.

5. Jeroboam's Sons

Jeroboam's two sons, Abijah and Nadab, did not increase the glory of Israel. The former died at a young age. When he became ill, Jeroboam sent his wife, disguised as a commoner, to Ahijah the prophet to inquire about the destiny of the young man. Having been informed of the whole venture by Jehovah, Ahijah predicted the death of Abijah. It occurred just as he had foretold.

Jeroboam lost several cities, including Bethel, in war with Judah, a defeat that so weakened the king that he died soon after (2 Chron. 13:20), having ruled for 22 years. Nadab ruled for two years in place of Jeroboam but did nothing of note. He did go to battle against the Philistines, but he and all the other descendants of Jeroboam were murdered by Baasha of the tribe of Issachar. Thus ended the first of the nine dynasties of Israel (1 Kings 15:29–30).

6. Baasha and Elah

The second dynasty consisted of two men also: Baasha, who ruled for 24 years, and Elah, his son, who ruled for two. Not favoring Shechem as a capital, Baasha replaced it by Tirzah, which remained the governmental center till the days of Omri. This was a town a few miles north of Shechem.

Asa, ruling as king of Judah, persuaded the Syrian king at Damascus, Benhadad, to enter into an alliance with him against Baasha. "And there was war between Asa and Baasha king of Israel all their days" (1 Kings 15:32). After Baasha's death Elah, his son, ruled over Israel for less than two full years.

7. Zimri

When Elah was holding a riotous feast in the house of his steward at Tirzah he was assassinated by Zimri, the captain of half his charioteers. The murderer then wiped out every member of Baasha's family and assumed the throne. He had completed only seven days of his reign when Tirzah was besieged by Omri, a captain of Elah's army just crowned as a counter-king by the Israelites at Gibbethon. When Zimri saw the besieging army around Tirzah he burnt the royal palace over his own head and perished. His brief rule of seven days constitutes the third dynasty of Israel (1 Kings 16:8–20).

8. Omri, Builder of Samaria

The Bible says very little about this founder of the fourth dynasty who ruled twelve years, six at Tirzah and six at Samaria; but the house of Omri and the house of Jehu are the two strongest of the dynasties who ruled in Israel. The Bible reveals that another claimant

for the throne vied with him for the chief spot, Tibni, with half
the people wanting Omri and half Tibni. However, Omri prevailed
over his opponents, and after Tibni's death there was no controversy
on this score. Omri bought a hill from one named Shemer and built
a city on it, naming it Samaria after the former owner. This remained
the capital until the fall of the Northern Kingdom in 722–721 B.C.
Omri "dealt wickedly above all that were before him" and walked
in Jeroboam's ways (1 Kings 16:21–28).

Inscriptions found in Assyria show that these people considered
Omri to be a powerful and influential ruler, for they designate Israel
as the "land of Omri." So even though the Bible does not relate
much concerning him, his reign is a very significant one due to
his diplomatic relations with foreign powers. He might even be considered a statesman-king. The Moabite Stone, found east of the Jordan
River in 1868, records his reconquest of Moab, a land held for
forty years and from which much tribute was exacted (2 Kings 3:4).
He also had trade relations with Phoenicia. The house of Omri
consisted of four kings: Omri, Ahab, Ahaziah, and Jehoram, the
last two being brothers.

9. Ahab and Jezebel

One of the most infamous of Israel's kings was Ahab, son of
Omri. "And Ahab the son of Omri did that which was evil in the
sight of Jehovah above all that were before him" (1 Kings 16:30).
He was completely dominated by his wife Jezebel, the strong-willed
daughter of Ethbaal (or Ithobaal), priest-king of the goddess Astarte,
who by revolution had become king of Sidon, a large city in
Phoenicia. Omri's alliance with Ethbaal was strengthened by the
marriage of his son Ahab with Jezebel, but the union of these two
brought the worship of Melkarth, the Phoenician Baal, into the land
of Israel. They set up the worship of Baal, with all its ritual and
intolerance, as the recognized religion of Israel. Ahab even established a house of Baal with an altar of Baal in Samaria. The persecution of those who were devoted to Jehovah worship became the
order of the day. The prophets of Jehovah were killed, except 100
of them who were hidden by fifty in caves and fed secretly. This
was done by Obadiah, Ahab's court chamberlain. Jezebel devoted

12.   Mount Ebal, Samaria

herself energetically to replacing the worship of Jehovah with
Baalism, and Ahab became a pliant accomplice in her endeavors.
The rivalry of these two religions became a violent issue in Israel.

10. Elijah the Tishbite

Elijah and his successor, Elisha, though nonwriting prophets,
made great imprints on the history of Israel. In fact, Elijah, colorful
and dynamic, was one of the greatest men in the Old Testament,
being the uncompromising champion of Jehovah worship. He came
from the town of Tishbeh, across the Jordan in the land of Gilead;
other than this we know nothing of his youth. This rough, uncouth
prophet of the desert appeared suddenly at court and announced
a severe drought as the result of the sin of Ahab and Jezebel: the
attempted destruction of Jehovah worship throughout Israel. He
declared to Ahab, "As Jehovah, the God of Israel, liveth, before
whom I stand, there shall not be dew nor rain these years, but
according to my word" (1 Kings 17:1). At God's direction he
departed and hid himself by the brook Cherith that flows into the
Jordan, where he was fed by the ravens and where he drank from
the brook. But in time even the brook dried up for lack of rain,
and Elijah departed for Zarephath, a town in the territory of Sidon
of Phoenicia.

In Zarephath Elijah found that the people were experiencing the
drought also. When he requested a widow of that place to set before
him water and bread, she replied that she had only enough meal
and oil to prepare a little food for her and her son, after which
she expected starvation and death. At the insistence of Elijah she
shared with him her sparse meal, only to find that henceforth her
supply of meal and oil never failed. She even prepared him an upper
room in her home, so that he might live comfortably. When her
son met death, Elijah carried the lad up to the room, stretched
himself upon him three times, and requested God to restore life.
When he delivered the living boy to his mother, she said, "Now
I know that thou art a man of God, and that the word of Jehovah
in thy mouth is truth" (1 Kings 17:24).

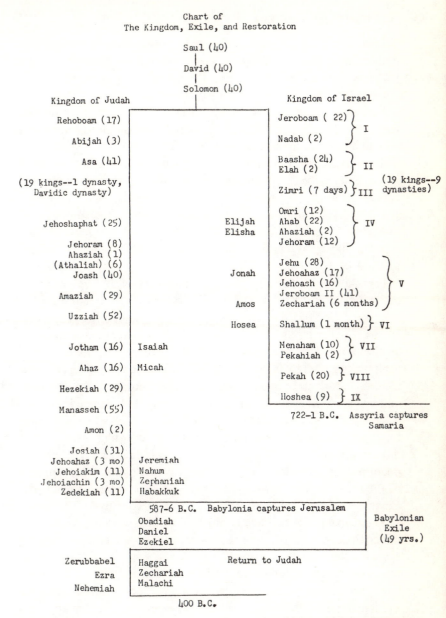

Chart of
The Kingdom, Exile, and Restoration

Saul (40)

David (40)

Solomon (40)

Kingdom of Judah   Kingdom of Israel

Rehoboam (17)   Jeroboam (22) ⎫
                                                 ⎬ I
Abijah (3)   Nadab (2)   ⎭

Asa (41)   Baasha (24)   ⎫
                                 Elah (2)   ⎬ II

(19 kings--1 dynasty,   (19 kings--9
Davidic dynasty)   Zimri (7 days) ⎬ III   dynasties)

                                 Omri (12)   ⎫
Jehoshaphat (25)   Elijah   Ahab (22)   ⎬ IV
                      Elisha   Ahaziah (2)   ⎭
                                 Jehoram (12)
Jehoram (8)
Ahaziah (1)   Jehu (28)   ⎫
(Athaliah) (6)   Jonah   Jehoahaz (17)   ⎪
Joash (40)   Jehoash (16)   ⎬ V
                                 Jeroboam II (41)⎪
Amaziah (29)   Zechariah (6 months) ⎭
                      Amos
Uzziah (52)
                      Hosea   Shallum (1 month) ⎬ VI

Jotham (16)   Isaiah   Menaham (10)   ⎬ VII
                                 Pekahiah (2)

Ahaz (16)   Micah   Pekah (20)   ⎬ VIII

Hezekiah (29)   Hoshea (9)   ⎬ IX

Manasseh (55)   722-1 B.C. Assyria captures
                                             Samaria
Amon (2)

Josiah (31)
Jehoahaz (3 mo)   Jeremiah
Jehoiakim (11)   Nahum
Jehoiachin (3 mo) Zephaniah
Zedekiah (11)   Habakkuk

                587-6 B.C. Babylonia captures Jerusalem   Babylonian
                Obadiah   Exile
                Daniel   (49 yrs.)
                Ezekiel

Zerubbabel   Haggai   Return to Judah
Ezra   Zechariah
Nehemiah   Malachi

                400 B.C.

13. Chart of National History

11. The Contest of Mount Carmel

According to Luke 4:25 the drought lasted three years and six months, near the end of which God commanded Elijah to return and show himself to Ahab, "and I will send rain upon the earth" (1 Kings 18:1). While Ahab and Obadiah, his servant, were separately wandering through the hills of Samaria in search of water for the herds, Elijah met Obadiah. He commanded Obadiah to return and send to him Ahab his master, which he reluctantly did. The meeting of these two bitter enemies was a very dramatic one. When Ahab called Elijah the "troubler of Israel," the latter returned the "compliment" by his harsh disapproval of the Baal worship established by Ahab and his house. Elijah challenged Ahab to come to Mount Carmel with "all Israel," plus the 450 prophets of Baal and the 400 of Asherah, "that eat at Jezebel's table" (1 Kings 18:16–19).

The clash of Elijah and the false prophets of Jezebel was one of the most colorful incidents in Hebrew history, for Ahab regarded the proposition of Elijah to be a fair one and yielded to his request. It was Elijah who alone represented Jehovah, with many lined up on the other side. The great man of God threw out his challenge to all Israel gathered on the mount: "How long go ye limping between the two sides? if Jehovah be God, follow him; but if Baal, then follow him." There was no reply. The prophets of Baal were to have a bullock, and Elijah a bullock. Each side was to prepare for a sacrifice but to put no fire to the wood. This was to be a day of decision, a day of crisis for Israel. It was to be proved once and for all who was God, Baal or Jehovah. The prophets of Baal were to call down fire from Baal to consume their bullock; Elijah was to call down fire from Jehovah to consume his.

The pagan prophets called unto Baal for fire unto the noon hour, but no fire came. Elijah even heaped upon them and their god stinging sarcasm that must have hurt. They cried and cut themselves in their frenzy until evening, and no fire! Elijah prepared his bullock and placed it upon an altar of twelve stones, newly made. He even drenched it all with water; three times he did so! When he appealed to Jehovah for fire, it fell on the sacrifice and consumed offering, wood, stones, dust, and even the water in the trench. The people said, "Jehovah, he is God; Jehovah, he is God." Elijah immediately took the prophets of Baal down to the brook Kishon at the base of Mount Carmel and slew all of them (1 Kings 18:20–40).

Elijah, announcing to Ahab that rain was soon to come, went with his servant to the top of Mount Carmel. While he prayed, the servant was to look out over the Mediterranean. Six times he reported seeing nothing, but the seventh time he discerned a cloud "as small as a man's hand." Elijah warned Ahab to flee in his chariot toward Jezreel, for Ahab had built there a summer palace in the beautiful valley of Jezreel. Ahab rode in his chariot to Jezreel, but Elijah "ran before Ahab to the entrance of Jezreel" (1 Kings 18:41–46).

12. Elijah's Flight

This was good running on Elijah's part, but he was not through. Jezebel, who evidently was not present at the tiff of Mount Carmel, sent a message to the victorious Elijah. "So let the gods do to me, and more also, if I make not thy life as the life of one of them by tomorrow about this time." To this feminine challenge the prophet "went for his life, and came to Beersheba," a place in the south of the kingdom of Judah. Leaving his servant, he traveled a day's journey into the wilderness and there fell exhausted and longed for death. Falling asleep under a juniper tree, he was awakened, fed, encouraged, and sent on his way. In forty days and as many nights he came to Mount Sinai. When God asked him why he was there, he answered in tones of utter failure, stating that he alone was left of those faithful to Jehovah. God spoke to him, not in the wind, not in the earthquake, and not in the fire, but in a still, small voice. (The literal Hebrew says "a sound of gentle stillness.") God commissioned Elijah to return to Israel with a threefold duty: to anoint Hazael as king of Syria, to anoint Jehu as king of Israel, and to anoint Elisha as his own successor. In this same divine revelation God also advised the prophet that he had 7,000 in Israel, "all the knees which have not bowed unto Baal, and every mouth which hath not kissed him" (1 Kings 19:1–18). This is the first hint of the idea of a faithful remnant, an idea made prominent later in the book of Isaiah. When Elijah returned to Israel, he found Elisha, son of Shaphat, plowing with oxen, he and eleven servants. When he threw his mantle over Elisha "he left the oxen, and ran after Elijah." After sacrificing a "yoke of oxen" he ministered to Elijah, becoming a follower in the fight for Jehovah against Baalism. Jehu and Hazael received their anointings later on (1 Kings 19:19–21).

13. Benhadad's War with Ahab

By good diplomacy and effective treaties Ahab was able to maintain peace throughout the early part of his reign. Then the Syrians attacked the Israelite kingdom (1 Kings 20:1–43). With the aid of 32 vassal kings Benhadad marched south from Damascus, the Syrian capital, toward Samaria. While besieging the city he sent a bold message with haughty demands to Ahab; in fact two embassies were dispatched to the Israelite king. After a conference with his elders Ahab returned word to Benhadad that they would defend the city, to which Benhadad declared his intent to level the capital with the ground. A prophet stood forth and predicted Ahab's victory with only a small contingent of men, and the Syrians were utterly routed.

The same prophet that had announced victory for Ahab warned him that the Syrians would return in the spring, which they did. Since the Syrians believed the last Israelite victory was due to their attacking in a hilly region a people whose "god was a god of the hills" (v. 23), they returned to do battle in the plain. So Benhadad went up to Aphek, a town in the level country east of the Jordan. When the two armies faced each other the Israelite host looked like two little flocks of kids compared to the vast battle array of the Syrians; but again a man of God assured Ahab of a victory. Again the victory was decisive for Ahab, and thousands of Syrians were slain. Ahab was very lenient with Benhadad, when the latter appealed for mercy, and spared his life. The Syrian king promised a return of many northern cities and a quarter in the Syrian capital itself for trade. This clemency on Ahab's part toward a formidable foe brought on Ahab a stern rebuke by a son of the prophets. He had spared a man whom Jehovah had devoted to destruction; he and his people must bear the punishment (1 Kings 20:22–43).

14. Naboth's Vineyard

Adjoining Ahab's palace at his "second capital," Jezreel, was a vineyard belonging to a man named Naboth, a piece of ground that Ahab desired to acquire and convert into a garden of herbs. When he asked Naboth to sell it or to trade for it, he refused, saying it was an inheritance from his forefathers. Ahab returned home displeased and actually pouted. "And he laid him down upon his bed, and turned away his face, and would eat no bread" (1 Kings 21:4). When Jezebel returned home, her husband's frustration was readily apparent; so she immediately set out in her unscrupulous way to acquire the vineyard. Arranging for the false accusation of Naboth by two base fellows and for his being stoned to death, she unmercifully attained what Ahab so ardently coveted. She announced to her self-centered husband, "Arise, take possession of the vineyard of Naboth the Jezreelite, which he refused to give thee for money; for Naboth is not alive, but dead." Ahab arose and took possession (1 Kings 21:5–16).

God not only informed Elijah that Ahab was in Naboth's vineyard but gave him a message for the king. Ahab's first words for Elijah were self-condemning: "Hast thou found me, O mine enemy?" These words form quite a contrast to Ahab's words at a previous meeting of the two, when he called Elijah "troubler of Israel." Elijah replied, "I have found thee," and then boldly indicted Ahab for his shedding of innocent blood. For punishment the Omri dynasty was doomed to destruction; all male descendants of Ahab would be wiped out. Dogs would lick Ahab's blood where they had licked Naboth's, and dogs would devour the body of Jezebel by the rampart of Jezreel, a prophecy which was literally fulfilled. This was the final encounter between Elijah and Ahab.

15. First Battle of Ramoth-gilead

After a space of three years hostility again broke out between Syria and Israel. Ahab, king of Israel, and Jehoshaphat, king of Judah, formed an alliance to fight the Syrians at Ramoth-gilead, for Ahab wished to recover this strategic city east of the Jordan (1 Kings 22:1–40), which Benhadad had failed to restore after the pact made at Aphek. Therefore Ahab took advantage of the good will that existed at this time between the Northern and Southern Kingdoms. Jehoshaphat, concerned about divine guidance in the venture, asked Ahab to seek God's advice. When Ahab summoned and questioned 400 prophets they unanimously assured the two kings of victory. The prophet Zedekiah even made horns of iron to demonstrate how the Syrians would be gored. When Jehoshaphat requested another prophet of Jehovah, Micaiah was brought forth; this one foretold tragedy for Ahab, that he would be killed in the battle and that Israel would be defeated. Ahab commanded that Micaiah be imprisoned and released only if he, Ahab, returned in peace. Micaiah's words, prior to his prediction are extremely noble for any one called to proclaim God's message: "As Jehovah liveth, what Jehovah saith unto me, that will I speak" (1 Kings 22:14).

Ahab, quite apprehensive, attempted to disguise himself during the battle, while Jehoshaphat very openly wore his royal robes. But "a certain man drew his bow at a venture," and the stray arrow pierced the joints of Ahab's armor, fatally wounding him. They held him up in his chariot and he died at evening. Returning from Ramoth-gilead, they washed the blood from the bottom of the chariot at the pool of Samaria, the dogs licking the blood of Ahab as Elijah had predicted. An evil and turbulent reign of 22 years was at last terminated (1 Kings 22:29–40).

16. Ahaziah's Short Reign

Ahaziah, son of Ahab, began his brief reign over Israel, ruling less than two years. He formed a partnership with Jehoshaphat, king of Judah, to build a fleet of merchant ships at Ezion-geber at the Gulf of Akabah to sail to Ophir for gold. This project ended in disaster, for the storms smashed the ships on the rocks (2 Chron. 20:35–37).

A second discouraging factor of his short career was the rebelling of Moab, which for years had been paying tribute to Israel. "And Moab rebelled against Israel after the death of Ahab" (2 Kings 1:1). This rebellion was probably fostered by the defeat that Benhadad handed Ahab and Jehoshaphat at Ramoth-gilead; at any rate, it is described on the famous Moabite Stone found at Dibon, east of the Dead Sea, in 1868. Before the Arabs broke it to pieces an impression was made, so the message was translated and read.

The account on the stone agrees remarkably with the biblical account in 2 Kings 3:4–27. Mesha, king of Moab, in very boastful words describes how he overthrew the Israelitic yoke, all of which he credits to Chemosh, his god. Ahaziah was unable to reclaim Moab.

A third unfortunate event in Ahaziah's reign was his fall through the lattice of an upper window in his palace in Samaria, after which he became very ill and sent to Baalzebub (lord of flies), god at Ekron, to inquire concerning his recovery. Elijah, meeting the king's messenger in the way, sent Ahaziah an announcement of his ensuing death. He endeavored twice to kill Elijah but failed, soon dying just as the prophet predicted (2 Kings 1:2–17).

17. Jehoram of Israel

Ahaziah's brother, Jehoram, succeeded him on the throne of Israel, last of the house of Omri. He destroyed the pillar (or obelisk) that his father Ahab had made, but he did not remove the old calf worship Jeroboam had established (2 Kings 3:2–3). His rule of 12 years was brought to a halt by Jehu, who endeavored to expunge the whole Omri dynasty. Athaliah, sister of Ahaziah and Jehoram, married Ahaziah, king of Judah, another indication of the friendly relations between Israel and Judah prevailing at this time. (Jehoram's name is written Joram.)

No mention is made in the Bible of any association of Elijah with Jehoram; the last appearance of this great prophet before a king was his short personal warning to Ahaziah that he could expect God's judgment. But there were many occasions where Elisha, Elijah's successor, met Jehoram; and Jehoram was greatly helped by the great prophet.

18. Elisha Succeeds Elijah

It will be recalled that Elijah was informed at Horeb, or Sinai, to return home and anoint his successor, Elisha. When he found Elisha plowing, he called him to follow him; and apparently Elisha obeyed. Master and student jointly established what were called "schools of the prophets," but what the "curriculum" of these schools contained would be hard to determine. One thing is certain:

one should never underestimate the significance of these schools on the thrust of prophecy in Israel and Judah in the ensuing years.

When Elisha realized that the end of his "prophetic apprenticeship" was nearing and that Elijah would soon be gone, he asked his master that he might have a double portion of the spirit that had rested upon him. Elisha followed Elijah from Gilgal to Bethel, then from Bethel to Jericho, and from Jericho to the Jordan. Here 50 of the sons of the prophets climbed a high cliff to watch the happenings below. At the bank of the river Elijah struck the water with his prophetic mantle, to have the waters divide and the two men to cross over on dry ground. It is at this point, at the invitation of the older man, that the younger wisely requested a double portion of his spirit. Elijah replied, "Thou hast asked a hard thing: nevertheless, if thou see me when I am taken from thee, it shall be so unto thee; but if not, it shall not be so" (2 Kings 2:10). Elisha saw a chariot of fire and horses of fire, and Elijah going toward heaven in a whirlwind. He cried out, "My father, my father, the chariots of Israel and the horsemen thereof!" He saw his master no more. Dramatically tearing his own clothes in two pieces and gathering up Elijah's mantle, he returned to the river and struck the water with the mantle, saying, "Where is Jehovah, the God of Elijah?" The waters parted, and he crossed over (2 Kings 2:1–14). The great champion of the worship of Jehovah over Baal had passed on to his reward. His paramount contribution to his people was the preservation of a trust in Jehovah at a time when the pull toward apostasy was tremendous.

The 50 sons of the prophets, seeing that truly Elijah's spirit rested upon Elisha, insisted on crossing the Jordan to hunt for Elijah. Elisha tried to dissuade them from doing so, but to no avail. Of course their search was in vain (2 Kings 2:15–18).

The successor to Elijah continued his master's unrelentless demand that Israel be loyal to Jehovah. Not quite so stern, not quite so dramatic as Elijah, he was still as uncompromising toward evil and toward the worship of Baal. He seemed quieter, calmer in his method of dealing with the people. With his schools of the prophets at Bethel, Gilgal, and Jericho he continued to exert a great influence as a teacher of other prophets.

Elisha was a great miracle worker, far surpassing Elijah in this respect; these miraculous episodes are recorded in 2 Kings 2—6. In the second chapter he healed the spring of water at Jericho and punished the boys who mocked him; in the third chapter he miraculously supplied water for the Israelite army; in the fourth chapter he provided oil for a widow, restored the life of a young boy, made the pottage sweet, and multiplied the loaves; in the fifth chapter he healed Naaman of his leprosy and punished Gehazi with leprosy; in the sixth chapter he made the axe head to swim and blinded the whole Syrian army, leading them into Samaria—many supernatural events in just five chapters! Though Elijah's miracles were fewer in number, they were just as effective in their purpose.

19. Jehoram and Moab

Jehoram, king of Israel, resolved to reclaim Moab as a vassal state; for the plentiful annual tribute had ceased back in the previous reign of his brother, Ahaziah. Enlisting the support of Jehoshaphat of Judah, he made a seven-day march to the south, where the king of Edom joined the alliance also. He planned to attack Moab not from the north but from the south, through Edomite territory. While encamped at the Moabite-Edomite border, in desert country, the combined armies were in desperate need of water. Elisha, being contacted, miraculously supplied the water; and the Moabites were repulsed in battle the following day. After a final but unsuccessful attempt on the part of the Moabite king to break through the allied army, he took his oldest son, heir to the throne, and sacrificed him on the wall in view of all the Israelites. After seeing such a sight the Israelite army departed for home (2 Kings 3:4–27).

20. The Shunamite Woman

In the village of Shunam lived a man and his wife who befriended Elisha by building for him a room atop their house, "a little chamber on the wall." In this room they provided all the essential furnishings for the man of God, that he might stay there whenever he wished. Calling for the woman one day, Elisha declared to her that she would become the mother of a son. The son was born, just as the prophet predicted; but the lad died one day a few hours after having been exposed to the hot sun with his father and the reapers. Elisha restored life in the child by stretching himself upon him, after which he presented him back to his mother (2 Kings 4:8–37).

21. Naaman the Leper

One of the most famous of Elisha's miracles was the cleansing of Naaman of the dreaded disease of leprosy, which the Jews called the "stroke" and the Greeks called the "first-born son of death." This man, a captain of the Syrian army living in Damascus, seemingly was able to retain his army position, due probably to the fact that he was a Syrian and not subject to the Mosaic law. Had he been a Hebrew he would have been required to live as an outcast and to yell "Unclean!" as anyone approached him. Due to a little captive Israelite maid residing in his home he learned of the healing ministry of "the prophet that is in Samaria." In true army style, Naaman secured a letter written by Benhadad of Syria to Jehoram of Israel and came to Samaria laden down with gold, silver, and fabrics. When Jehoram received the letter he rent his clothes, saying, "Am I God, to kill and to make alive, that this man doth send unto me to recover a man of his leprosy?" He interpreted the letter to be an attempt on the part of the Syrian king to start a quarrel (2 Kings 5:7). Elisha sent word to Jehoram to send Naaman to him, and Naaman arrived with his whole cavalcade before Elisha's house.

Naaman became disgusted with Elisha on two scores. For one, Elisha did not present himself personally but sent Gehazi his servant outside with a message of directions for effecting the cure. Second, the "prescription" for the cleansing was so simple that it appeared to Naaman to be ridiculous, for Elisha told him to go and dip seven times in the Jordan River. Did he not have clear mountain streams near his own city of Damascus, the Abanah and the Pharpar? He could wash in these, could he not, and be clean? "So he turned and went away in a rage." But his servants persuaded him to do as Elisha had directed. Dipping himself seven times in the Jordan, he came up clean; then he returned to the prophet to offer him a reward. Elisha, refusing to be rewarded, sent Naaman on his way; but not so was it with Gehazi, his servant. Secretly following

Naaman and coveting the rich gifts originally proffered Elisha, he used deceit in begging for the gifts. When they were generously given to him, he returned home with them, hiding them. However, his act of greed was known to Elisha, who transferred the leprosy of Naaman to Gehazi. "And he went out from his presence a leper as white as snow" (2 Kings 5:1–27).

22. Jehoram and Syria

The king of Syria renewed his warfare against Israel and Jehoram (2 Kings 6:8–23), endeavoring to invade the Northern Kingdom; but all his plans and strategy of war were revealed to Jehoram by Elisha. Therefore Benhadad knew he must capture the prophet if he were to have any military success in Israel. Learning that Elisha was at Dothan, six miles north of Samaria, he sent an army to surround the city; but Elisha called upon Jehovah to blind the entire Syrian army, after which he led them to Samaria, even into the city itself. Jehoram would have executed them, saying, "My father, shall I smite them? shall I smite them?" Elisha dissuaded him from doing so, but suggested he feed them bountifully and return them to Benhadad. This he did.

Benhadad's next move was to attempt to conquer Samaria, so he besieged the city for three years, during which the inhabitants suffered tremendously, even to the point of eating human flesh. The story of the two mothers who resolved to eat their two sons vividly depicts the arduous living conditions within the city. When one child was boiled and eaten by the two women, the mother of the second son hid hers away and would not fulfill her part of the agreement. When Jehoram heard from the lips of the first mother her complaint, he rent his clothes, only to reveal that he wore sackcloth beneath. Jehoram, burning with anger at Elisha for permitting the Syrian army to return home when he had once had them in his grasp, decided to take Elisha. But Elisha predicted an immediate end to the siege, and the next day God caused the Syrians to hear the sound of horses and chariots. Thinking it was advancing Egyptians and Hittites hired by the Hebrews, they fled, leaving their camp deserted; and the Israelites went out "and plundered the camp of the Syrians" (2 Kings 6:24 to 7:20).

After Samaria was miraculously saved Elisha made a visit to the city of Damascus, where Benhadad, the king, was sick. When Benhadad sent Hazael to inquire of Elisha if he would recover, the prophet announced to the king's messenger that the king would recover, but that he, Hazael, would rule in his stead. The very next day Hazael suffocated Benhadad and replaced him as king (2 Kings 8:7–15).

23. Second Battle of Ramoth-gilead

You will recall that Ahab and Jehoshaphat at one time fought with the Syrians at Ramoth-gilead in an endeavor to restore the city to Israel (1 Kings 22). Again the northern king and the southern king united in a siege upon the city, this time the monarchs being Jehoram of Israel and Ahaziah, his nephew, king of Judah. (Ahaziah's mother was Athaliah, sister of Jehoram of Israel and daughter of Ahab and Jezebel.) The combined armies marched toward Ramoth-gilead east of the Jordan and laid siege to the city. Jehoram, being wounded, returned to the summer palace at Jezreel to recuperate, where Ahaziah came to visit him in his sickness (2 Kings 8:25–29).

Israel, Jehu Through the Fall of Samaria
(2 Kings 9—17)

1. Jehu, Bloody Revolutionary

Two of Elijah's three anointings having already occurred, it became time for the third, for Jehu to take over as king of Israel. Elisha sent one of the sons of the prophets to Ramoth-gilead to Jehu, son of Jehoshaphat and one of Ahab's guards. Asking for a private interview, the young prophet poured oil on Jehu's head, announced that he would be king and that he would smite the house of Ahab, and then opened the door and fled. Jehu's fellow officers soon ratified what the young prophet had done by placing their peer on a rude carpet of state, blowing the trumpet, and shouting "Jehu is king" (2 Kings 9:1–13).

Having been ordered to destroy the family of Ahab, Jehu drove his chariot toward the fords of the Jordan and then directly toward Jezreel. The watchman in the tower of Jezreel declared that the approaching one drove like Jehu, "for he driveth furiously." When Jehoram (also called Joram) and Ahaziah, kings of the dual monarchies, went out to meet him, the former asked, "Is it peace, Jehu?" His query was immediately met by a vivid denunciation of the idolatries of Jezebel, his mother, at which time both kings turned and fled toward Jezreel. Jehu shot an arrow into the chest of Jehoram and had his body cast over into the field of Naboth, the Jezreelite. Fleeing after Ahaziah, the famous charioteer shot him also, but the Judean king managed to get as far as Megiddo before he died. His servants bore his body back to Jerusalem for burial in the royal tomb (2 Kings 9:14–28).

With this double killing Jehu's slaughters had just begun, for he proceeded to Jezreel for his next victim, the queen-mother Jezebel. As the revolutionary entered the city, Jezebel "painted her eyes, and attired her head, and looked out at the window." She called him "Zimri," for Zimri had murdered a former king and had taken his place. Jehu ordered her cast from the window. "So they threw

201

14. Esdraelon Plain from ruins of Megiddo

her down; and some of her blood was sprinkled on the wall, and on the horses: and he trod her under foot." At the close of his meal Jehu commanded that Jezebel be buried, but all they could find were "the skull, and the feet, and the palms of her hands." Scavenger dogs had played their part in the drama of divine justice. Jehu, hearing of this, interpreted it as the fulfillment of Elijah's prophecy (1 Kings 21:23): "The dogs shall eat Jezebel by the rampart of Jezreel." The infamous queen, the one making Baalism such an effective part of Israel's religion, was gone at last (2 Kings 9:30–37).

Jehu then turned his face toward Samaria, the capital, where sons and grandsons of Ahab to the number of 70 persons resided. He sent a boastful letter to the elders of Samaria telling them to put a royal son on the throne and then to prepare to defend him, to which they replied in the negative and vowed loyalty to Jehu. A second letter to the elders of Samaria demanded that the seventy sons be beheaded and their heads brought to Jezreel. When this atrocious command was fulfilled, Jehu ordered the heads piled at the gate in two heaps till morning, at which time he viewed the gory scene and said, "I conspired against my master, and slew him; but who smote all these?" He then proceeded to exterminate all of Ahab's kinsmen remaining in Jezreel, his friends, and his priests. On the way to Samaria Jehu met 42 princes of Judah traveling to visit their kinsmen in Israel; these he killed also. Arriving in Samaria he repeated his deed at Jezreel by wiping out all the remainder of the house of Ahab (2 Kings 10:1–17).

2. Jehu and Baal Worship

Israel's new king struck a blow at Baal worship by calling together to the house of Baal all the prophets of Baal, the worshipers of Baal, and the priests of Baal. "And they came into the house of Baal; and the house of Baal was filled from one end to another." He even ordered a search to see that no worshipers of Jehovah were there. Then at the conclusion of the pagan worship he ordered the guard to enter and to slay every person, after which the house and its heathen furnishings were destroyed. "Thus Jehu destroyed Baal out of Israel" (2 Kings 10:18–28).

Jehu had made a remark to Jehonadab, son of Rechab, while on his way to Samaria for his mass murders there: "Come with me, and see my zeal for Jehovah!" (2 Kings 10:16). This zeal is easily discerned in his gigantic move against Baal worship at the house of Baal in Samaria, but his "zeal for Jehovah" was not sufficient to bring devastation to the golden-calf shrines set up at Dan and at Bethel, the abominations of Jeroboam the son of Nebat. His religious reform was incomplete; "He departed not from the sins of Jeroboam, wherewith he made Israel to sin." Nor did he return to Jehovah worship, the worship that his forefathers knew and followed (2 Kings 10:29–31). The prophet Hosea brought condemnation upon the name of Jehu for his intense cruelty (Hos. 1:4); and did he not "overwork" his commission? He was commanded by the prophet who anointed him to blot out the house of Ahab, and this he did. But he included as well a horrible massacre of Ahab's nobles, friends, and priests.

3. Jehu's Decline

The Scriptures present very little detail about Jehu's reign of 28 years other than his bloody and savage beginning. Second Kings devotes two verses (10:32–33) to relate how Hazael of Syria ravished the part of Israel east of the Jordan and reduced it to serfdom, with the Moabite territory also thrown in. But the Black Obelisk of Shalmaneser III, king of Assyria, depicts "Jehu, son of Omri" prostrate on his face before the Assyrian monarch and behind him thirteen of his servants loaded with valuable gifts for the new Assyrian overlord. The monument, made of black basaltic rock and set up by Shalmaneser in his capital at Nimrud before 825 B.C., shows how archaeology can supplement the account in the Scriptures. This monument, discovered in 1846, also shows four other nationalities bringing tribute to Assyria, thus revealing the growing might of the cruel nation on the Tigris in Mesopotamia. Jehu died a natural death and was buried in Samaria; Jehoahaz, his son, became the next king in Israel (2 Kings 10:32–36).

4. The House of Jehu

Jehu's dynasty consisted of five kings: Jehu, Jehoahaz, Jehoash (or Joash), Jeroboam II, and Zechariah. The time covered by the reigns of these five men might be described as one of revolution, of decline, of recovery, and of the initial phase of another decline. Concurrent with this dynasty of almost a century (longer than any other of the nine dynasties of Israel) was a growing Assyrian aggressiveness. Under Jehu Israel suffered territorial losses, reducing it to its smallest geographical area; but under Jeroboam II Israel reached its peak, not only in territory claimed but also in wealth and in international prestige. In less than three decades this prosperity and honor began to fade before Assyrian dominance.

5. Jehoahaz and Syria

Jehoahaz had to contend with the same Syrian king that disturbed Jehu, Hazael of Damascus. Hazael extended his dominance even into the hill country of Ephraim, to the point that Israel's army was reduced to 50 horsemen, 10 chariots, and 10,000 footmen. Hazael even conquered Gath, and, when he looked toward Jerusalem, was bought off by the southern king. After a reign of 17 years Jehoahaz died and was succeeded by Jehoash, his son (2 Kings 13:1–9).

6. Jehoash and Elisha

In spite of the warning of the aged Elisha Jehoash practiced idolatry, as did his predecessors, throughout his reign of 16 years. Hazael died sometime during his reign, and Israel's upward surge was begun during Jehoash's leadership.

The silence of the Scriptures in the matter would be good evidence for the belief that neither Jehu nor Jehoahaz had much to do with Elisha. Not so was it for Jehoash. When Elisha was struck with his fatal illness, Jehoash went down to see him and wept over him. Elisha instructed him to shoot an arrow out of the open window facing east, after which the prophet termed it "the arrow of victory over Syria." Then he told him to shoot arrows into the ground; shooting three in number the king was informed of three future victories over the Syrians (2 Kings 13:10–19).

Elisha's final miracle occurred even after his death and burial. During a Moabite invasion a dead man was cast over into the sepulchre of Elisha; when he touched the bones of the dead prophet, the man was revived and stood up (2 Kings 13:20–21).

Hazael, king of Syria, died and was replaced by his son, Benhadad II. When Jehoash marched against the new king he regained the cities of Israel that Hazael had captured from his father Jehoahaz. Probably the territory east of the Jordan was recovered later, during the time of Jehoash's successor (2 Kings 13:22–25).

7. Jehoash and Amaziah

Amaziah, king of Judah and contemporary of Jehoash, initiated a conflict with Israel. After Amaziah's victory over Edom, in which he killed 10,000 of the Edomites, he challenged Jehoash to do battle. "Come, let us look one another in the face." Jehoash, answering by means of a parable, advised Amaziah to glory in his recent victory, return home, and remain there. But Amaziah, not willing to heed, was not only defeated by Jehoash but had his own territory invaded. The king of Israel broke down the wall of Jerusalem for a length of 600 feet, plundered the palace and the Temple, and returned to Israel with hostages. Jehoash died after a reign of 16 years and was buried in Samaria (2 Kings 14:7–16).

8. Jeroboam II and Prosperity

Jeroboam II, fourth ruler in Jehu's dynasty, was probably the most outstanding of all the 19 kings of Israel. His reign of 41 years, though characterized by evil, brought a wealth, splendor, and magnificence that proved to be the climax of glory for Israel. Omri was the next strongest king in Israel's span of history, and for both these kings the scriptural accounts are brief. Second Kings devotes only seven verses to the history of Jeroboam II (14:23–29). Jonah, the son of Amittai, who must be the Jonah of Jonah 1:1, predicted that Jeroboam would restore Israel from the border of Hamath in the north to the Dead Sea (sea of the Arabah) in the south, which he was indeed able to do (2 Kings 14:25). He restored to Israel all the territory held previously by David, with the exception of Judah, of course, and brought great military and commercial prosperity to his country. At the same time Uzziah, reigning as king in Judah, led his country to a zenith in power and prosperity also. All this was due chiefly to the inactivity of Assyria, the powerful nation with its capital on the Tigris River. All during Jeroboam's reign of 41 years he never pulled his country out of the low religious depth created by Jeroboam the son of Nebat, first king of Israel.

9. Zechariah's Brief Reign

When Jeroboam II died, he was succeeded by his son Zechariah, the fifth and last member of the house of Jehu. After a short rule of six months he was assassinated by one named Shallum, who took over the throne (2 Kings 15:8–12). Thus ended the dynasty of Jehu, some of whose kings were brilliant but most defiant of principles of right and wrong.

10. The Last of Israel's Kings

The great prophets, Amos and Hosea, had been preaching throughout Israel that God would bring judgment on the evil nation; the people little realized how soon that devastating day would come! After the fall of Jehu's dynasty Israel survived for only three more decades, going down to Assyrian might never to arise again. During these three decades revolution and murder prevailed. Four dynasties, including a total of five kings, ruled over Israel. One of the prophets described the era with the words "blood toucheth blood."

Shallum reigned only one month and was assassinated, his rule being the shortest except for Zimri's seven-day record. Menahem, Shallum's murderer, took over the realm, dying ten years later and leaving the throne to his son, Pekahiah. Pekah, captain in Pekahiah's guard, assassinated his master after a brief reign of two years and put himself on the throne, ruling 20 years in Israel. "And Hoshea the son of Elah made a conspiracy against Pekah the son of Remaliah, and smote him, and slew him, and reigned in his stead" (2 Kings 15:30). Hoshea's control of the kingdom lasted for nine years, at the end of which Samaria the capital was captured by the Assyrians and Israel existed no more (722–721 B.C).

11. Assyrian Aggression

It was during the reign of Menahem that Tiglath-pileser (or Pul, as he was called) began to rule in Assyria as one of the strongest kings of that nation. He began the policy of conquering a people and then exporting the strongest citizens, executives, and political officials to his own country and replacing them by foreigners—all with the idea of discouraging any possible rebellion. Tiglath waged a war against eastern Israel, taking away many people as captives (1 Chron. 5:26). Menahem paid Tiglath-pileser 1,000 talents of silver in tribute, after which the Assyrian monarch returned home (2 Kings 15:19–20).

During the days of Pekah, Tiglath-pileser took more cities in northern Israel, again carrying away a captive horde (2 Kings 15:29). Pekah aligned himself with Rezin, king of Syria, against the Assyrians to the north and against Ahaz, king of Judah, to the south. These two kings even made war against Jerusalem but could not overcome Ahaz (2 Kings 16:5). This is known as the Syro-Ephraimitic War and is found in 2 Kings 16:5–9 and in Isaiah 7:1 to 8:8. Ahaz appealed to Tiglath-pileser for help, after which the Assyrian king conquered many towns in the vicinity of Damascus and then Damascus itself (732 B.C.).

12. Fall of Samaria

Hoshea, last king of Israel, weary of sending tribute to Nineveh, rebelled, and withheld the annual money. Shalmaneser V, the new monarch on the Tigris, besieged Samaria, the capital city; but he died before it was taken. The three-year siege was completed by Sargon II in 722–721 B.C., and Israel collapsed and was no more. It became a small part of the vast Assyrian empire.

Captive Israelites were deported far to the north, even to Persia, probably to be swallowed up by intermarriage. Assyria brought in large numbers of people from the more inland portions of the empire, placing them in and around Samaria, where they intermarried with the remaining Israelites. The Samaritans mentioned in the New Testament were descendants of this mongrel race.

Judah, Rehoboam Through Ahaz
(1 Kings 12—2 Kings 17; 2 Chronicles 10—28)

1. The Kings in Judah

In the kingdom of Israel there were nine dynasties and nineteen kings. In Judah there was one dynasty composed of nineteen kings, all of the family of David except the usurper-queen Athaliah. Her brief reign of six years is considered as not breaking the line; it was merely an unfortunate interlude that shoved aside temporarily the Davidic descent. As the whole history of Israel was the continuing influence of Jeroboam, the whole history of Judah was the continuing influence of David. Israel lasted a little over 200 years, while Judah lasted about 345 years. Though all the kings of Israel were more or less evil, Judah had some that were good and some that were evil. One of Judah's kings, Manasseh, was extremely wicked and vicious.

2. Rehoboam, First King of Judah

We have already seen how Rehoboam's "suicidal policy" lost for him the ten northern tribes. The story of the encounter of Rehoboam, son of Solomon, and Jeroboam, former tax gatherer for Solomon, at Shechem has already been depicted in detail. Jeroboam's activities were merely "bringing to pass" what the prophet Ahijah had predicted, that he, Jeroboam, would rule over the ten northern tribes.

The northern tribes revolted under Jeroboam's leadership, with Jeroboam becoming the first king in Israel and Rehoboam being driven back to the territory of Judah to be content (or discontent) to reign there (1 Kings 12:1-24). Rehoboam was not even permitted of God to send his 180,000 men marching north to punish the recalcitrant people of Israel. The foolish behavior of Solomon's son became known as "Rehoboam's folly" and constitutes the direct or immediate cause of the split of the kingdom. The indirect or background cause of the division was the deeply rooted jealousy between

Judah in the south and some of the tribes in the north, especially Ephraim. The rift seen in the early years of David's reign became a never-to-be-filled breach after Solomon's death. In fact, the rumblings of discontent were heard even before Solomon died; the "straw" of Rehoboam's tyranny "broke the camel's back."

The new boundary between the two countries was a line running east and west about ten miles north of Jerusalem, with the greater part of the population and about three fourths of the land falling to Israel. Even the best of the land was in the north, with the fine pastures and plains. Added to all this was the fact that a divided people meant a diminished strength in the face of a common enemy. The break came about 931 B.C.

The Scriptures speak of continuous warfare between Rehoboam and Jeroboam (1 Kings 15:6), but no details of any battles are given. And when Jeroboam set up his golden calves at Dan and at Bethel in the territory of Israel, he made the priests and Levites of Jehovah leave the land. Returning to Judah, they strengthened the realm of Rehoboam; and for the first three years of Rehoboam's reign there was religious zeal in the land (2 Chron. 11:13–17). But then he took unto himself many women (18 wives and 60 concubines), and his kingdom declined during his latter days.

3. Shishak's Invasion

One of the most embarrassing things that occurred during Rehoboam's tenure was that Shishak (or Sheshonk I), king of Egypt, invaded Judah with great disaster. This was in Rehoboam's fifth year as king. He took many of the fortified cities, even entering Jerusalem itself. Israel did not even escape unharmed, for Shishak took some cities there, including Megiddo. When Shishak raided Jerusalem, he appropriated the Temple treasures and the palace treasures, even taking the golden shields Solomon had made, which Rehoboam replaced with brass ones (1 Kings 14:25–28). Shemaiah the prophet interpreted this as Jehovah's judgment upon Judah because of its sin (2 Chron. 12:5–8). Now Jeroboam, Rehoboam's rival, had been a refugee in Shishak's court prior to the death of Solomon. Whether there is any connection between that visit and Shishak's invasion is a debatable question.

After a reign of 17 years Rehoboam died and was buried in Jerusalem. There were no outstanding achievements during his time as king in Jerusalem.

4. Abijah and Continuing Idolatry

This son of Rehoboam by Maacah, daughter of Absalom, is called Abijah in Chronicles and Abijam in Kings. "And there was war between Abijah and Jeroboam" (2 Chron. 13:2). Abijah activated the ill-feeling between Israel and Judah by challenging Jeroboam within Ephraimite territory. By a circling movement the Israelite troops were able to get into an advantageous position; but, even though Abijah had half the number of troops, in the ensuing conflict the forces of Judah were victorious. Judah weakened Israel by capturing three cities with their surrounding villages (2 Chron. 13:3–20).

Idolatry became stronger during his days, for he did not wipe out the worship of the foreign gods but followed the example of his father and grandfather. He had 14 wives and many children. Abijah died after three years and left the throne to his son Asa.

5. Asa and Religious Reform

Asa ruled in Jerusalem for 41 years, the first ten of which were in peaceful times. His mother also, as was the case with Abijah, was named Maacah (2 Chron. 11:20,22; 1 Kings 15:10). "And Asa did that which was right in the eyes of Jehovah, as did David his father" (1 Kings 15:11). He is noted for the religious reform that he initiated, desiring to wipe out all signs of pagan and idolatrous worship that had obtained such a footing in Judah and to revive Jehovah worship in its stead. He drove the sodomites out of the land and destroyed all the idols his predecessors had installed. He demoted Maacah his mother "from being queen" and publicly burnt her idol at the brook Kidron east of Jerusalem. His aim was to make a strong appeal to the people to turn back to the worship of Jehovah, the one true God. The religious festivities in Jerusalem during the reign of Asa were greater than any held there since Solomon's dedication of the Temple.

6. Wars of Asa

Along with his religious reforms Asa showed himself to be strong militarily. He fortified the frontier towns and equipped a large army, which probably gave him the strength to withstand an invasion from the south by Zerah, the Ethiopian (probably Osarkon I of the Libyan dynasty in Egypt), who swept into the land with a million men and 300 chariots. Asa, having the favor of Jehovah, met Zerah in the low country of Judah and completely defeated and routed his army. The retreating forces left much booty for the Judeans. This story is found in Chronicles (2 Chron. 14:9–15), but is not found in Kings.

Besides Zerah, Asa had to contend with another enemy, Baasha, king of Israel. Israel had been defeated by Judah during the days of Abijah, and at this time the people were migrating from Israel to Judah. Therefore Baasha built Ramah (2 Chron. 16:1) five miles north of Jerusalem.

Asa must have interpreted Baasha's act as one of aggression; for he formed an alliance with Benhadad of Damascus, paying him with silver and with gold. "And Benhadad hearkened unto king Asa, and sent the captains of his armies against the cities of Israel" This is the first instance of a Hebrew king seeking an alliance with a heathen nation while in a great national crisis (2 Chron. 16:1–6).

When Baasha left Ramah to go north to fight the Syrians, Asa moved into his southern territory at Ramah and also fortified two other cities for himself. When Hanani the prophet rebuked Asa for this ungodly alliance with Syria, Asa put Hanani in prison. Hanani predicted wars for Asa (2 Chron. 16:7–10). Two years before his death Asa suffered a severe foot disease; he died and was buried in Jerusalem, having reigned 41 years.

7. Jehoshaphat, Good Administrator

Jehoshaphat, son of Asa, succeeded his father as king and ruled 25 years over Judah. He was not only an able statesman; he was also a competent religious leader, for he was vitally interested in seeing that his people worshiped Jehovah. "And Jehovah was with Jehoshaphat, because he walked in the first ways of his father David"

(2 Chron. 17:3). "And his heart was lifted up in the ways of Jehovah" (17:6). He not only put away the high places and the Asherim in the land; he sent out a commission of princes, Levites, and priests throughout the kingdom to teach the people the law (2 Chron. 17:6–9). He was held in high respect not only by his own people (17:5), but also by the surrounding nations (17:10–11). While Asa had been at odds with the Israelite king, during Jehoshaphat's reign peace was restored between Israel and Judah. Ahab's good sense and Jehoshaphat's good religion brought peace. Besides, Jehoshaphat's son, Jehoram, married Ahab's daughter, Athaliah; this marital bond tended to establish harmony between the two Hebrew nations. Jehoshaphat built up a large army (1,160,000) and fortified many cities in Judah and Ephraim (17:2,12–13). He was truly one of the great kings of Judah, a more worthy ruler than his father Asa.

8. Jehoshaphat's Wars

Jehoshaphat accepted the invitation of Ahab, king of Israel, to form a military alliance with him, resulting in a war with the Syrians at Ramoth-gilead. This account has been presented in chapter 13 under the heading "First Battle of Ramoth-gilead." The very fact that Jehoshaphat asked Ahab to inquire first "for the words of Jehovah" relative to the proposed battle was characteristic of this able king of Judah. Accordingly Ahab called in 400 prophets, all of which said that he, Ahab, would be victorious. The lone prophet Micaiah predicted disaster, that Ahab would be killed (1 Kings 22:1–28). In the battle Jehoshaphat did not divest himself of his kingly robes, but Ahab did. Even though disguised, Ahab was killed. At the end of the day a cry went forth, "Every man to his city, and every man to his country" (1 Kings 22:29–36). When Jehoshaphat returned home to Jerusalem he was rebuked by a prophet named Jehu for his alliance with Ahab (2 Chron. 19:1–3).

A coalition of southwestern peoples—Moab, Ammon, and Edom—swept around the lower end of the Dead Sea and up into Judah, headed for Jerusalem. Jehoshaphat called for a national fast and in an assembly of Judah prayed for the help of Jehovah in a long prayer. To this request in prayer he received a favorable reply through the prophet Jahaziel. As Cromwell's army did in England they marched forth to battle singing, but they soon found that there would be no need for a battle. Quarreling among themselves, the enemy had fallen upon one another and annihilated themselves. Jehoshaphat and his army found the field strewn with dead bodies, and three days were required for gathering the booty (2 Chron. 20:1–30).

A third military venture of Jehoshaphat has also been discussed in chapter 13 under the heading "Jehoram and Moab." This event occurred near the end of Jehoshaphat's reign and is related in 2 Kings 3:4–27. After the death of Ahab Moab ceased paying tribute to the Northern Kingdom, Israel. Apparently Ahaziah did nothing about it, but Jehoram his brother, the next to sit on Israel's throne, decided to venture forth and correct the situation, inviting Jehoshaphat to help him in his march through Edom to defeat Moab. Again Jehoshaphat was found in an alliance with an ungodly king. Edom also was involved in the union against Moab, as they marched up toward the Edomite-Moabite border. They lacked water desperately; and because of the presence of Jehoshaphat in the coalition (2 Kings 3:14) Elisha miraculously supplied the water, thus saving the three armies. The Moabites were routed the next day in battle.

9. Jehoshaphat's Business Tragedy

The Judean king aligned himself commercially with Ahaziah, king of Israel, to manufacture ships at Ezion-geber on the Persian Gulf for the purpose of sailing to Tarshish. Eliezer prophesied that, due to Jehoshaphat's joining himself with the unholy northern king, Jehovah would destroy the venture. "And the ships were broken, so that they were not able to go to Tarshish" (2 Chron. 20:35–37). An invitation from Ahaziah for a second attempt in such a venture was declined by Jehoshaphat (1 Kings 22:48–49). When the latter died, having reigned 25 years, he was succeeded by his son Jehoram on the throne in Jerusalem.

10. Jehoram and Idolatry

The peaceful rule that existed under wise Jehoshaphat soon changed to one of bloodshed and idolatry under Jehoram his son.

As soon as Jehoram secured the throne he killed his six brothers and all other possible rivals for the kingship (2 Chron 21:1–4). He married Athaliah, the daughter of Ahab and sister to Ahaziah and Jehoram of Israel, and thereby walked in the ways of the kings of Israel, "for he had the daughter of Ahab to wife" (2 Chron. 21:6). He restored the high places and forms of idolatry that his father Jehoshaphat had removed.

Edom and Libnah rebelled against his yoke and refused to pay tribute. And Elijah sent him a letter of rebuke, stating that because he had led Judah into idolatry and because he had killed his brothers, he would be struck with a terrible, incurable disease (2 Chron. 21:12–15). Added to these afflictions was a raid by Philistines and Arabians, who entered Jerusalem and carried away treasures of the palace as well as the family of Jehoram. His sons and his wives were led away captive, all except Athaliah and the youngest son, Ahaziah (2 Chron 21:16–17). Two years before his death he was stricken with a mortal disease. He had ruled eight years at the time of his death (2 Chron. 21:18–20).

11. Ahaziah's Short Reign

The only son of Jehoram left by the raiders was Ahaziah, the youngest, who became the next king. Naturally he followed in the ways of his father, Jehoram, and his wicked mother, Athaliah.

Jehoram of Israel, ruling at the same time, was his uncle, being Athaliah's brother (2 Kings 8:25–27). The young king aligned himself with his uncle, Jehoram of Israel, to fight the Syrians at Ramoth-gilead. This second battle of Ramoth-gilead also has been discussed in the section entitled "Second Battle of Ramoth-gilead" in chapter 13. Hazael had just replaced Benhadad as king of Syria. In the disastrous battle, Jehoram of Israel was wounded and returned to Jezreel to recuperate. Ahaziah came to visit his ailing uncle (2 Kings 8:28,29), and it was here that Jehu struck violently, killing both the reigning kings. Jehu himself took over in the north, while Athaliah, the queen mother, took the reins in Judah. Ahaziah was twenty-two years of age when he started to reign, a reign that had endured only one year when he was murdered by the famous charioteer of Israel's army.

12. Athaliah, Infamous Queen Mother

When the news reached Athaliah in Jerusalem that her son Ahaziah had been killed, she immediately proceeded to destroy all the ones remaining of the royal line, that she herself might occupy the throne unmolested. This infamous deed included murdering her own grandchildren. As Jezebel slew the prophets of Jehovah in Israel, Athaliah slew the descendants of David in Judah, who were also her own descendants. However, one little boy, a year old, was secreted away by his aunt, sister of his father Ahaziah, and was hidden "in the house of Jehovah six years." The aunt's name was Jehosheba, whose husband was Jehoiada the priest; and the name of the little prince was Joash. During these six years Athaliah reigned in Jerusalem, having usurped the throne (2 Kings 11:1–3), and Baal worship was promoted there. It could very well be that Jehu's persecution of Baalism in Israel made Athaliah all the more determined to establish it firmly in Judah.

Jehoiada, a priest who had lived during the revival days of Asa and Jehoshaphat, was the man who successfully planned and executed the replacing of the Davidic line on the throne. Having secured the faithful and loyal support of the guard, composed of priests and Levites, he divided them into three groups to protect the little king at the moment of coronation, for little Joash had now reached the age of seven years. On the sabbath day at the changing of the guard the little prince was brought out of hiding and crowned king, as the people all shouted, "Long live the king!" Athaliah, hearing the shouting of the people and the blaring of the trumpets, started for the Temple. She came to the entrance but was barred; here she rent her clothes and shouted, "Treason! treason!" The captains followed her to the palace and slew her there. A degrading period of rule by three wicked monarchs, in which the pernicious and evil ways of Israel penetrated into Judah, had at last ended (2 Kings 11:4–16).

13. Joash and Jehoiada

Jehoiada the high priest renewed the covenant between Jehovah and his people. The house, altar, and images of Baal were destroyed, and the priest of Baal, Mattan, was killed. Joash (sometimes called Jehoash in the biblical record) was seven at the time, and therefore greatly in need of counsel, advice, and training. This the aged priest and his good wife, Jehosheba, were able to give, at least for the first half of Joash's reign, or until the death of Jehoiada at 130 years. After that it was a different story.

During the years of terror the Temple and its services had suffered from great neglect; repairs were greatly needed. As a result the priests were instructed to collect funds from throughout the nation; but this project failed. In Joash's twenty-third year of reign a chart was placed in the Temple at the side of the altar and near the entrance. Money placed in this chest provided for both the repair of the Temple and the needs of the priests.

When the aged Jehoiada died, a change in the government took place. The princes who had been suppressed by the party of priests appealed to the king. Overturning the priestly party they forsook the house of Jehovah to serve the Asherim and the idols; "and wrath came upon Judah and Jerusalem for this their guiltiness." When God sent prophets to reproach them, they would not hear (2 Chron. 24:15–19). When Zechariah, son of Jehoiada, called them to time, they stoned him to death in the very court of the Temple. He cried, "Jehovah look upon it, and require it" (2 Chron. 24:20–22).

This cry was soon fulfilled. The army of Hazael, king of Syria, came to Judah and Jerusalem and killed the royal princes. When Joash paid them off with treasures from the Temple and from the palace, Hazael and his army retreated from Jerusalem (2 Kings 12:17–18; 2 Chron. 24:23–24). Joash's lapse into idolatry embittered his close friends of early years. His own servants killed him upon his own bed, and his reign of 40 years came to an end.

14. Amaziah and Apostasy

Amaziah, son of Joash, commenced his rule over Judah by punishing the murderers of his father; these he killed, but their children he spared. His next move was against the Edomites, whom he defeated with great slaughter in the Valley of Salt just south of the Dead Sea. He captured their capital, or fortress, named Petra (or Sela) and then returned home to set up in Jerusalem the idols of the nation he had just conquered. To these Edomite gods he bowed down and burned incense. God sent to him a prophet to rebuke him for his apostasy (2 Chron. 25:1–16).

Amaziah's second military venture, not so successful, was waged against Jehoash of Israel; this campaign has been fully depicted in chapter 14 under the heading "Jehoash and Amaziah." Amaziah boldly challenged Jehoash and, though advised by the king of Israel to remain at home, marched forth with his army to meet Jehoash. "And Judah was put to the worse before Israel; and they fled every man to his tent." Jehoash captured Amaziah himself, took him to Jerusalem, broke down the wall, plundered the Temple and palace, took hostages, and returned to Samaria. Amaziah became so discredited with his own people following his apostasy that he fled to Lachish, where they followed and slew him. After a reign of 29 years he was buried in Jerusalem (2 Chron. 25:17–28).

15. Uzziah (or Azariah) and Prosperity

When only sixteen years of age, Uzziah, son of Amaziah, was made king by "all Judah" (2 Kings 14:21 calls him Azariah). His reign proved to be a long one, 52 years in all. Establishing himself as an able administrator and organizer, he helped Judah tremendously in many ways. He had a personal adviser in a prophet named Zechariah; as long as he followed the counsel of this man of God he did well and prospered. He fortified Jerusalem to a greater extent by the addition of towers and catapult machines. He even built towers in the desert and hewed out cisterns for his herds. His love of agriculture and for vineyards was great. His fighting force was well organized; he waged successful warfare against the Philistines, the Arabians, and the Meunim, and the Ammonites paid him tribute. He built Elath on the Gulf of Akabah. All of these enterprises brought him great prosperity at home and great fame abroad. Conditions in Judah were certainly quite different from those during the days of Amaziah, when defeat at the hands of Jehoash of Israel left a breach in the walls of Jerusalem and a confiscation of the treasures of Jerusalem. "And his name spread far abroad; for he was marvelously helped, till he was strong" (2 Chron. 26:1–15).

The key words here are striking: "till he was strong." In his latter years Uzziah became vain and arrogant. Entering the Temple and assuming the role of a priest, he burnt incense on the altar, a function assigned by the Mosaic law only to the priesthood (Ex. 30:7; Num. 18:1–7). When this act was protested by Azariah the high priest, backed up by 80 other priests, Uzziah became angry and defied them. Instantly, as a result of divine judgment, he turned leprous. For the rest of his life he could enter neither the palace nor the Temple, and Jotham his son had to function as ruler (2 Chron. 26:16–23). However, these years in which Jotham was co-regent are part of the 52 years allotted to Uzziah as ruling monarch.

16. Jotham, Son of Uzziah

Jotham, son of Uzziah, is credited with a reign of 16 years of duration. Most scholars believe that many of these 16 years overlap with the 52 years of Uzziah his father, when he actually reigned as regent with his father. In that case Jotham ruled alone for only a short time. Be that as it may, he was an able ruler, entering into an extensive building program. He constructed cities in the hill country for Judah and erected castles and towers in the forests. He also conquered the Ammonites, from whom he received tribute for several years (2 Chron. 27:1–9).

17. Ahaz, an Evil King

Ahaz, son of Jotham, succeeded his father on the throne of Judah, ruling for a span of 16 years; "and he did not that which was right in the eyes of Jehovah, like David his father." He rejected the worship of Jehovah and promoted the very obnoxious idol worship found in Israel and in surrounding nations. This even included child sacrifice, for "he burnt his children in the fire." He made images of Baal and burnt incense in the iniquitous high places, pagan altars of worship (2 Chron. 28:1–4). All this took place in spite of the preaching and counter-advice of the great prophet Isaiah of Jerusalem. Ahaz stubbornly ignored this great man of God.

Being twenty years of age when he began to reign, and being faced with many international difficulties, his reign was far from a smooth one. Assyria, with its capital Nineveh on the Tigris in Mesopotamia, aspired to control the entire Fertile Crescent. Pekah,

king of Israel, and Rezin, king of Syria, had banded together to
resist Tiglath-pileser, the aggressive ruler of Assyria. Apparently
Ahaz refused to join their pact, and Isaiah at some time or other
admonished the king not to fear "these two tails of smoking
firebrands," but to trust in Jehovah (Isa. 7:1–9). What did Ahaz
care for Jehovah, however?

Syria and Israel invaded Judah and carried away many captives,
the Syrians even regaining Elath, the city that Uzziah had built
up for Judah. The two allied nations even tried to conquer Jerusalem
but were unable to do so (2 Kings 16:5–6; 2 Chron. 28:5–15). Added
to all this was the fact that the Edomites and the Philistines had
invaded Judah's southern territory, wreaking havoc there. Ahaz
was paying dearly for his wanton rejection of Jehovah (2 Chron.
28:17–19).

As a result Ahaz appealed to Tiglath-pileser for help, saying,
"I am thy servant and thy son: come up, and save me." He even
bribed the great monarch with gold and silver from the Temple
and the palace. Fulfilling his request, Tiglath-pileser captured
Damascus and killed Rezin (2 Kings 16:7–9). Ahaz, on visiting in
Damascus and viewing there a pagan altar, ordered Urijah, his high
priest, to construct a similar one and place it in Jerusalem; and
when this was accomplished, he ordered the altar of Jehovah moved
and this one put in its place, with the morning and evening sacrifices
being offered thereon (2 Kings 16:10–16). Ahaz's idolatry even
increased through the years through further decrees and practices
(2 Chron. 28:22–25). Ahaz, after a reign of 16 abominable years,
died and was buried in Jerusalem, but not in the sepulchres of the
kings.

Judah, Hezekiah Through the Fall of Jerusalem
(2 Kings 18—25; 2 Chronicles 29—36)

1. Hezekiah, Man of Reform

The prophets and worshipers of Jehovah naturally rebounded from the iniquitous religious debauch of evil Ahaz, wishing for a return of the customs of the days of Jehoshaphat and Uzziah. They found a champion in the man Hezekiah, who ruled Judah for 59 fruitful years and who heeded the advice of the great prophet Isaiah as much as Ahaz had ignored it. In fact, Isaiah 36—39 must be read, along with Kings and Chronicles, in a study of the life of this outstanding king who brought religious reform to Judah. His reign shines out as a bright interlude between two evil kings, Ahaz and Manasseh.

In the first year on the throne he reopened the doors of the Temple of Jehovah, which Ahaz had closed, and repaired them. He instructed the priests and Levites in reorganizing the worship of Jehovah and to cleanse the Temple of Jehovah. All the pagan equipment found there was thrown in the brook Kidron east of Jerusalem. Then, after 16 days of cleansing, sacrifices were offered, with great rejoicing and singing (2 Chron. 29:3–36). This was the most extensive reform in the history of the Southern Kingdom.

Hezekiah sent out invitations into all Israel and to all Judah to come to Jerusalem to celebrate the Passover unto Jehovah. Many responded to his plea, people from the tribes of Asher, Manasseh, Ephraim, and Issachar, as well as Judah. The feast was so successful that it was lengthened to include two full weeks. All the pagan altars of incense throughout Jerusalem were cast into the brook Kidron. There was more joy in Jerusalem than at any time since Solomon's dedication of the Temple (2 Chron. 30:1–27). Hezekiah then extended his religious reform to include all of Judah, wiping out the pagan altars and high places. He also revived observances of the laws concerning tithes and offerings (2 Chron. 31:1–21).

2. Hezekiah as King

It was in the fourth year of the reign of Hezekiah of Judah that the city of Samaria fell to Sargon II of Assyria, and Hoshea the king and thousands of his subjects were deported to Mesopotamia as captives. Israel ceased to be a nation. Many people from throughout the Assyrian empire were brought in and placed in and around Samaria to intermarry with the remaining Israelites. This was in 772–721 B.C. No doubt this catastrophe in Israel had a great effect upon Judah's young king.

"And Hezekiah had exceeding much riches and honor." As a wise ruler he built treasuries, and storehouses, and stalls, and provided himself with cities. He built up his flocks and herds and strengthened Jerusalem. His great engineering feat was the construction of a tunnel from the Virgin's Spring under the east side of the city of David to the pool of Siloam within the walls of the south end of Jerusalem. This tunnel was 1,758 feet long, six feet high, bored in solid rock many feet below the surface of the ground. Workmen started from either end and met in the middle with the cuttings almost exactly in line with each other, quite an engineering accomplishment for those days. On the wall at the Siloam end of the tunnel an inscription was engraved in the Hebrew language telling the story of how the two groups of workmen met in the middle. In 1880 a schoolboy, absenting himself from school to roam around the walls of Jerusalem, adventurously entered the tunnel and, groping along the side, felt the letters. He reported his discovery, and archaeologists found it to be the oldest piece of Hebrew writing in existence. The section of the wall bearing the inscription was carefully cut out, removed, and translated. It was placed in the Ottoman Museum in Constantinople (2 Chron. 32:2–4, 27–30).

3. Hezekiah's Sickness

When Hezekiah became ill with a very painful skin disease, he almost died. "And Isaiah the prophet the son of Amoz came to him, and said unto him, Thus saith Jehovah, Set thy house in order; for thou shalt die, and not live." With this Hezekiah prayed and humbled himself before God, and God's answer came soon by way of the great prophet. Isaiah announced to the king that God would heal him and would add 15 years to his life, and that he would

15. Pool of Siloam in Jerusalem at lower end of Hezekiah's Tunnel

deliver Jerusalem out of the hand of the Assyrians. The remedy for the inflammatory condition of his skin was a poultice of figs, which was soon applied and a cure effected (2 Kings 20:1–7). When Hezekiah asked of Isaiah a sign that God would heal him and that he would go up into the Temple the third day, Isaiah asked him if he wanted the shadow on Ahaz's sundial to go forward ten steps or backward ten steps. He chose the latter; and when Isaiah cried to God the shadow went backward ten steps (2 Kings 20:8–11). Isaiah records a very moving song of thanksgiving that Hezekiah uttered for the sparing of his life (Isa. 38:10–20).

4. Hezekiah and Merodach-baladan

Merodach-baladan had seized the city of Babylon from the Assyrians, and Sargon II was getting ready to recapture it. Merodach sent messengers to Hezekiah to congratulate him on his recovery, but probably with the intent to spy out his strength and to determine whether or not he could aid him. Hezekiah, with gladness at their arrival and pride in his possessions, showed them his entire treasures. For this Isaiah rebuked him and predicted the carrying away into Babylon of the very treasures that had been so proudly displayed as well as of his male descendants (2 Kings 20:12–18; Isa. 39:1–8). Later Sargon II put down Merodach-baladan and removed him from Babylon.

5. Hezekiah and Sennacherib

In 701 B.C. Jerusalem was saved from destruction by the Assyrians, and all due to Hezekiah's heeding the advice of Isaiah the prophet; otherwise Jerusalem and Judah would have fallen to the Assyrians just two decades later than Samaria's inglorious end. Sennacherib, son of Sargon, had succeeded his father on the throne. Hezekiah, along with a general uprising of all southwest Asia against Assyria, in 702 cut off payment of tribute; and the Hebrews rejoiced over throwing off the shackles of Assyrian might. Sennacherib turned his attention toward the Mediterranean and took city after city as he proceeded down the coast. Coming to Lachish in Philistia he was delayed due to a necessitated prolonged siege. In the meantime he captured fortress after fortress in the surrounding countryside

16. Mount of Olives, foreground, and Jerusalem

of Judah and took many captives. Realizing the danger Hezekiah sent messengers to Lachish to say to him, "I have offended; return from me: that which thou puttest on me will I bear." To this humble remark Sennacherib demanded vast amounts of gold and silver. This Hezekiah paid, both from the treasuries in the Temple and palace and by stripping the gold from the Temple itself (2 Kings 18:13–16).

But this did not satisfy Sennacherib, for his next demand, in 701 B.C., was for Jerusalem itself. (Isa. 10 gives a vivid description of this Assyrian threat to the security of Jerusalem.) Sennacherib sent three envoys to Jerusalem to demand surrender: Tartan, Rab-saris, and Rabshakeh. These envoys talked to Hezekiah's representatives in very arrogant terms demanding surrender. The Hebrew envoys asked the Assyrians not to talk to them in the Hebrew language, lest the people on the wall hear the discussion; but they would not heed. They continued to talk with them. When Hezekiah's tactful diplomats returned with the doleful message, Hezekiah immediately sent them to Isaiah the prophet. He in turn sent them back to Hezekiah with the prediction that Sennacherib would return home to Assyria and be killed there (2 Kings 18:17 to 19:7).

Sennacherib, getting no result from the first embassy, sent a second to Jerusalem, this time with a letter to Hezekiah demanding the surrender of the city. Hezekiah took the letter to the Temple, spread it before Jehovah, and prayed urgently. Isaiah soon brought God's message, that God would turn Sennacherib back by the way he came; not even an arrow would be shot into the city. That night "the angel of Jehovah went forth" and destroyed 185,000 of the Assyrian army. Sennacherib returned to Nineveh and was killed as he worshiped in his pagan temple (2 Kings 19:8–37). Sennacherib's inscriptions are of course silent about any such defeat in the southwest; but the famous English poet, Lord Byron, has captured the mood of this miraculous defeat of the Assyrians in his poem "The Destruction of Sennacherib," one of his greatest works. Finally, after a reign of 29 years, Hezekiah died and was buried in Jerusalem.

6. The Four Eighth-century Prophets

The four great prophets who prophesied in Israel and Judah during the 700's were Amos, Hosea, Isaiah, and Micah; the first and second in Israel and the third and fourth in Judah. The message of Amos and Hosea evidently had little effect on corrupt Israel, for they failed to influence that nation to return to the worship of Jehovah. Isaiah and Micah were the pillars of loyalty to Jehovah in Judah, preaching just a little later than Amos and Hosea did in Israel. Both witnessed the downfall of Samaria, and both proclaimed doom for the sinners in Judah. They openly condemned the priests and judges for their hypocrisy in worship and heaped words of degradation upon the idols still found in Judah. Nor did the abundant social evils escape their denunciation. Though Ahaz rejected the advice of Isaiah, the mighty statesman prophet of Jerusalem, Hezekiah leaned heavily upon him. The contrast of conditions during the two reigns is very apparent. The fact that Isaiah's message was accepted gave Judah well over a century more to continue as a nation.

7. Manasseh, Worst of the Kings

The most evil king to sit on a throne in either Israel or Judah was Manasseh, son of Hezekiah, who took over at the death of the good king. This ruler, as notorious in his evil as Hezekiah was famous in his goodness, started reigning at twelve years of age and continued for 55 years, the longest of any king, north or south. He endeavored to revert Judah to the conditions found during Ahaz's devastating years.

Turning from the religion of his father he indulged immediately in idolatry and pagan rites. The devotees of the corrupt cults were probably just biding their time, waiting for the right moment to bring back their abominations and evil practices. The accession to the throne of a young boy, plus the probability that Isaiah was becoming aged, gave them their chance. There was a more general adoption of heathen modes of worship than had existed during Ahaz's harmful era. Manasseh restored the high places and established altars to Baal. He made an Asherah and placed it in the Temple itself. He worshiped all the host of heaven, as well as setting up altars for all the host of heaven in the Temple courts. He made his son to pass through the fire, as well as bringing back augury, enchantments, and wizardry. He and the people indulged in almost every kind of worship but that of Jehovah; for he endeavored to stamp out Jehovah worship, persecuting and destroying the true prophets. "Moreover Manasseh shed innocent blood very much, till he had filled Jerusalem from one end to another; besides his sin wherewith he made Judah to sin" (2 Kings 21:1–16). Tradition says that Isaiah the prophet was "sawn asunder" in a tree during this iniquitous period (compare Heb. 11:37).

8. Manasseh's Religious Reversal

When Sennacherib died in 681 B.C., Esarhaddon his son began to reign on the Assyrian throne. This aggressive king instituted a military campaign in Palestine and the surrounding countries. He even conquered Egypt as far up the Nile as Thebes, the first Assyrian king ever to subdue this nation in Africa. After a reign of military conquest he died, and Asshurbanipal his son became monarch in Nineveh. He too marched south in conquest, quelling a rebellion in Egypt and traveling up the Nile even to Thebes. He left Thebes unhurt, but he had to return later, this time destroying the city. In about 648 B.C., for some reason, he carried Manasseh as a captive in chains to Babylon—not Nineveh, as might be expected. Here sinful Manasseh, being in great distress, pleaded with Jehovah his God and humbled himself greatly; God heard his prayer and brought him back to Jerusalem. Here he not only removed the foreign gods, but the idol and the altars he had built in the Temple of Jehovah, casting them out of the city. He restored the altar of Jehovah to its rightful place and offered sacrifices thereon, commanding the people to worship Jehovah, the God of Israel. In the few remaining years of his life he attempted the gigantic task of undoing all the gross wickedness of his early years, an almost impossible feat in so few years. When he died, he was buried in his own house in Jerusalem (2 Chron. 33:10–20).

9. Amon and Apostasy

Amon, son of Manasseh, succeeded his father on the throne but occupied that position for only two years. And well this was, for he reverted to the idolatrous and pagan rites of the major part of

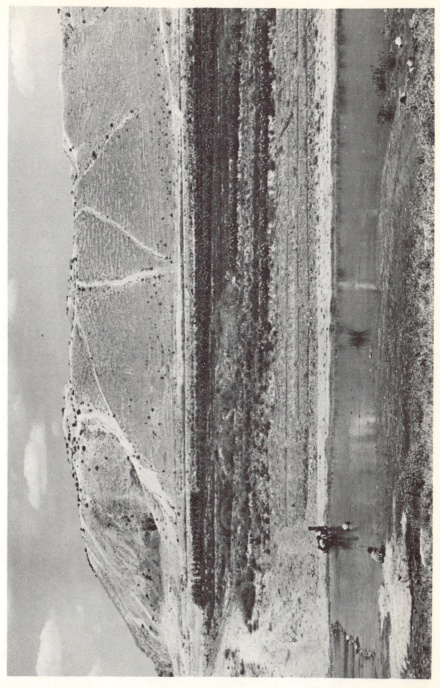

17. Ruins of Nineveh

Manasseh's kingship. Evidently Manasseh's reforming activities during his late career did not carry over to his son; the earlier years had the greater impression, and Judah was led in the degrading spiritual practices of certain previous periods. Some servants killed Amon in his own house (2 Kings 21:19–26).

10. Josiah and Waning Assyrian Power

At the early age of eight Josiah was crowned king in the place of his murdered father, Amon, himself to be killed 31 years later in battle at Megiddo. This span of almost a third of a century was one of religious reformation and increased nationalism. Assyria's power was waning, with Nineveh finally falling in 612 B.C. to the Medes and Babylonians. Therefore, Judah was able to extend its power northward into the territory previously occupied by Israel and to gain complete freedom from Assyrian domination.

During the early part of Josiah's reign, the religious conditions in Judah were probably no different from those during the early part of Manasseh's reign and during Amon's two years, but as the young king grew to manhood he reacted against the intolerable spiritual abominations of his country. In the eighth year of his regal career he began to seek after the God of David, and in the twelfth year of his reign "he began to purge Judah and Jerusalem from the high places, and the Asherim, and the graven images, and the molten images." He removed the altars dedicated to Baal, destroyed the sun images, and performed many other things of a reforming nature, his zeal extending even up into the territory of the northern tribes (2 Chron. 34:1–7).

11. The Book of the Law and Reformation

In the eighteenth year of his reign Josiah ordered a general repair of the Temple with the money brought into the house of God. This was in 621 B.C. (2 Chron. 34:8–13). In the course of the repairs Hilkiah the priest found "the book of the law of Jehovah given by Moses." This he showed to Shaphan the scribe, who in turn carried it to Josiah, before whom he also read it. "And it came to pass, when the king had heard the words of the law, that he rent his clothes." Josiah sent a delegation to inquire of Jehovah concerning the words in the book, for he knew that God's wrath lay upon the nation for its utter neglect of God's demands found in the book. Therefore Hilkiah and the remaining members of the delegation went to Huldah the prophetess. She assured them that divine judgment would certainly be fulfilled and that God would bring evil upon the place, but not during the days of Josiah. His humility would defer the disaster till after his death (2 Chron. 34:14–28). Calling a general assembly of all the priests, the prophets, and the people the king read the book before them and covenanted publicly before Jehovah to obey all the commandments and demands of God's word, the people agreeing to the covenant also (2 Chron. 34:29–33).

The reformation that ensued was drastic and is vividly described in 2 Kings. The land was purged of all pagan symbols of worship and the Temple of Jehovah thoroughly cleansed of all heathen influences. Josiah forbad sacrificing children to Molech in the valley of Hinnom, as well as destroying Jeroboam's golden calf and high place at Bethel. His reformation even extended to the cities of Samaria (2 Kings 23:4–20). He ordered an observance of the Passover feast and urged the people to participate. "And there was no passover like to that kept in Israel from the days of Samuel the prophet" (2 Chron. 35:1–19).

12. Jeremiah the Prophet

Jeremiah, one of the greatest prophets of the Old Testament, began his work in 626 B.C., just five years preceding Josiah's reformation. He was a native of Anathoth, a little village just north of Jerusalem, but spent most of his life in Jerusalem. Here, through a long ministry of approximately fifty years, he exerted a tremendous influence for Jehovah, especially during the closing years of the Southern Kingdom. He fearlessly condemned the wickedness he observed, whether by kings or by people; therefore he was not always popular or held in high esteem. He was the one steady influence in Jerusalem during this period of crisis and waning power. His book is highly biographical, so we know considerable about the character and personality of the man himself. A reading of his book shows that he was highly influenced by the laws and ethical codes found in the book of Deuteronomy.

13. Egypt and the Death of Josiah

At this period Assyria was on the brink of falling, and Babylonia was rising in influential might, with Media to the east of Mesopotamia willing to be her ally. The Medes under Cyaxares and the Babylonians under Nabopolassar (father of Nebuchadnezzar) destroyed Nineveh in 612 B.C., with the remainder of the Assyrian army fleeing to Haran in western Mesopotamia to set up a temporary capital. Egypt was recovering somewhat of former glory through a powerful king named Necho, who, wishing to aid tottering Assyria, marched north to join in the fight against the Babylonians and the Medes. As he was advancing through Palestine he was met at Megiddo in the valley of Jezreel by Josiah, who, in spite of the pleas for peace on the part of Pharaoh Necho's envoys, drew up his forces for battle. Though he disguised himself, Josiah was shot by the Egyptian archers, was returned to Jerusalem, and there died. "And all Judah and Jerusalem mourned for Josiah," as well as the great prophet Jeremiah (2 Chron. 35:20–27). One of Judah's most beloved kings was gone.

14. Jehoahaz, Three-month King

The people put a younger son of Josiah on the throne, Shallum, and changed his name to Jehoahaz. Pharaoh Necho, with his headquarters at Riblah in Syrian territory, summoned Jehoahaz to appear before him, bound him with chains, and sent him to Egypt for the remainder of his days (Jer. 22:10). Necho fined Judah "a hundred talents of silver and a talent of gold" (2 Chron. 36:1–3).

15. Jehoiakim

On sending Jehoahaz to Egypt, Pharaoh Necho seated his older brother, Eliakim, on the throne in Jerusalem and changed his name to Jehoiakim. He ruled for eleven years and died a natural death. In 605 B.C., a few years after Jehoiakim's accession to the throne of Judah, Necho's Egyptian army met the Babylonians under the command of a prince named Nebuchadnezzar at Carchemish. The Babylonians were victorious; Necho returned to Egypt, and all

Assyria, Syria, and Palestine came under Babylonian control. When Nebuchadnezzar advanced into Judah, he captured Jerusalem, put Jehoiakim in chains, robbed the Temple, and took captives to Babylon, including Daniel and his three friends: Hananiah, Mishael, and Azariah. (These three were better known by their new Babylonian names of Shadrach, Meshach, and Abednego.) This happened in 605 B.C. (Dan. 1:1–6) and might be considered the first deportation of Hebrews to Babylonia in the Judean captivity. When Jehoiakim promised loyalty to the Babylonian monarch, he was permitted to retain his own kingly position—at least in name. This continued for several years, when Jehoiakim rebelled and withheld his tribute to the Babylonians. Nebuchadnezzar did not come down himself; instead he incited raids on Judah by the Chaldeans, Syrians, Moabites, and Ammonites. At this time Jehoiakim died, leaving the throne to his son, Coniah (2 Chron. 36:5–8; 2 Kings 23:36 to 24:7).

16. Jeremiah and Jehoiakim

Just as Ahaz rebelled against Isaiah, Hezekiah gave him his utmost cooperation; also, just as Josiah heeded diligently the advice of Jeremiah, Jehoiakim rejected his every word of counsel. While standing in the Temple Jeremiah predicted the forthcoming Babylonian captivity for the inhabitants of Jerusalem and the destruction of the temple, for which the priests, the prophets, and the people laid hold on him to kill him. Only when some of the elders came to his aid did he escape being murdered and his life spared (Jer. 26).

A very dramatic incident in the life of Jeremiah occurred in connection with "the roll of a book" which Jeremiah dictated to Baruch, his scribe, containing all the words that God spoke unto him "against Israel, and against Judah, and against all the nations," from the days of Josiah on. The prophet commanded Baruch to read it in the Temple, which he did. Then the princes heard it, and finally the king himself. Jehoiakim became so filled with wrath that he "cut it with the penknife, and cast it into the fire that was in the brazier, until all the roll was consumed in the fire that was in the brazier." The king ordered that Baruch and Jeremiah be taken, "but Jehovah hid them." Jeremiah was immediately commanded to take a second roll and write the same words again, which he

not only did but added many more words besides (Jer. 36). Most
scholars believe that this is principally what is now the biblical book
of Jeremiah. Besides these incidents Jeremiah performed many
"object lessons" to depict God's message to Judah and Jerusalem.

17. Jehoiachin, Another Three-month King

Jehoiakim's son, Coniah, ascended the throne at the death of
his father but reigned only three months. He took the name
Jehoiachin. (He is called Coniah in Jer. 22:24 and Jeconiah in Jer.
27:20.) Nebuchadnezzar and his army again besieged Jerusalem,
at which time Jehoiachin and all his family gave themselves up.
The Babylonian king took 10,000 captives to Babylon, including
the royal family, Ezekiel the prophet, the craftsmen and the smiths,
and the leaders of the army, as well as much of the wealth of the
temple and the palace. This was in 597 B.C., being the second deportation to Babylon (2 Kings 24:8–17). Jehoiachin was imprisoned
for 37 years.

18. Zedekiah, Last of Judah's Kings

Nebuchadnezzar then put Mattaniah, son of Josiah and brother
to Jehoahaz, on the throne, changing his name to Zedekiah. He
ruled eleven years, a puppet king to Babylon's monarch, and with
only the lower class of people left in Jerusalem due to Nebuchadnezzar's purge of all the leadership (2 Kings 24:18–20).
Some envoys came to Zedekiah from Edom, Moab, Ammon,
Tyre, and Sidon with an appeal for the king to join them in a coalition
against the Babylonians (Jer. 27:1–11). The false prophets predicted
an early release from Babylon's power, but Jeremiah gave just the
opposite word. He advised submitting to the yoke of the great city
on the Euphrates (Jer. 27:12 to 28:17). Jeremiah also sent a letter
to the exiles, telling them to settle down, cultivate the land, and
build houses for themselves (Jer. 29).
In the fourth year of his reign Zedekiah made a trip to Babylon,
evidently proving his loyalty, for he was allowed to return to
Jerusalem to continue his reign (Jer. 51:59–64). But things in Judah
became worse and worse, both socially and religiously. Pagan gods
and pagan cults held sway in the courts of the house of Jehovah.

Moral laws were violated. When a new king, Hophra, came to the throne of Egypt in 589 B.C., Zedekiah rebelled against Nebuchadnezzar "in sending his ambassadors into Egypt, that they might give him horses and much people" (Ezek. 17:15). The Babylonians descended upon Judah, for Zedekiah openly rebelled against Babylon (2 Kings 24:20).

19. The Fall of Jerusalem

There had been many who had foretold the destruction of Jerusalem: Isaiah, prophets in the days of Manasseh, Huldah the prophetess, and Jeremiah, both to Jehoiakim and then to Zedekiah (Jer. 25:9–11; 34:22). Jeremiah advised surrender, but Zedekiah ignored his counsel. After the start of the siege the king and the people agreed to free all Hebrew slaves. Soon after this an Egyptian army appeared on the southwestern horizon, to which Nebuchadnezzar was forced to give his attention and therefore lift the siege. Then Jerusalem broke out with joy at the relief, but Jeremiah chilled their hopes by stating that the Babylonians would return to take Jerusalem and burn it (Jer. 37:1–10).

The prophet was ignored; the people disregarded their oath and seized the slaves they had just liberated. Reproving the slaveholders for their violation of oath, Jeremiah again predicted destruction for Jerusalem and urged surrender to Babylon. Jeremiah was arrested and put down in a miry cistern, which almost caused his death. He was pulled out by an Ethiopian slave and his helpers but was then put in the court of the guard with other prisoners (Jer. 38:1–13). Zedekiah secretly sent for Jeremiah to seek his advice; but the advice was just the same as it had been, for the prophet pictured the awful disaster that would follow for both king and people. He advised surrender (Jer. 38:14–28).

The Egyptians were defeated, and the Babylonians then continued the siege. This went on for about 16 months, and the famine was intense (2 Kings 25:3). Finally a breach was made in the wall and the invading army poured into the city. Zedekiah and some of his troops escaped by night; the troops were scattered and Zedekiah captured in the plains of Jericho. He was taken to Nebuchadnezzar, headquartered at Riblah. Here, after seeing his sons executed, he himself was blinded and taken in fetters to Babylon (2 Kings 25:4–7).

The devastation of Jerusalem was complete in every way. The walls were broken down; the Temple, palace, and great houses were burnt; the people were taken as captives to Babylon, with only "the poorest of the land to be vinedressers and husbandmen" remaining. The brass, the gold, and the silver of the Temple were taken as spoils of war. The chief priests were executed (2 Kings 25:8–21). This was the third deportation of captives to Babylon, occurring in the year 587–586 B.C. It is estimated that about 25,000 people were deported.

Over the people left in Judah Nebuchadnezzar appointed Gedaliah as puppet governor, with his headquarters at Mizpeh, a strong fortress six miles north of Jerusalem (2 Kings 25:22). Jeremiah was given the choice of remaining in Jerusalem or of departing with the captives. He chose the former, resolving to share the sufferings of the miserable lot staying in Judah (Jer. 40:1–6). Gedaliah was treacherously assassinated by a man named Ishmael, along with ten others. Though Ishmael was pursued by Johanan, a Judean army captain, the former made good his escape to the country of the Ammonites (Jer. 41:15). "And all the people, both small and great, and the captains of the forces, arose, and came to Egypt; for they were afraid of the Chaldeans" (2 Kings 25:26). Tradition says that Jeremiah died as a martyr in Egypt.

After Nebuchadnezzar died, Evil-merodach began to rule in Babylon. He freed Jehoiachin from prison and gave him a living allowance the remaining years of his life in Babylon (2 Kings 25:27–30).

The Captivity and the Restoration
(Jeremiah, Ezekiel, Daniel, Ezra, Nehemiah Esther, Haggai, Zechariah, Malachi)

1. Desolation of Jerusalem

Around 50,000 Hebrews were removed through successive deportations from Jerusalem and its environs to Babylon, each time the leaders and executives being chosen to go. This left only the "poorest sort of the people" in Jerusalem, and after the death of Gedaliah at the ruthless hands of Ishmael the most desirable of the remaining ones fled to Egypt to escape the wrath of the Babylonian king. The neighboring nations, such as the Philistines, the Ammonites, the Moabites, and the Edomites, capitalized on this weakened condition of Judah and moved in to possess as much of the land as possible. Jerusalem remained in ruins and desolate, as the whole book of Lamentations, written by the prophet Jeremiah, testifies. This great prophet of God, choosing to remain in Jerusalem rather than go with the exiles to Babylon, became known as the weeping prophet. Listen as he laments in 1:1–2:

> How doth the city sit solitary, that was full of people!
> She is become as a widow, that was great among the nations!
> She that was a princess among the provinces is become tributary!
> She weepeth sore in the night, and her tears are on her cheeks.

The Hebrews who fled to Egypt found a better lot, for they were hospitably received and seemed to have prospered. They probably lived off to themselves, segregated from the native population, as was the case wherever they fled throughout the Roman Empire. The ones who settled at Elephantine, an island in the Nile at the foot of the first cataract, built a temple for their worship very similar to the old Temple of Jehovah at Jerusalem. The Hebrews continued to live in Egypt and to multiply there. During the third century B.C. there were so many Jews in Alexandria, Egypt, that they called forth the Septuagint, the Greek translation of the Hebrew Scriptures.

237

2. The Greatness of Babylonia

The country to which the Jews were transplanted presented a striking contrast to the land of Judah, their previous home. From a merely local and provincial type of government they came face to face with a great imperial state of affairs. Instead of their picturesque mountain city of Jerusalem, looking down into deep and steep ravines with their scanty mountain streams, the defeated Hebrews entered the huge, square, level city of Babylon, lying on both sides of the mighty Euphrates River and surrounded by immense plains stretching far into the distance, intersected by long straight irrigation canals bordered by rows of willows. Instead of their beloved Temple, standing in the midst of its courts on the brow of a high precipice, small but highly finished and adorned, they viewed the colossal temple of Bel, rising from the plain with its eight stories or towers, all to the height of 600 feet. Even the palace of the Babylonian king was more than twice the size of their Jerusalem; it contained the famous Hanging Gardens, which were built on arched terraces, each rising higher than the other and rich in luxuriant foliage and cultivation. These gardens, one of the seven wonders of the ancient world, were constructed at tremendous expense by Nebuchadnezzar in honor of his wife to help relieve her homesickness for her native hills. The city itself was surrounded by four walls, each fifteen miles in length. Twenty-four streets ran north and south, and twenty-four ran east and west. There was a gate where each street met the wall—100 gates in all. The city was thus made up of 600 square blocks with a garden in the center of each square. There were many elaborate and expensive buildings besides the palace and temple. The city was fortified by a moat and a double wall. All of this adds up to the fact that Babylon was one of the most beautiful and famous of the cities of ancient times. Nebuchadnezzar made the arrogant boast that he built the city by his might and for his glory (Dan. 4:30).

Out from Babylon extended a very elaborate system of canals used for irrigation and water transportation, thus insuring fertile plains and rich harvests. The Babylonians also enjoyed a high degree of civilization, with their libraries, well-developed literature,

18. Ruins of "Hanging Gardens" of Babylon

astronomy, the production of textiles and pottery, engineering feats, commercial expansion, and military might. Great armies and royal pageantry added to the magnificence of the empire, an empire that controlled the destinies of hundreds of thousands of people.

3. Nature of the Captivity

The exiles from Judah were located in a rich plain on the river Chebar, a canal that connected Babylon with Nippur (Ezek. 1:1–3). Even though it appears the Hebrew people were segregated from the native Babylonians, they apparently had great freedom in their mode of living. They were not slaves, as their forefathers had been in Egypt, with forced labor as part of their lot; instead they were more like colonists. All that their conquerors demanded was loyalty to the Babylonian government. In a general way they were allowed to govern themselves, having more or less an internal jurisdiction over their own members. They received grants of land, either agricultural or pastoral. They increased in numbers and in wealth. A few attained positions of prominence (Dan. 2:48). They preserved their genealogies and were allowed to retain their positions of rank. Although their Temple was gone, thus preventing any form of a sacrificial system, they observed as much of the Mosaic law as possible.

Archaeologists have found some 300 Babylonian tablets, written in cuneiform and dated about 595–570 B.C., which name the nations furnishing captives to Babylon. Among these nations is listed Judah. Even more significant is the mention of the name of Jehoiachin and his five sons, or princes. Therefore, the Babylonians recognized Jehoiachin as the rightful heir to the throne in Jerusalem as well as did the Hebrews.

The main drawback to the captivity, as far as the Hebrews were concerned, was the disgrace of the whole ordeal. There was homesickness mixed with resentment toward their captors. Psalm 137:1–6 vividly portrays their feeling of despair.

> By the rivers of Babylon,
> There we sat down, yea, we wept,
> When we remembered Zion.
> Upon the willows in the midst thereof

> We hanged up our harps.
> For there they that led us captive required of us songs,
> And they that wasted us required of us mirth, saying,
> Sing us one of the songs of Zion.
> How shall we sing Jehovah's song
> In a foreign land?
> If I forget thee, O Jerusalem,
> Let my right hand forget her skill.
> Let my tongue cleave to the roof of my mouth,
> If I remember thee not;
> If I prefer not Jerusalem
> Above my chief joy.

They had lost their freedom and had become a people without a country; they had become subjects of a strange people in a strange land.

4. A Religious Problem

The exile posed for the Hebrews a religious crisis, a crisis that was twofold in nature. There was the danger that they might be swayed away by the materialism and prosperity of Babylon and be tempted to drift from the faith that had made their forefathers great. Commerce flourished and things were in abundance; financial security, making life easy and comfortable, bid for first place in their purposes and plans. Could the advantages of Jehovah worship compete with such enticing allurements?

Also, could Jehovah be worshiped in a foreign land? Was their concept of Jehovah as an almighty, all-present God strong enough that they should experience his presence hundreds of miles from their homeland? Among most people of their day the various gods were thought of as tribal or national deities, with the presence, power, and influence of a certain god going to the boundary allotted to him and no further. For instance, the Edomite gods were to be worshiped in Edomite territory alone, Moabite gods in Moabite territory, and so forth. No doubt many Hebrews thought of Jehovah as a national God who could be worshiped only in Palestine. "How shall we sing Jehovah's song in a foreign land?" (Ps. 137:4). The great prophet Ezekiel helped the Hebrew people learn that Jehovah, their God, could be worshiped anywhere, for he is a God near to all. He is the one supreme God over all the world.

5. Prophets of the Exile

The three prophets who prophesied during the time of the exile were Jeremiah, Daniel, and Ezekiel. Most of Jeremiah's influence was felt in Jerusalem in the years prior to the fall of the great city, but he continued to be a tower of strength to the bewildered captives even in distant Babylonia. As far as is known Jeremiah never went to Babylonia, but he preached courage and faith in God to the Hebrew exiles by means of a famous letter (Jer. 29). He advised them to build houses, plant gardens, rear families, and live at peace with their captors. He also advised them to ignore the false prophets among them and to pray to God instead; God would in time again bring them back to Jerusalem. Tradition says Jeremiah died a martyr's death in Egypt.

The two prophets who were carried away into exile and prophesied there were Daniel and Ezekiel. Daniel and his three friends—Hananiah, Mishael, and Azariah—were carried away in the first deportation in 605 B.C. (Dan. 1:6–7). These names were changed to Babylonian ones: Belteshazzar, Shadrach, Meshach, and Abed-nego, respectively. (In the biblical account Daniel continues to be called by his Hebrew name, but the other three are called by their new Babylonian names.) These four were so steadfastly loyal to Jehovah and his way of life and so determined to maintain their personal ideals of chastity that they were found in the best of physical condition at the end of three years, thus being appointed to positions of responsibility. Daniel seems to have been the leader of the group; it appears that he was of royal blood (Dan. 1:3) and that he was very talented (Dan. 1:4). All four were of the tribe of Judah (Dan. 1:6).

Several very remarkable occurrences are recorded in the book of Daniel. (1) He interpreted the dream of Nebuchadnezzar announcing the doom of his kingdom. Instead of receiving punishment for his announcement, Daniel was paid the highest tribute by Nebuchadnezzar, who gave him costly gifts and elevated him to the head of all his wise men (Dan. 2). (2) Shadrach, Meshach, and Abed-nego were miraculously delivered from the fiery furnace after having been

placed there for being loyal to Jehovah (Dan. 3). (3) Daniel interpreted Nebuchadnezzar's dream of the tree (Dan. 4). (4) Daniel
interpreted the writing on the wall seen during Belshazzar's feast
(Dan. 5). (5) Daniel, due to being loyal to Jehovah rather than to
the laws of the Medes and Persians, was placed in a den of lions,
where he was miraculously saved from death (Dan. 6).

6. Beginning of the Synagogue and Judaism

During the centuries prior to the exile there had been the Temple,
historic center of worship in Jerusalem. To this imposing structure
the Hebrews came year after year to fulfill all the exactness required
of them by the Mosaic law. Not only was it now a crumpled mass;
the people of Israel were in a foreign land amid a foreign culture.
As a result, and somewhat of a makeshift, the installation of the
synagogue evolved. These were smaller houses, not only serving
as places of worship but as centers of instruction in the law. There
were no priests offering sacrifices; instead the rabbi, or teacher,
came into prominence. Here the assembly, or congregation, of the
people convened to read and to discuss the law. The word
"synagogue" is derived from a Greek term meaning "assembly"
or "meeting."

In the various synagogues in Babylonia, Judaism, as a highly
legalistic religion, sprang into being. The Hebrews came to
appreciate more and more the real values of the law, but in so
doing they surrounded it and engulfed it with many and multitudinous
interpretations of what the various statements found in this law
required. The letter of the law came to be very important. Every
phase of the law was to be obeyed meticulously. They came to
love the law, but it was a love that was to enslave them in its
details.

As a result, the synagogues and Judaism grew simultaneously
and were destined to play very important roles in the future life
of the Jews. When the Jews returned from the exile, they brought
the synagogue concept with them, and synagogues sprang up in
all the Jewish communities throughout the Mediterranean world.
Even though the Temple was rebuilt at their return—and glorified
in structure later by Herod the Great, the synagogues continued

to exert a tremendous effect upon the life of the Jews.

The reader should notice that this is the first instance in which the term "Jew" has been used in the writing of this book, the terms "Hebrew" or "Israelite" have been employed up to this point. The terms "Jew" and "Judaism" go hand in hand, for a Jew is one who has Judaism for his religion. The term "Jew" is a religious one, while the term "Hebrew" is one denoting bloodline. It denotes one who has a direct descent from Jacob; since Jacob's name was changed to Israel, a Hebrew is also an Israelite. A Gentile, in accepting Judaism as his religion, might become a Jew, but he could never become a Hebrew. When a Gentile became a Jew, he was known as a proselyte, a term used by Jesus in Matthew 23:15.

7. A New Language

When the Hebrews entered the world of Babylonian culture, they found themselves confronted with a new language, Aramaic. Their Hebrew gave place to the language of their conquerors, and Aramaic became for them the language of the home, the street, and the marketplace. Those that returned later to Jerusalem brought the Aramaic with them as their vernacular language, and there it replaced the Hebrew as the spoken language also. Therefore at the time of Christ, Aramaic, not Hebrew, was the common language of Palestine. (Syriac and Aramaic were the same.) Yet Hebrew remained as the religious language, for all the sacred scrolls in the Temple and the synagogues were written in Hebrew. This remains true for all the scrolls in the Jewish synagogues of the modern world. Though the Jews of today have no temple, they have thousands of synagogues.

8. An End to Idolatry

One very beneficial effect of the exile upon the Hebrews was a cessation to the tendency toward idolatry. They were thoroughly cured of this chief sin responsible for their bitter experience of being deported to a foreign soil. Never again did the Jews resort to foreign gods and pagan idols. Ezekiel 36:24–28 depicts God's promise to bring them back to their own land and to cleanse them from their filthiness and from their idols. This passage also portrays God's promise that their religion would be more spiritual and personal in nature, which is what would be expected with a ceasing of idolatry.

9. Cyrus and the Persian Empire

Cyrus the Great, one of the most remarkable of the kings of this period of history, influenced the lives of millions of people by a new alignment of the nations in the sixth century B.C., setting up a new empire covering more territory than any previous empire. The Babylonian Empire and many other nations were swallowed up by his invading armies. Just as Tiglath-pileser had built the Assyrian Empire, and just as Nebuchadnezzar had built the Babylonian Empire, Cyrus the Great built the Persian Empire. Appearing as a man of royal blood about thirty years of age in the province of Anshan in Media, he began a revolt that led to the defeat and capture of the Median king. Then he took in Persia to the south, forming the Medo-Persian kingdom. He did not march against Babylon at this time but went against northern Mesopotamia and Armenia, then Asia Minor. Within twenty years from his military start he was master of almost all the territory from the Indus River in the east to the Aegean Sea in the west. Then he returned to lay siege to Babylon in 539 B.C., capturing it in 538 B.C. This meant the cessation of the mighty empire built by Nebuchadnezzar in years past and its replacement by one of vastly greater proportions.

10. Proclamation of Cyrus

Cyrus the Great was a very unusual man, one with keen insight and skill in administering the affairs of so large a realm. Being extremely considerate of his subjects and concerned with their welfare, he broke with the traditional manner of dealing with the various captivated peoples throughout his domain. Beginning with Tiglath-pileser (or Pul) the Assyrians had used a ruthless policy of removing terrorized subjected nations to distant lands, a policy subsequently repeated by the Babylonians. An example of this is the manner in which the Assyrians carried off the kingdom of Israel. Another example is that in which the Babylonians deported the people of Jerusalem and its environs. Cyrus, however, made a general public proclamation that all displaced people in his realm could return to their homelands, there to worship their gods in their own sanctuaries.

Such was a liberal policy indeed!

Cyrus' proclamation for the Jews (Ezra 1—6) came in 538 b.c., two copies of which are found in the book of Ezra (1:2–4 and 6:3–5). "Thus saith Cyrus king of Persia, All the kingdoms of the earth hath Jehovah, the God of heaven, given me; and he hath charged me to build him a house in Jerusalem, which is in Judah. Whosoever there is among you of all his people, his God be with him, and let him go up to Jerusalem, which is in Judah, and build the house of Jehovah, the God of Israel (he is God), which is in Jerusalem. And whosoever is left, in any place where he sojourneth, let the men of his place help him with silver, and with gold, and with goods, and with beasts, besides the freewill-offering for the house of God which is in Jerusalem" (Ezra 1:2–4).

The tone of this decree would have one to think that Cyrus was one who believed in Jehovah, the God of Israel; but after scholars were able to decipher the various inscriptions of Cyrus he is seen to have been a polytheist, a believer in many gods, who probably desired the favor of all his gods. Without a doubt, however, this outstanding man was the agent of God whereby Israel was able to accomplish the divine purpose. In Isaiah 44:28 he is called God's "shepherd," and in Isaiah 45:1 he is termed God's "anointed." Such a proclamation made it possible for all Israelites who desired to do so to return to their homeland, as some of them did.

11. Three Returning Groups

There is no way of knowing how many Jews there were in Babylonia at the time of Cyrus' decree, but the fact that time for three or four generations had elapsed since their arrival there would lead to the thought that they had multiplied considerably. However, not a large number desired to return to Palestine; Babylonian ways were too enticing, as well as Cyrus' lenient policy toward their citizenship too comforting. Many had doubtlessly become firmly entrenched in business ventures, while some had intermarried with those of the new land. Besides, those living two or three generations removed from the originally deported ones had never experienced living in the land of their fathers made hallow with the Temple and the footprints of the patriarchs and other Hebrew personages.

Their knowledge of the Land of Promise was merely secondhand. The glories of the temple and ritual of Marduk, the god of Babylon, were too strong and enticing. Many lacked the faith and fortitude required to leave an economically secure condition and undertake a journey of 800 miles back to the devastated and bleak hills of Judah. Scholars estimate that about 60,000 in all returned, a surprisingly large number considering the discouraging factors surrounding a return. The first group was led by Zerubbabel, the second by Ezra, and the third by Nehemiah.

12. The First Return

The first group to migrate back was led by Zerubbabel, a prince of the house of David and grandson of King Jehoiachin. This was in 537 b.c., about a year after Cyrus' decree. Eleven leaders are named (Ezra 2:2) for the return, but the main one after Zerubbabel was Joshua, the high priest. (The name Shesh-bazzar occurs frequently, as in Ezra 1:8–11; 5:14–16. The preferred view of scholars is that this is the Chaldean name for Zerubbabel, and that it therefore does not represent another person.) According to Ezra there were about 50,000 in this first return (Ezra 2:64–67).

What inspired these people to make such a long journey back to Jerusalem, with all the hardships it entailed? For one thing, there was the religious impulse, the desire to worship Jehovah at the site of the old temple built by Solomon, surrounded as it was with ancient lore and hallowed in their sacred writings. There was an intense ambition to restore the ancient place of worship in Jerusalem. This religious impulse was probably the strongest factor in their desire to return. Second, national pride figured predominantly in their motivation to return to the land of the patriarchs—Abraham, Isaac, Jacob, and Joseph—and to the land of the kingdom made great by David and other prominent kings. Third, the prophets predicted the return of some of the Hebrew exiles to the place of their forefathers. These predictions are found in Isaiah 14, 44, 45, 46; Jeremiah 28, 29, 50, 51; and Ezekiel 20. Would the people not remember these predictions, and therefore feel that God's providential purpose demanded their return? Fourth, they were encouraged in their return by gifts from all who were so minded (Ezra 1:6) and by a command from Cyrus that his provincial heads in the west contribute to their support. Cyrus also gave back to them the vessels of gold and of silver that Nebuchadnezzar had carried out of the Temple at the time of its destruction and had put in the house of his gods. ''All the vessels of gold and of silver were five thousand and four hundred'' (Ezra 1:7–11).

13. Conditions in the Homeland

A very discouraging situation faced the faithful Jews who trekked their way back to Palestine in the sixth century B.C. The destruction of Jerusalem in 587–586 B.C. had not left much either in the way of people or resources. Some of the Hebrews had fled to Egypt. Edomites, Moabites, and Ammonites had pushed into the territory of Judah made weak by the devastation wrought by the invading hordes of Babylonians; and, since the Israelites conceived of the land as their very own possession, the influx of other peoples was regarded as an undesired intrusion. Some of the invaders had intermarried with the Hebrews left in Judah at the time of the fall of the historic capital, producing a mongrel race. The Samaritans, already a mongrel race due to Assyrian policy, had pushed south into much of the territory previously occupied by Judah. Jerusalem itself, thoroughly sacked and razed by Nebuchadnezzar, was a mass of rubble and debris. Their beloved temple was no more and the formidable wall was a thing of the past. Only those well over fifty years of age could remember any of the former glories of the city of David; most knew it merely through report. It was a very discouraging scene, one that needed great planning, immense fortitude, and a deep faith in the providence of God.

14. Beginning of the Second Temple

Soon after they returned all the people gathered into Jerusalem from the cities where they had settled for the purpose of worship. There they set up the altar of burnt offering upon its base and, under the direction of Zerubbabel and Joshua the priest, offered burnt offerings morning and evening. Daily the sacrifices required in the Mosaic law were kept; the set feasts were observed; and the people brought a freewill offering to Jehovah (Ezra 3:1–5).

Rebuilding the Temple seems to have been the main objective of their return, so they secured masons, carpenters, and other workmen for such an enterprise. They also secured workmen from Phoenicia to cut and transport cedar logs from the forest of Lebanon by way of the Mediterranean to Joppa, so they could then be brought by land to Jerusalem (Ezra 3:6–7). Cyrus even gave them a grant of money for the rebuilding enterprise. In the second year after their return they laid the foundation of the new Temple, with the old men weeping and the young people shouting for joy. The older ones wept because they were reminded of the ornate and glorious structure that Solomon had erected, quite a contrast to the new house going up. But in spite of this "the people shouted with a loud shout, and the voice was heard afar off" (Ezra 3:8–13). The new Temple had at last been started, and this in the second month of the second year of their return, or in 536 B.C.

Soon, however, there was trouble brewing. The people of Samaria of mixed blood, called in the Scriptures, "the adversaries of Judah and Benjamin," came to Zerubbabel and the other leaders, offering their aid in rebuilding the Temple. They stated that they had been sacrificing unto Jehovah since Esarhaddon (681–668 B.C.) had placed them there. Zerubbabel, Joshua, and the leaders answered, "Ye have nothing to do with us in building a house unto our God; but we ourselves together will build unto Jehovah, the God of Israel, as king Cyrus the king of Persia hath commanded us" (Ezra 4:3). When their request was thus denied, they began a policy of frustrating the workers of the struggling colony of Jews. They even "hired counsellors against them, to frustrate their purpose, all the days of Cyrus king of Persia" (Ezra 4:4–5). These counselors probably misrepresented the Jews at the court of Persia; at any rate the Samaritans successfully hindered the work of Zerubbabel and his associates on the Temple for the remainder of the reign of Cyrus, throughout the reign of Cambyses, and to the second year of Darius' reign, or until 520 B.C.

15. Prophets of the Restoration

Again God was to use prophets with which to make known his purpose to his people. In 520 B.C. a prophet named Haggai stepped forth with God's message for the occasion, accusing the people of becoming so absorbed in building their own houses that they had neglected the house of worship. He so stirred up the people that in less than a month Zerubbabel and Joshua (called Jeshua in the book of Ezra) had led the people in a renewed effort of rebuilding (Hag. 1:1–15). Shortly after this the prophet Zechariah emerged to help in his stimulation of the building program (Zech. 1:1). According to this younger prophet Jehovah stirred up the spirit of Zerubbabel, and the spirit of Joshua, and the spirit of the people to cause them to work on the house of Jehovah of hosts, their God (Zech. 1:14). As Daniel and Ezekiel became known as the prophets of the exile, Haggai and Zechariah became known as the prophets of the restoration. The preaching of Haggai and Zechariah must have been effective. "And the elders of the Jews builded and prospered, through the prophesying of Haggai the prophet and Zechariah the son of Iddo" (Ezra 6:14).

16. The New Temple

Again the Jews experienced a little interference, this time on the part of Tattenai, an officer for the Persians located in Syria. He and his colleagues came to Jerusalem to investigate the building program, then sent word to Darius reporting their findings. They seemed to be questioning Cyrus' permission for the Jews to rebuild. A search of the archives in Babylonia and Ecbatana was made, and in the latter a copy of the decree of Cyrus was found. Tattenai was not only told not to interfere; he was also told to grant to the Jews royal revenue from the province of Syria, as well as animals for sacrifice (Ezra 5:3 to 6:13).

The Temple was completed in 516 B.C. (Ezra 6:14–15) and made ready for dedication. The ceremony was performed with great solemnity, numerous sacrifices being offered. Also, the priests were set up into courses of duty, and this Passover was celebrated amid great rejoicing of spirit (Ezra 6:16–22). By this time their future did not seem so forlorn. They not only had houses of their own; they had a Temple ready for service. The good hand of God had settled over the little colony of Jews.

Although it was erected on the very site of Solomon's Temple, it did not equal the former Temple in either beauty or workmanship. David's elaborate preparation and Solomon's unequaled resources permitted the former structure to be much more magnificent. The holy place still contained the three same objects: the altar of incense, the table of showbread, and the seven-branched lampstand. But the holy of holies did not contain the ark of the covenant, for it was probably destroyed along with Solomon's Temple. Josephus says there was a slab of stone marking the former position of the ark. Here the high priest placed his censor on every Day of Atonement.

17. The Length of the Captivity

Since there were three deportations to Babylonia and three groups to return to Jerusalem it is hard to determine the length of the Babylonian exile. From which deportation to which return is to be measured as the time involved? If the last group went to Babylonia in 586 B.C. and the first group returned in 537 B.C., the duration of the stay away from their homeland would be 49 years. This is the time given by many scholars.

Jeremiah predicted that the captives would be on Babylonian soil for 70 years. "For thus saith Jehovah, After seventy years are accomplished for Babylon, I will visit you, and perform my good word toward you, in causing you to return to this place" (Jer. 29:10). From the first deportation in 605 B.C. to the first return in 537 B.C. would make 68 years, a little short of 70. From the last deportation in 587–586 B.C. to the completion of the Temple in 516 B.C. would make exactly 70 years, which would be the time during which there was no temple in operation in Jerusalem. Was Jeremiah thinking of the temple in his prediction? Or, is it possible to interpret Jeremiah's 70 years in a liberal manner, as not depicting a literal 70 years at all, just a long span of time?

18. The Story of Esther

The story of Esther, found in the book of the Bible by that name, concerns the welfare of the exiles who did not return to Jerusalem with Zerubbabel to rebuild the Temple. The scene is laid in the reign of Xerxes (485–465 B.C.), who is called Ahasuerus in the biblical account. The name of God is not mentioned in the entire book of Esther, but divine providence is apparent throughout the story. The Feast of Purim, commemorating the deliverance of the Jews, finds its explanation in the events recorded in Esther. It is not known when and by whom the book was written. The events took place in Susa, or Shushan, the capital of Persia in the province of Elam. (A mound, still called Shush, is probably the present site of the old capital.) Here the palace of Xerxes occupied two and one-half acres on the acropolis, but Susa had been a royal city since the days of Cyrus, ranking along with Nineveh and Babylon.

The story opens with a great feast given by Ahasuerus at his magnificent palace, a seven-day celebration of drinking and banqueting. On the seventh day the intoxicated king ordered Queen Vashti to display her crown and beauty before his visiting dignitaries. Her refusal angered the king tremendously, and a conference with his wise men led to her dismissal as queen. She was banished from the royal court. After this, and at the advice of his servants, Ahasuerus ordered that beautiful maidens be selected from throughout the empire and be brought to the royal palace that he might select one for his queen.

There was a certain Jew in Shushan the capital named Mordecai. Having no children of his own he had adopted his cousin, Esther, a Jewish orphan, as his own daughter. Esther was not only one of the maidens selected and brought to the palace; she was the one further selected to be the next queen. She had concealed her racial origin. In the seventh year of the reign of Ahasuerus she was acknowledged queen at a royal banquet.

Just before Esther's elevation to the queenship Mordecai, lingering near the palace gate, overheard that two of the guards were planning to assassinate the king. This he reported to Esther, who in turn reported it to the proper authorities. The conspirators were hanged and the whole event recorded in the official writings, or chronicles, with Mordecai receiving the credit for the disclosure.

Haman, influential in the royal court, was advanced above all his associates in royal rank. In his new position he received honor on the part of others by the act of bowing down. "But Mordecai bowed not down, nor did him reverence" (Esther 3:2). As a Jew he refused to do so; Haman, angered by such an attitude, sought to do Mordecai harm. Learning that the latter was a Jew, Haman devised a scheme that would destroy not only his rival but all the Jews throughout the kingdom. He appealed to the Persian king, in a very diplomatic way, to execute all the Jews of the kingdom. He represented them as very dangerous, as well as adding that much gain would come into the treasury by the confiscation of all Jewish property. This double appeal instantly pleased Ahasuerus, who gave Haman the authority to annihilate all the Jews and to take over their property. An edict was issued and the date set for the execution; the date of the edict was the thirteenth day of Nisan, and the date of the execution set for the thirteenth day of Adar, a span of eleven Jewish months.

Such an edict issued in sorrow for the Jews, and fasting and mourning immediately followed. Mordecai appeared at the palace gate in sackcloth and ashes, alerting Esther concerning the dire threat to the very existence of the Hebrew people and informing her that the only hope for them lay in her intercession with the king. Esther immediately spoke of the danger of approaching the king uninvited; and Mordecai answered with the famous words, "Who knoweth whether thou art not come to the kingdom for such a time as this?" (Esther 4:14). Esther requested that the Jews fast for her three days and three nights and said, "So will I go unto the king, which is not according to the law: and if I perish, I perish" (Esther 4:16).

When she appeared before the king, she was received, for he extended to her his golden scepter and asked her of her request. Her petition was that the king and Haman attend a banquet that she had prepared for that very day. He agreed. At this banquet he again asked her for her request, to which she issued another invitation for the king and Haman to attend another banquet on the following day. On the evening prior to the second banquet Haman was bragging to his friends and to his wife Zeresh of all the royal favors that the king and queen had shown him, but bemoaning the fact that Mordecai still sat at the king's gate. His wife suggested that he build a gallows seventy-five feet high and secure the king's permission to execute Mordecai. He immediately had the gallows erected.

That very night the king, unable to sleep, ordered that the royal chronicles be read to him, at which time he found that Mordecai had never been rewarded for exposing the plot of the palace guards. At this very moment Haman appeared, seeking entrance to the king to make request that Mordecai be hanged on the newly constructed gallows. When Haman was permitted to enter, Ahasuerus asked, "What shall be done unto the man whom the king delighteth to honor?" (Esther 6:6). Haman, thinking this could be none other than himself, suggested that such a man be honored by putting upon him royal robes and a royal crown, placing him upon the king's own horse, having him led through the street by one of the highest of the royal nobles, and having him proclaimed as one so honored. Promptly accepting his suggestion the king announced that Mordecai was the one to be so honored and that he, Haman, was to deck him out in such apparel and lead him through the street. This command Haman had to obey, and it was all done prior to the second banquet.

When Haman and the king were dining with Esther, the king again requested what should be granted to the queen, at which time she recounted to Ahasuerus the story of Haman's plot to destroy her and all her people. Instant anger came over the king. Being informed of the gallows Haman had built at his home for Mordecai, the king ordered that Haman be hanged on it himself.

The king's edict that the Jews be slain had been approved and was being announced throughout the domain. When Esther requested of her husband that this decree be reversed, he replied that "the writing which is written in the king's name, and sealed with the king's ring, may no man reverse" (Esther 8:8). However, he wrote a new edict which allowed the Jews to defend themselves against any enemy who would attack them. When the fighting broke out, the Jewish defense was so effective that they killed 800 of their adversaries at Susa and 75,000 in the provinces (Esther 9:6–16). They also killed the ten sons of Haman. In all this they took no spoil. Peace was soon restored, and the Jews instituted a two-day feast, the Feast of Purim, or Feast of Lots, to commemorate their deliverance, the thirteenth and fourteenth days of Adar (our month of March). It was so called because Haman had determined the thirteenth day by casting the lot, or Pur (Esther 9:26).

19. The Second Return

The second and third returns were not far apart, but they were quite some time after Zerubbabel's group. In fact, little is known about events in Jerusalem from the dedication of the second Temple till Ezra's return, a space of 58 years; so there is a span of 58 years between Ezra 6 and Ezra 7. The second group was led in 458 B.C. by Ezra, a man who was both a priest and a scribe as well as a descendant of Hilkiah, the high priest in the time of Josiah. If the main concern of Zerubbabel was a reconstruction of the Temple, the main concern of Ezra was a desire to see the laws of Moses taught and observed in the homeland. "For Ezra had set his heart to seek the law of Jehovah, and to do it, and to teach in Israel statutes and ordinances" (Ezra 7:10). Artaxerxes Longimanus, king of Persia at that time, gave Ezra authority to receive contributions from the Jews in Babylonia for the purpose of adorning the Temple in Jerusalem, authority to establish magistrates and judges in the Jewish province, and authority to claim help from the rulers of the provinces through which the caravan would pass (Ezra 7:11–26). He persuaded 6,000 of his countrymen to return to Jerusalem with him, among whom were many priests. They fasted for three days at the river Ahava, seeking God's blessing on the trip. Twelve men were "set apart" to carry the silver, the gold, and the vessels of precious metal to Jerusalem for the Temple. After a journey of four months they finally arrived at their destination, the city of David.

20. Conditions in Jerusalem

As soon as Ezra's band of Jewish travelers arrived in Jerusalem they offered burnt offerings unto Jehovah and presented themselves to the Persian officials. Ezra immediately discovered that the Jews had neglected the law of Moses and had declined into a state of religious lethargy. They had flagrantly violated the law against mixed marriage, even including the priests, the Levites, the princes, and the rulers. "And when I heard this thing, I rent my garment and my robe, and plucked off the hair of my head and of my beard,

19. Jerusalem; west wall of Temple area with Dome of the Rock above

and sat down confounded" (Ezra 9:3). Ezra fell upon his knees and offered to God a zealous prayer, confessing the sins of his people and requesting a forgiveness of their open violation of God's expectations of them. This had a tremendous effect upon the people gathered unto him out of the surrounding countryside, "for the people wept very sore" (Ezra 10:1). Shecaniah, speaking for the people, suggested that they make a new covenant with Jehovah and that they put away their foreign wives and the children born to them. He pledged full support to Ezra in correcting this problem. Three days later Ezra met with the people in the open square before the Temple and addressed the fearful congregation concerning the seriousness of the matter. Expressing their willingness to conform to Ezra's demands, the Jewish state agreed to a three months' examination of all guilty parties. A long list of priests, Levites, and laymen were found guilty of intermarriages; the mixed marriages were abandoned (Ezra 10:9–44). Ezra's book closes with the list of those who consented to put away their foreign wives.

21. The Third Return

The third return followed on the heels of the second, being led by Nehemiah in 444 B.C. This was merely 14 years later than Ezra's return. This man, one of the most colorful figures in the restoration period, was willing to forfeit his position in the Persian court in order to return to his homeland and help in the reconstruction. Zerubbabel the prince, then Ezra the scribe, and now Nehemiah the governor—those are the three great leaders who led migrating groups back to Palestine.

Nehemiah must have been a forceful character to have risen to the position of cupbearer to King Artaxerxes I of Susa. He was not only an able and distinguished man, but one of piety and loyalty to his people. Hanani, his brother, and certain Jews from Jerusalem brought Nehemiah word of the distressing conditions prevailing in Jerusalem, of the great affliction of the people, and of the fact that the walls were broken down and the gates burnt with fire. "And it came to pass, when I heard these words, that I sat down and wept, and mourned certain days; and I fasted and prayed before the God of heaven" (Neh. 1:4). His prayer to God, following his period of mourning (Neh. 1:5–11), shows his familiarity with Israel's history and with the covenant and the law connected with Sinai. He asked that God grant him favor with the king of Persia.

After three months' time Artaxerxes noticed that Nehemiah was very dejected. To his inquiry Nehemiah expressed grief over the chaos that prevailed in Jerusalem. To a further inquiry of what he desired, Nehemiah boldly requested that he be allowed to return to Jerusalem to build again the city of his father. The king asked him how long he would be gone, and Nehemiah set him a certain time. The request of the cupbearer was not only granted; the king issued letters to the governors beyond the Euphrates that they permit Nehemiah to pass and that they supply him with building materials for the walls and the gates and for his own private house. The king even provided him and his small party a royal cavalry escort for the 1,000-mile trip from Susa to Jerusalem (Neh. 2:1–9).

22. Rebuilding the Wall

Among the governors that Nehemiah encountered on the way down to Jerusalem, to whom he presented his official letter, were two that were very unhappy over his arrival with a desire to aid the Israelites. These were Sanballat the Horonite and Tobiah the Ammonite (Neh. 2:10).

When Nehemiah had entered and been in Jerusalem three days, he did a very dramatic thing. Taking with him a few men and riding upon a beast he made a nightly inspection of the crumbled wall and the charred gates. Of this nocturnal ride the rulers knew nothing. Assembling the people and challenging them to rebuild the wall, he was met with instant support on the part of the people. "And they said, Let us rise up and build. So they strengthened their hands for the good work." But three people laughed at the idea: Sanballat the Horonite, Tobiah the Ammonite, and Geshem the Arabian. Nehemiah told them that God would help his people to build, but that they would have no portion in Jerusalem (Neh. 2:10–20).

Very efficiently Nehemiah assigned various groups of the people, each group being under one head, to various gates and to various sections of the wall (Neh. 3:1–32). It should be remembered that the previously used stones were available and that the foundations of the past wall were still there. It may have been that even a few tiers of the previous wall were still standing. As the wall began to rise Sanballat became very angry; he and Tobiah even mocked the Jews. Sanballat and others decided "to come and fight against Jerusalem, and to cause confusion therein." But the people of Israel prayed and set up a watch day and night. Nehemiah placed half of the people working and half with weapons to defend and to fight. Even the workers themselves had weapons for defense. There were trumpeters ready to sound an alarm for any place that suddenly was attacked. Neither Nehemiah nor any of the workers put off their clothes the entire time; they even took their weapons with them to get water (Neh. 4:1–23).

But the rebuilding program was especially hard for the poorer people, as they found it difficult to pay their taxes and their interest and to provide necessities for their families while they were having to work on the wall. Some were even faced with the possibility of enslaving their children due to their debts. Nehemiah's skill as an administrator is shown in the excellent manner in which he solved this economic crisis so that the building program could continue (Neh. 5:1–19). As the walls were nearing completion in spite of all opposition, Nehemiah's enemies tried to ensnare him; four times Sanballat and Geshem invited Nehemiah to meet with them in one of the villages. Nehemiah refused. The fifth invitation was a stronger one, being accompanied by a threat. Again he refused. They did not stop here but continued in their endeavor to thwart Nehemiah in his plans, but Nehemiah constantly resorted to God in prayer and pleaded for his help (Neh. 6:1–19). At last the wall was completed, and this in just 52 days (Neh. 6:15). Nehemiah then reorganized the administration of the city with a view toward defense, placing his brother Hanani in charge (Neh. 7:1–4).

23. Reformation Under Ezra

With Jerusalem fully secured Nehemiah the governor turned his attention to other things. During the religious reformation that ensued, Nehemiah faded into the background while Ezra the priest came forward (Neh. 8–10). Ezra was deeply concerned that the proper worship services be reinstated, with the proper priests officiating and the exact ritual observed. The great need, however, was that Israel be taught the laws of Moses. The people, assembling themselves in the broad place, requested that Ezra read to them from the book of the law of Moses. This Ezra did. "And he read therein before the broad place that was before the water gate from early morning until midday, in the presence of the men and the women, and of those that could understand; and the ears of all the people were attentive unto the book of the law." This he did before a pulpit of wood that they made for him. All the people rejoiced and worshiped with shouts of Amen, Amen. There were also interpreters to give the sense of that which was read (Neh. 8:1–12). Then the people went out into the hills and brought in branches to make booths, so that they could observe the Feast of Tabernacles. This observance proved to be the greatest since the days of Joshua at the time of the conquest. The law was read each of the seven days, with the eighth day being a holy convocation (Neh. 8:13–18).

After two days the people assembled with fasting and the wearing of sackcloth. They read the law, confessed their sins, and worshiped (Neh. 9:1–4). There was a long prayer of public confession of sin (Neh. 9:5–37), followed by the account of a written covenant in which the people bound themselves to keep the law of God given to Moses on Mount Sinai. This covenant was signed by Nehemiah and other representatives of the people (Neh. 9:38 to 10:39).

24. Nehemiah's Policies

Nehemiah wished to increase the population of Jerusalem so as to provide greater security for the city, being sure this met with divine approval. He even resorted to the genealogical register at the time of Zerubbabel that the people of his day "might be reckoned by genealogy" (Neh. 7:5–73). He cast lots so that one tenth of the Jewish population outside Jerusalem could be brought into the city in order to increase the number there (Neh. 11:1–2). The register of those living in Jerusalem and the surrounding towns during Nehemiah's time is found in Nehemiah 11:3–36.

There was a dedication of the wall that involved the whole Jewish province. There were two processions, headed by Nehemiah and

Ezra, that finally met at the Temple for a great service of thanksgiving, all with orchestra and choir. Abundant sacrifices were made. It was a festive occasion with much joy and rejoicing (Neh. 12:27–43).

Nehemiah organized the priests and the Levites to care for the tithes sent in by the people from the various towns, so that there would be plenty for the priests and Levites and they could perform their duties (Neh. 12:44–47).

During his twelfth year as governor of Judah, which was about 432 B.C., Nehemiah returned to Persia, stayed for some time, and then came back again to Jerusalem (Neh. 13:6–7). When he arrived back in the Jewish capital, he found that there was somewhat of a spiritual decline. Eliashib the high priest had even granted Tobiah the Ammonite a room in the court of the Temple, one that had previously been used to store provisions for the Levites. Nehemiah threw out the furniture and had the room renovated for its proper use.

Nehemiah charged the officials with neglect of the Temple by failing to collect the tithes. He appointed trustworthy men over the storehouses. Then he started on the laws for the sabbath, for the Jews were working and selling on the sabbath day. He ordered the gates of Jerusalem closed on the sabbath and put guards to stop all commerce on that day. Mixed marriages were next dealt with, for the Jews had married women from Ashdod, Moab, and Ammon. Nehemiah seemed to have lost his temper. "And I contended with them, and cursed them, and smote certain of them, and plucked off their hair, and made them swear by God, saying, Ye shall not give your daughters unto their sons, nor take their daughters for your sons, or for yourselves." He reminded them of what foreign women had done to Solomon and how they had caused him to sin (Neh. 13:4–31).

Thus it is seen that Nehemiah is one of the great men of Hebrew history. He was a man of high rank and noble character, very pious, courageous against the enemies of God's plan, and defiant against all factors that would discourage and thwart God's work and God's people. The social and economic welfare of his people was at the center of his thoughts; he was a champion of the poor. His courage is revealed in his reply to the threats of his enemies: "Should such a man as I flee?"

Some scholars think that Nehemiah made a second return to Susa, this time about 413 B.C., but this is debatable. At any rate the Old Testament period ends about 400 B.C.

25. A Late Prophet

Malachi is the last book of the Old Testament in English. (Chronicles holds this spot in the Hebrew Scriptures.) Although little is known about the author, the name Malachi means "my messenger." Most scholars believe that he prophesied during the time of Ezra and Nehemiah; the second Temple and the altar were in use, as well as the fact the people were under a Persian governor. This would place him after the time of Haggai and Zechariah but would not determine whether he was prior to Ezra's return or during the time of Nehemiah.

He proclaimed Israel's peculiar relationship to God but proceeded to relate Israel's disrespect for God—even to the point that the people had offered imperfect or stolen animals to God. The priests were denounced for their unfaithfulness in responsibility and the people for their intermarriage with the heathen. The foreign wives practiced idolatry. Sorcery and adultery were present. There was also a failure to bring the tithe unto the storehouse. Social injustices were rampant. In conclusion, he exhorted his people to be faithful to the law of Moses.

Hebrew Prophecy and Poetry

1. Significance of the Prophets

The prophets of Israel were a class of men who exerted a tremendous influence on the life of the Hebrew people. Therefore a brief survey of their work is vital to an understanding of the Old Testament. Their work covered several centuries, extending from the time of the judges to the close of the Old Testament era about 400 B.C.; yet their greatest activity centered in the years of the monarchy. They were powerful leaders religiously, socially, and politically, each with a message from God at a time it was vitally needed.

Other terms are used in the Old Testament to refer to these important leaders: watchmen, men of God, messengers of Jehovah, men of the Spirit, seers, interpreters, servants of Jehovah. There are three Hebrew terms in the Old Testament all of which are translated with the English word "prophet." Two of these are not used so much; they mean "to see" and therefore carry the idea of a "man of vision." The term "seer" would also be a good translation for these two terms. But the term translated "prophet" that is found more than 300 times means "to announce." This term represents the prophet as a "speaker," or "forthsayer." Therefore the prophet is one who speaks forth for God. He is one who has received a vital message from God in some special way and must declare that message to the people. He is God's messenger, God's medium for revealing himself and his will to the people. "Thus saith the Lord" is his recurrent theme.

2. Call of a Prophet

The prophet of Israel was one who had experienced a call from Jehovah; this was the source of his motivation and his authority. This call was received in different ways. God might speak audibly or in a vision. Isaiah described his call in the sixth chapter of his book (6:1–13). He saw the Lord sitting majestically in the Temple high upon a throne, with seraphim flying and singing of his holiness. In this vision of glory Isaiah received both forgiveness and an invitation. "Whom shall I send, and who will go for us?" To this he responded, "Here am I; send me." Then God gave him his commission, very difficult though it was to be.

Ezekiel described his call in the first two and a half chapters of his book (1:1 to 3:15). While he was a captive by the river Chebar in Babylonia, the heavens were opened, and he saw visions of God; "and the hand of Jehovah was there upon him" (1:3). There was a vision of four living creatures, or cherubim, as well as a vision of four wheels with eyes in the rims. In this picture of divine brightness and divine glory Ezekiel received his call; the Spirit said to him, "Son of man, I send thee to the children of Israel, to nations that are rebellious, which have rebelled against me." He was commanded to eat the roll of a book, which when he did so, tasted "as honey for sweetness." Then God gave him his commission. Jeremiah's call and commission are presented in his first chapter. "Before I formed thee in the belly I knew thee, and before thou camest forth out of the womb I sanctified thee; I have appointed thee a prophet unto the nations" (v. 4). Amos received his call when God roared like a lion. "The lion hath roared; who will not fear? The Lord Jehovah hath spoken; who can but prophesy?" (3:8). Many other prophets did not feel led to reveal psychologically just what they experienced when God called them, but every "Thus saith the Lord" that issued from their mouths bore witness to God's hand upon them.

The call brought to the prophet the consciousness of God's authority, so that every word he spoke was done courageously and fearlessly. Since God was speaking through him, he could voice his message without compromise. There was the comforting assurance that his every word was the word of God; therefore the true prophet did not shrink even before kings and nobles. Nathan's accusation of David, "Thou art the man," was followed by a sermon of reproof because he had taken Bathsheba as a wife. Yet Nathan did not alter the force of his message.

3. Denouncers of Evil

The prophets of Israel were the denouncers of evil practices both by the individual and by the nation. Carnal sins, social sins, sins of pride and arrogance, sins against the poor, high-handed sins as well as sins of ignorance—all came within their scathing speech. Just as Nathan denounced David, Elijah denounced Ahab. Amos declared that Israel desired to "buy the poor for silver, and the needy for a pair of shoes" (Amos 8:6). He advised them: "Hate the evil, and love the good, and establish justice in the gate" (Amos 5:15). Hosea told Israel that there was "no truth, nor goodness, nor knowledge of God in the land." Instead there was nothing "but swearing and breaking faith, and killing, and stealing, and committing adultery; they break out, and blood toucheth blood" (Hos. 4:1–2).

As a result of Israel's sins and evil practices the prophets predicted destruction and captivity. Doom awaited them. "Israel is swallowed up: now are they among the nations as a vessel wherein none delighteth. For they are gone up to Assyria" (Hos. 8:8–9). Doom awaited Judah also, for they would be carried away to the Euphrates. "Behold, I am Jehovah, the God of all flesh: is there anything too hard for me? Therefore thus saith Jehovah: Behold, I will give this city into the hand of the Chaldeans, and into the hand of Nebuchadrezzar king of Bablyon, and he shall take it." The Chaldeans shall "set this city on fire, and burn it, with the houses, upon whose roofs they have offered incense unto Baal, and poured out drink-offerings unto other gods, to provoke me to anger" (Jer. 32:27–29). The prophet Jeremiah gave the reason for the calamity: "For the children of Israel and the children of Judah have done only that which was evil in my sight from their youth." They have even "set their abominations in the house which is called by my name, to defile it" (Jer. 32:30,34).

One prophet, Jonah, was commanded of God to travel to far-off Nineveh, the capital of the Assyrian empire on the Tigris River, and there proclaim a message urging the people to repent. Jonah refused, endeavoring to run away from God. After great difficulty God finally got him to the foreign capital, where he marched through the streets preaching his message of woe: "Yet forty days, and

Nineveh shall be overthrown'' (Jonah 3:4). To this message the entire city, including the king, responded favorably. They believed God, ''from the greatest of them even to the least of them.'' When they turned from their evil, God reversed his intended doom and did not destroy the city. Jonah, failing to realize that his message was conditional, pouted, because he thought God had not supported him in his proclamation to the inhabitants of the city. God then taught him a lesson by means of a gourd. The book of Jonah is one of the greatest missionary books of the Old Testament.

4. Schools of the Prophets

From the days of the judges references are made in the Scriptures to what are termed ''schools'' of the prophets. These communities seemed to have been especially connected with Samuel, and then later with Elijah and Elisha. Saul at one time met ''a band of prophets,'' after which the Spirit of God came upon Saul and he prophesied (1 Sam. 10:5,10). Samuel had a ''company of prophets'' at his own home in Ramah, where Samuel was ''head over them'' (1 Sam. 19:20). The ''sons of the prophets'' at Bethel came forth to meet Elisha and to speak to him (2 Kings 2:3). The ''sons of the prophets'' at Jericho also came forth to Elisha and also spoke to him (2 Kings 2:5). This group must have been large, for fifty of them went down to the Jordan with Elijah and Elisha (2:7). When Elisha was at Gilgal, the ''sons of the prophets were sitting before him'' (2 Kings 4:38). One of them called him ''man of God.'' Though very little is known about the training of these men by their very prominent leaders, their influence upon later prophecy in Israel should never be underestimated. It must have been tremendous for the cause of righteousness and for the fulfilling of God's purpose among his people.

5. Classification of the Prophets

Many of the prophets of Israel did not put their messages in book form, although they exerted a great impact for Jehovah. Some of these were men like Elijah and Elisha, who figure prominently page after page in the historical books; others were heard from only once or twice and then passed off the scene, such as Nathan,

Gad, Ahijah, Obed, Azariah, and Hanani. These prophets became known as nonwriting prophets, while those who left behind a book, or scroll, of their work became known as writing prophets. Examples of writing prophets are Isaiah, Jeremiah, Amos, Hosea, and all others whose name heads a book of the Bible. There are sixteen of these books of prophecy in the Old Testament, of which four are known as major prophets and twelve are known as minor prophets. However, the terms "major" and "minor" refer to the relative length of the books and not to their relative importance. Although most of these scrolls were probably written down by the prophets themselves, Jeremiah seems to have had a personal scribe named \Baruch who recorded his message for him. When Baruch's first roll was destroyed, Jeremiah dictated again; and Baruch for the second time wrote down the words of the prophet (Jer. 36:4,32). It is believed by most scholars that this second roll is virtually what is now the book of Jeremiah.

6. Nature of Prophecy

The word "prophet" means one who "speaks before," which conveys the idea of one standing before a person or a group to which he proclaims a message. He is a "forth speaker." Therefore the prophet of Israel was one who spoke forth God's message before the people, a message geared to the spiritual needs of that time. He was Jehovah's messenger, proclaiming Jehovah's will for Israel. His message was related to the past, the present, and the future.

As the prophet recorded and interpreted the work of God with his people in the past he was the historian. Most of his message, however, related to the day in which he lived. He called people to repentance and to obedience of Jehovah's laws and commands for them. He urged them to obey his will. He gave advice to rulers and to those in command. He endeavored to give men a greater knowledge of God. But sometimes his message predicted future events, promises of rewards and threatenings of punishment. He told of things to come, of what Israel could expect from the Lord, as when Amos tried to warn the people of the terror of the day of Jehovah lying out ahead. "Shall not the day of Jehovah be darkness, and not light? even very dark, and no brightness in it?"

(Amos 5:18–20). Jeremiah not only informed Judah that they would be carried away into a Babylonian exile, but that it would last seventy years, after which God would bring them back to their homeland (Jer. 29:10). Micah predicted that the coming Messiah would be born in Bethlehem (Mic. 5:2).

It is at this point many people derive their erroneous idea of the work of a prophet, for they believe that the main burden of the prophet is predicting the future. Their concept of prophecy is that it is an unveiling of happenings yet to be, concepts revealed to the proclaimer by the Lord who desires that they be in turn revealed to his people. But the future part of a prophetical utterance is only incidental; it may or may not refer to the future. In fact, the major part of the messages of the prophets of the Old Testament era concerned the desires for God at that time for the people of that day. Just as rhyme is not the main characteristic of poetry but an incidental one instead, so the future element in prophecy is merely incidental. The essential factor in prophecy is that it conveys God's message to man. A prophet is a "forthsayer" more than a "foreteller."

7. Prophecies About Christ

In the Old Testament are found many statements of hope, hope concerning a Coming One who will champion the cause of a sinful and dejected people, bringing light to a world of chaos and of sorrow. These passages that specifically refer to the coming of a Messiah are termed messianic passages. Genesis 3:15 tells of the seed of woman that shall bruise the serpent's head. Micah says that he will be born in Bethlehem (5:2). Isaiah says that his name will be called Immanuel, or "God with us" (7:14) and "Wonderful, Counsellor, Mighty God, Everlasting Father, Prince of Peace" (9:6), and that his kingdom of peace, justice, and righteousness shall be forever (9:7). Jeremiah avows that he will establish a new covenant, a spiritual covenant, one that is eternal and with forgiveness of sin at its center (Jer. 31:31 ff). The fifty-third chapter of Isaiah views him as one who will give himself in substitution for sinful humanity, bearing blame for the sins of fallen man. These and many other passages predicting the coming of this magnificent Redeemer must be the ones brought forth and discussed by Jesus on the road to Emmaus. "And beginning from Moses and from all the prophets, he interpreted to them in all the scriptures the things concerning himself" (Luke 24:27). He himself was a prophet, the consummation of all prophets. Walking the streets, paths, and byways of Palestine he was both the Messenger and the message.

8. Poetry in the Old Testament

If one were to read only from the King James Version of the Bible, he would never be aware of the fact that some of the Old Testament was originally written in Hebrew poetry, rather than in Hebrew prose; the King James translators produced an English version that appears to be all prose. That which is prose in the Hebrew should be prose in English, and that which is poetry in the Hebrew should be poetry in English. The books that are poetry are Job (except for the first two chapters and part of the last chapter), Psalms, Proverbs, Ecclesiastes (about one fourth poetry), Song of Solomon (also called Song of Songs and Canticles), and Lamentations. In addition to these books there are other poems found in many of the early books, as Genesis 4:23,24; 49:2–27; Exodus 15:1–18; Balaam's four prophecies in Numbers; the Song of Moses in Deuteronomy; the Song of Deborah in Judges; and many, many more. Just as with other nations, the earliest Hebrew literature was in poetry form, for these early peoples expressed their emotions in song. Especially would this be true for victory in war, for marriages, and for other great events. Some of these early poems have become lost, for it was mainly the ones of religious significance that were included in the Old Testament books. The writers of the early books in the Old Testament canon refer to such works as the "Wars of Jehovah" (Num. 21:14) and the "Book of Jashur" (Josh. 10:13); the quotations from these books reveal that they were probably collections of poems.

Poetry of the Hebrew language differs from poetry in English and other modern languages in that there is no rhyme and no meter, making it resemble what is known as free verse. All this makes the translation of Hebrew verse into English verse much simpler in terms of sense but quite different regarding form.

9. Varieties of Hebrew Poetry

There are four kinds of Hebrew poetry occurring in the Old Testament. (1) There is lyric poetry, or that which expresses the emotions or deep feelings. The sentiments, or overflow of the heart, can be felt in line after line. The Psalms are examples of this type. (2) There is dramatic poetry, or that which deals with a drama of some sort. Job is an example of this. (3) There is proverbial poetry, or that which states a proverb or aphorism, a short, pithy saying full of wisdom. Proverbs constitutes an example of this type. (4) There is elegiac poetry, or that expressing a mournful or sorrowful theme. Lamentations is a good example of such.

10. Parallelism in Hebrew Poetry

Parallelism, one of the distinguishing marks of Hebrew poetry, involves the use of the couplet and is found in four varieties, or types.

(1) In synonymous parallelism the same thought is repeated in the second line of the couplet but in different words or phrases.

> Love not sleep, lest thou come to poverty;
> Open thine eyes, and thou shalt be satisfied with bread
>   (Prov. 20:13).

Also,

> Oh how love I thy law!
> It is my meditation all the day (Ps. 119:97).

This is probably the most common type.

(2) In antithetical parallelism the opposite thought, or contrast, is found in the second line of the couplet.

> A wise son heareth his father's instruction;
> But a scoffer heareth not rebuke (Prov. 13:1).

Also,

> A good man shall obtain favor of Jehovah;
> But a man of wicked devices will he condemn (Prov. 12:2).

(3) In synthetic parallelism the thought expressed in the first line of the couplet is completed or supplemented in the second line.

> In my distress I cried unto Jehovah,
> And he answered me (Ps. 120:1).

Also,

> I was glad when they said unto me,
> Let us go unto the house of Jehovah (Ps. 122:1).

This type of parallelism is also termed progressive parallelism, as well as ascending parallelism.

(4) In comparative parallelism something in the first line is compared with something in the second line.

> As the hart panteth after the water brooks,
> So panteth my soul after thee, O God (Ps. 42:1).

Also,

> As cold waters to a thirsty soul,
> So is good news from a far country (Prov. 25:25).

This type of parallelism is the least common of all.

11. The Book of Psalms

The Psalms, loved by millions of people, are probably read and cherished more than any other book of the Bible as a source of spiritual strength and as a book of meditation and personal worship. Therefore to many people the book of Psalms is probably the most familiar part of the Old Testament. Not having time to delve into the books of law, history, or prophecy, the busy reader will frequently turn to the psalms for his consolation, inspiration, and spiritual strength. Here he finds easily and quickly the things he needs most, for these great devotional poems help him to draw closer to God.

There are 150 of these poems, written over a vast span of time. One is ascribed to Moses, seventy-three are ascribed to David, twelve to Asaph, eleven to the sons of Korah, two to Solomon, and one to Ethan. Fifty have no name attached to them. These ascriptions, found in the titles, or superscriptions, are rejected by some scholars as not being trustworthy. They say they are not part of the original text but were added later by some editor. Supporting this view is the fact that in the Hebrew language the same preposition may be translated with the English "to," "of," or "for." Therefore it follows that a psalm ascribed to David may mean that it is one dedicated to David, or one written by David, or one written for David, or simply one that he possessed. At the same time the significance of these names found in the superscriptions should not be underestimated. It is reasonable to suppose that David composed a large nucleus of the Psalms, even to the point that his name comes readily to mind when the Psalms are mentioned. He is called "the sweet singer of Israel."

The moods expressed in the Psalms vary greatly, for every emotion and feeling of the human heart is encountered somewhere in the Psalter. Some are poems of thanksgiving; some are songs of praise; some express adoration; some reveal triumph; some manifest penitence and remorse; some show grief; and others express the utmost desolation. The frailty and weakness of human life is there, as is a love for the law of Jehovah. The extreme joy of forgiveness is present, as is an abiding confidence in the strength of the Lord. Some of the psalms express patriotism, as well as the abuses citizenship receives at the hands of ungodly men. The psalmist ponders deeply the true meaning of life and the problem of death. The number of the psalms dealing with personal spiritual experience is large; so it is with Psalm 23, the Shepherd Psalm and most famous of all. Also deeply personal is Psalm 51, the greatest of the penitential psalms.

12. The Book of Job

The book of Job, one of the most remarkable pieces of literature ever written, is dramatic poetry dealing with some of the most profound issues of life. It is conversation, consisting of arguments and responses in very exalted style. Scholars have marveled for years at its depth and beauty, considering it one of the greatest poems of all the ages. In the original Hebrew the writer uses such an extensive vocabulary that he has been referred to as the Shakespeare of the Old Testament. The style of expression is superb, and the display of resources of knowledge is vast. Noble ideals and a high standard of ethics are discerned in the contents of the book.

The problem of human suffering, the theme of the book, is a very old one, for it continues to be one of man's unsolved perplexities. And the book of Job, though still failing to provide a final solution, does present some significant thoughts on suffering. More specifically the theme might be termed "Why do the righteous suffer?"

The first two chapters, the first five verses in chapter 32, and the last eleven verses of the last chapter (chap. 42), are in prose. The vast majority of the book is exalted poetry. Job and his friends do not possess knowledge of the reason for his apparent misfortune, for they do not know of the events recorded in the prose of the first two chapters. Here the writer gives an account of Job's righteous character, his great prosperity—all to the point that he is "the greatest of all the children of the east" (Job 1:3).

The next scene, laid in heaven, depicts a conversation between Jehovah and Satan, one in which God asserts the piety of Job. Satan implies that Job is righteous because it has paid him to be such. When Satan is permitted to afflict Job, great calamities come upon the righteous man—to the loss of everything! Yet Job remains faithful to God. At a second meeting between Jehovah and Satan, Satan is given permission to afflict Job further; the first time he was told not to touch him personally, but this time he is permitted to afflict him with bodily suffering. Satan implies that if his bone and flesh are affected he will renounce God. Job, struck with boils from head to foot, sits among the ashes and scrapes himself. Even his wife suggests he renounce God and die. "In all this did not Job sin with his lips" (Job 2:10). His loyalty to Jehovah is stedfast.

Job's three friends—Eliphaz, Bildad, and Zophar—come to see him in order to comfort him. Rending their clothes they sit and stare at him for seven days and seven nights. Job breaks the silence by cursing the day he was born. Then follows a very extensive argument, Job presenting his view and one friend answering, then Job speaking again and another answering, and so on time after time. Then Elihu, a very boastful young man, comes to present his view of the matter. In chapter 38 God steps in and answers out of the whirlwind, continuing his address to Job through chapter 41. In the epilogue, the last chapter, God rebukes the three friends and vindicates Job. Job is rewarded with more prosperity than he had previously and becomes the father of seven other sons and three other daughters. The book endeavors to disprove the theory that all suffering or misfortune is due to man's sin and is therefore an indication of God's displeasure. Since Jesus presents this same view in his masterful teaching the book of Job is far ahead of its time.

Nothing is known of the time the book was written or who the author might have been. The date of writing has been placed all the way from Moses down to the Babylonian exile. Moses, Elihu, Solomon, Jeremiah, Ezra, and many other Old Testament personalities have been set forth by scholars as the probable author. The writer could easily have lived much later than the characters of whom he wrote.

13. The Book of Proverbs

A proverb is a short, wise saying. It is a self-evident truth in a short, crisp form used to stimulate thinking. It is common-sense wisdom drawn from past experience and stated in a way easily remembered. It is a very old form of literature found universally among the peoples of the world. The modern world has accumulated thousands of them, but the people of both the Near East and the Far East are especially noted for their collections. The Hebrew people used them freely. Though most of the proverbs in the Old Testament are found in a book by that name, proverbs suddenly appear here and there in the prose sections. One example is in 1 Samuel 10:12. "Therefore it became a proverb, Is Saul also among the prophets?" Another is in Ezekiel 18:2. "What mean ye, that ye use this proverb concerning the land of Israel, saying, The fathers have eaten sour grapes, and the children's teeth are set on edge?" First Kings 4:32 says of Solomon: "And he spake three thousand proverbs; and his songs were a thousand and five."

The book of Proverbs is a collection of these pithy sayings covering a long period of time and representing the work of more than one man. It is an anthology, a collection, of proverbs, possibly even a collection of collections of these concise sayings. Yet Solomon's name is associated with this book of the Old Testament more than with any other book, and it is quite probable that he did write the nucleus of the wisdom sayings found there. The headings that occur in the book list two other names as providers of proverbs: Agur and King Lemuel. It is quite probable that parts of the book were added as late as King Hezekiah's time.

The book of Proverbs is more practical in nature than it is theological or speculative. It concerns itself with everyday conduct, with wise daily behavior, especially for young men. Its purpose seems to be to inspire young men to honest, ethical, and industrious living. Many proverbs start with the words "My son." Purity of living is stressed, along with a right relation to God. The young man is warned to flee from sinners and to depart from evil. He is warned against strife, lying, wicked purposes, false witnessing, mischief, laziness, and the strange woman. The evil of drinking is made plain, and the instruction of a father and a mother are highly extolled. True friendship is praised. Many proverbs have a great praise for wisdom. The book ends with a very beautiful poem depicting a virtuous woman (Prov. 31:10–31).

14. Other Books of Poetry

The three important books of poetry have now been considered. There are three less significant books to be dealt with: Ecclesiastes, Song of Solomon, and Lamentations.

The word "Ecclesiastes" comes from the Greek, but it translates a Hebrew word *koheleth,* meaning "preacher," or "proclaimer." Tradition says that Solomon wrote it, but most scholars believe that it was written by one living in the late days of the kingdom, or even later. He seems to have used other passages from the Old Testament as he wrote of his investigation of life. Even though the book is only about one-fourth poetry, it is classed with the poetry books, as well as being classed along with Job and Proverbs as Wisdom Literature. It was publicly read at the Feast of Tabernacles.

The author of Ecclesiastes talks freely of both the ventures and the failures of man. After very carefully observing and weighing life situations, he draws his inferences. He investigates things done "under the sun" and comes to the conclusion that "all is vanity"— two recurring phrases found throughout the book. Man's duty is to fear God and keep his commandments (Eccl. 12:13–14).

Song of Solomon, also called Song of Songs and Canticles, has drawn forth a wide variety of interpretations. As the title indicates, it was associated with Israel's famous king; but it is hard to ascertain whether it was written by or for Solomon. It seems best to infer that it pertains to Solomon. It is a love song, or maybe a collection of love songs, a type of literature greatly admired by the people of that time and that area of the world. It contains an abundance of metaphors and seeks to describe physical beauty and charm in glowing terms. Of the many interpretations, no one interpretation seems to satisfy all or even a vast segment of Old Testament scholars. But there is agreement that it does express the warm feeling of human love. However, the Hebrews must have sensed a spiritual value in their interpretation, since the book was read annually at the Passover; it must have reminded them of God's love in delivering them from Egyptian bondage.

Lamentations, an elegy over the desolation of the debris that was once Jerusalem, was written by Jeremiah after Nebuchadnez-zar's total destruction in 587–586 B.C. It was once a part of the book of Jeremiah; therefore it follows his book in the canon. Though written entirely in poetry, it is placed among the prophetic books and not among the poetical books. The book not only describes the wretched condition of the ruined city; it depicts vividly the horror of the siege itself. The writer gives the reason for the destruction: the sin of Israel against Jehovah, their God.

THE KINGDOMS OF ISRAEL
AND JUDAH

Scale of Miles

0 5 10   20   30   40

Mediterranean Sea

Sidon

Zarephath

Tyre

Accho

Dor

Megiddo

Taanach

Dothan

Samaria

Joppa

Aphek

Beth-horon

Gezer

Ekron

Ashdod

Ashkelon

Timnah

Zorah

Beth-shemesh

Adullam

Gath

Lachish

Gaza

Gerar

Ziklag

Raphia

Beer-sheba

MT. CARMEL

Plain of Sharon

P H O E N I C I A

MOUNT LEBANON

Leontes R.

MT. HERMON

Dan

Kedesh

Hazor

Chinnereth

Sea of Chinnereth

Hammath

Kishon

Plain of Jezreel

+Mt. Tabor

Shunem

Jezreel

Beth-shan

Abel-meholah

Jabesh-gilead

Mahanaim

Tirzah

Succoth Penuel

Mt. Ebal+ +Shechem

Mt. Gerizim

Shiloh

Bethel

Mizpah

Ramah

Jericho

Gibeon

Gilgal

Jerusalem

Bethlehem

Tekoa

Hebron

Ziph En-gedi

I S R A E L

River Jordan

G I L E A D

Jabbok R.

Heshbon

+Mt. Nebo
Medeba

Wilderness of Judah

Dead Sea

Arnon R.

Dibon

J U D A H

P H I L I S T I A

Valley of Salt

Kir-hareseth

Zered R.

M O A B

E D O M

S Y R I A

Abana R.

Damascus

Ashtaroth

B a s h a n

Aphek Yarmuk

Edrei

Ramoth-gilead

A M M O N

Rabbath-ammon

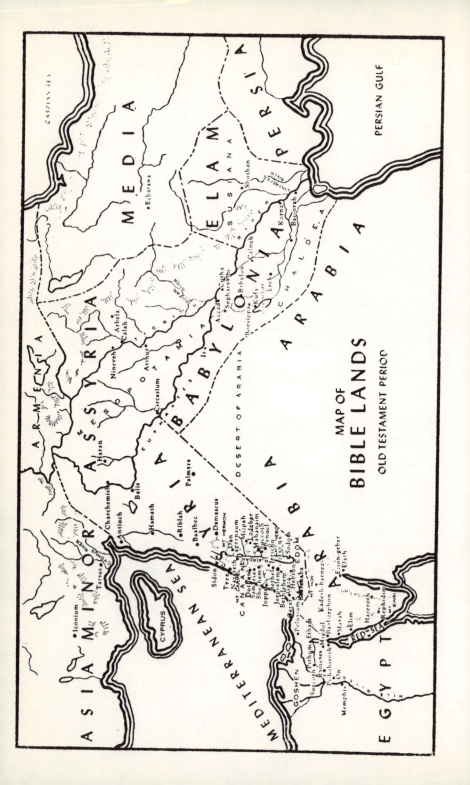

MAP OF
BIBLE LANDS
OLD TESTAMENT PERIOD

INDEX

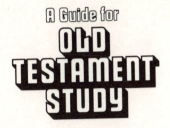

A Guide for
**OLD
TESTAMENT
STUDY**

Student Manual

Student Manual

1
The Significance of the Bible

I. Significant Questions

1. What is the earliest date and the latest date for any of the actual writing of the Bible?

2. What is the probable number of all the contributing writers of the Bible?

3. What is the theme of the Bible that runs from beginning to end?

4. What constitutes God's ultimate, or supreme, revelation?

5. What is the difference between "revelation" and "inspiration"?

6. Briefly stated, what are the three theories of inspiration?

7. Why is the idea of the covenant so important in a true understanding of the Bible?

8. What is the date after which all debate concerning the inclusion or exclusion of any book in the New Testament canon ceased?

9. What is the place of the Aramaic language in the history of the Hebrew people?

10. Who were the Jews of the Dispersion?

11. Why did the Septuagint become so important in the lives of the early Christians?

12. What is the difference in the attitude of Protestants and Roman Catholics in regard to the Apocrypha?

13. Who were Josephus and Philo?

14. When do the "rainy" and "dry" seasons occur in Palestine?

15. What are the four natural divisions in Palestine?

1

II. Word Studies

1. What is the source of our word "Bible"?
2. What is the root meaning of the word "inspired"?
3. Why is the word "covenant" rather than the word "testament" a better term with which to translate the Hebrew and Greek terms?
4. Why is the term "canon," as used relative to the Scriptures, an appropriate word?
5. How did we get the word "Torah," as is used in biblical books?
6. What is the meaning of the term "Pentateuch"?
7. What is the meaning of "Septuagint"?
8. What is the meaning of "Apocrypha"?
9. What is the meaning of "Mesopotamia"?
10. What is the Mediterranean Sea called in the Bible?
11. What is the probable explanation for the term Palestine? Is it a biblical term?

III. Inspiring Lessons

1. A book so significant as the Bible, so filled with God's revelation of himself and of his desire for man's life, should be read and applied more in daily living.
2. To endeavor to force the Bible to do what it does not purport to do is to do it an injustice. It is primarily a religious book, dealing with man's relation to God.
3. Archaeology can be used as an aid in the study of God's ancient people.

IV. Key Concepts

1. Man's high role in God's creative and providential activities is seen clearly in the fact that God has revealed himself to man and that we have the record of that revelation, the Bible.
2. The basic concept underlying both Judaism and Christianity is that God has revealed himself to man and man is able to receive that communication.

V. Enrichment Suggestions

1. Read further about the various theories of inspiration of the Bible in one of these books: J. McKee Adams, *Our Bible*, Convention Press, pp. 10-20. Olin T. Binkley, *How to Study the Bible*, Convention Press.

Doran McCarty, *Rightly Dividing the Word*, Broadman Press.

2. Study a good book on archaeology in biblical lands: Stephen L. Caiger, *Bible and Spade*, Oxford University Press. H. H. Rowley, *Rediscovery of the Old Testament*, Westminster Press, pp. 33-82.

3. Secure a copy of the Apocrypha and read some from it. Compare Ecclesiasticus with Proverbs in the Old Testament. Read some from 1 and 2 Maccabees.

4. Read about the great significance of the Old Testament for the Christian of today in H. Wheeler Robinson, *The Religious Ideas of the Old Testament*, Duckworth, pp. 212-235.

2
The Creation and Early Happenings

I. Significant Questions

1. What two important things should be remembered about the word "create" as used in Genesis?

2. What in the creation of man makes it more significant than the other phases of creation?

3. Where was the probable location of Eden? Why?

4. What three things, normally thought of as good, were the basis of the serpent's appeal?

5. What punishment was given to the man, the woman, and the serpent?

6. What three theories have been set forth by scholars for the extreme length of the lives of men prior to the flood?

7. What was the sign of God's covenant with Noah?

8. What does Genesis 11:4 seem to indicate as the reason for the building of the tower of Babel?

II. Word Studies

1. What is significant about the name "Adam"?

2. Why is "Genesis" appropriate for the name of the first book in the Old Testament?

3. What is the meaning of "sabbath"?

4. Give the meaning of the names of the three sons of Noah?

5. Why is "Babel" a good name for the tower of Genesis 11?

III. Inspiring Lessons

1. God as the sole source of creation should be the conviction of every believer.

2. Endeavoring to "play god," being a "god unto oneself," is the basic sin.

3. The picture of temptation as found in Genesis 3 is appropriate for the individual as well as the human race.

4. The tendency to blame others for one's own faults or inadequacies is universal.

5. The power of jealousy to bring on other sins, such as murder, is very evident.

IV. Key Concepts

1. Creation is the work of God alone. Only God creates, brings into existence that which is nonexistent.

2. God is sovereign by virtue of his creation.

3. Monogamy has been God's intent for man and the home since the days of creation.

4. There is a progressive order in God's creation, from the lower to the higher forms, man being the apex.

5. Sin results in punishment, unhappiness, and death.

6. The very best people sometimes sin (Noah).

7. Rebellion against God's commands means self-destruction.

V. Enrichment Suggestions

1. Read further about God's creating the world, for instance, L. Craig Ratliff, *Because We Believe*, Broadman Press, pp. 29-35.

2. Study false views about how the world came into existence; see William W. Stevens, *Doctrines of the Christian Religion*, William B. Eerdmans Publishing Co., pp. 65-67.

3. Study about evidence pertaining to the flood. Alfred M. Rehwinkel, *The Flood in the Light of the Bible, Geology, and Archaeology*, Concordia Publishing House. Andre Parrot, *The Flood and Noah's Ark*, Philosophical Library. Frederick A. Filby, *The Flood Reconsidered*, Zondervan Publishing House.

3
Abraham and Isaac

I. Significant Questions

1. Did the city of Ur, in Chaldea, have a high culture for its time? Explain your answer.

2. What relation was Abraham to Sarah prior to their marriage?

3. What are the four features of God's promise to Abraham?

4. What are the twin peaks of Samaria?

5. What ancient custom of ruling monarchs got Abraham into trouble in Egypt?

6. What fact made Egypt the "granary" for all surrounding nations in a time of famine?

7. Lot's separation from Abraham was due to what factor?

8. What dread prediction did God add to the wonderful promise he made to Abraham?

9. From where did the Ishmaelites come?

10. What became of the sign and token of the covenant relationship God made with Abraham, and therefore with all the Hebrew people?

11. What was Abraham's "acid test" of faith?

12. Who became Abraham's wife after the death of Sarah?

13. What six people were buried in the Cave of Machpelah?

14. Who became the wife of Isaac?

15. Contrast the character of Esau with that of Jacob.

II. Word Studies

1. Define "patriarch," and why is it an appropriate title?

2. What two rivers are involved in the name "Mesopotamia"?

3. What is significant about the change in the name Abram to Abraham?

4. How did Shechem get its name?

5. What is the biblical name for the Dead Sea?

6. What is the meaning of the name "Melchizedek?"

7. Why was Isaac so named?

III. Inspiring Lessons

1. The deep and abiding faith in God on Abraham's part needs to be emulated on our part.

2. Abraham's faithfulness in worshiping God became a source of spiritual strength and a key to his character.

3. Even the great characters of the Old Testament had their weak moments; yet God used them mightily in his providential workings.

4. Esau's selling his birthright for a dish of red bean soup is the supreme example of bad judgment concerning values.

IV. Key Concepts

1. God has a deep concern for all humanity, as seen in his promises to Abraham contained in the covenant made with him.

2. The inevitable result of sin is destruction and punishment.

3. The Old Testament presents the sins and sordid events of Hebrew history as openly as it does the courageous and noble ones.

4. God does things in his own order and in his own time, as in the birth of Isaac.

5. God does not want us to forget his promises of grace, as seen in the renewal of his covenant promises to the patriarchs.

V. Enrichment Suggestions

1. Make your own chart of the family of Terah to show the relationship of Abraham with others in this important family.

2. Study more about Abraham for an appreciation of his character; see a Bible dictionary or *A Nation in the Making*, Page Kelley, Convention Press.

4
Jacob and Joseph

I. Significant Questions

1. What part did Rebekah play in Jacob's receiving his father's blessing?

2. Where did Jacob go to seek a wife?

3. What kin were Leah and Rachel to Jacob by birth?

4. What was Jacob's business deal with Laban in order to secure the two girls?

5. How long was Jacob in Paddan-aram?

6. What was Rachel's sin that caused her own destruction?

7. In what special way did Jacob prepare to meet his brother Esau so that all his family would not be killed?

8. What was the sin of Simeon and Levi at Shechem?

9. Where was Rachel buried?

10. What were three reasons for the jealousy of Joseph's half brothers?

11. What were the dreams of the butler and the baker in the Egyptian prison?

12. Which one of Jacob's sons received from him the blessing due Reuben, the first son?

13. What two Hebrews were embalmed according to the Egyptian custom?

II. Word Studies

1. How did Jacob live up to the meaning of his name?

2. Why did Jacob change the name of the place called "Luz" to that of "Bethel"?

3. What is the meaning of "Peniel"?

4. What is the meaning of the word "teraphim"?

5. What is significant about Jacob's new name "Israel"?

6. What was the meaning of Joseph's Egyptian name?

7. What was the name of the rich Nile delta where Jacob's family settled down?

III. Inspiring Lessons

1. Anger and wrath hurt mostly the one expressing them, not the one upon whom they are laid (Esau).

2. God's blessings are given many times in unexpected places and in unexpected ways (Jacob's Bethel experience.)

3. Many of our worries never materialize (Esau's vow to kill Jacob, a twenty-year worry to Jacob).

4. God is willing to bless those who earnestly seek his blessings (Jacob and the angel).

5. Joseph's interpretation of his brothers' ungracious act of selling him into slavery as an act of God for the preservation of the family reveals the magnitude of his character.

IV. Key Concepts

1. God sometimes uses unusual signs to fulfill his purpose with his people—for example, Jacob's ladder.

2. A man's sins have a way many times of returning upon him. (Jacob's early deception was visited upon him later by his own children).

3. The righteous suffer just as the unrighteous do (Joseph).

V. Enrichment Suggestions

1. Look further into art, music, and poetry inspired by the Old Testament. *The Old Testament and the Fine Arts,* ed. Cynthia Pearl Maus, Harper and Row.

5
Moses and the Deliverance

I. Significant Questions

1. What is the generally accepted date of the Exodus?

2. Who was the Pharaoh of the oppression?

3. What three attempts did the Pharaoh of the oppression make to curtail the multiplying of the Hebrew population in Egypt?

4. In what two ways did God providentially train Moses for his future task of delivering his people?

5. Why did Moses flee to the land of the Midianites?

6. What are the five excuses given by Moses for not obeying God's request?

7. What three signs did God give Moses to take to Pharaoh and the Egyptians?

8. What were the three great obstacles confronting Moses in getting the Hebrews out of Egypt?

9. What relation is there between the "hardening" of Pharaoh's heart and the sovereignty, or supremacy, of God?

10. What connection is there between the plagues and the various Egyptian gods?

II. Word Studies

1. What is the appropriate meaning of the word "Exodus"?

2. What was the Nile called by the Egyptians? by the Israelites?

3. How was Moses' name appropriate?

4. Pharaoh's heart was "hardened". What is the real meaning of the Hebrew word behind the English "hardened"?

5. What is significant about the word "passover"?

III. Inspiring Lessons

1. As God delivered the Hebrews from the bondage of sin he will deliver the present-day sinner from his spiritual enslavement (Col. 1:13).

2. God will aid in the training and education of his called-ones of today just as he did for Moses.

3. God still speaks through "burning bushes" and "still small voices" when his people are receptive to his messages.

IV. Key Concepts

1. In no other place in the Scriptures is the providential hand of God seen more dramatically and openly than in the deliverance of his people from a land of bondage to a rich and promising country.

2. The holiness of God is not mentioned in the Bible until the burning-bush episode; then it becomes an important factor among the attributes of God.

3. The God of the Hebrews was unique in that he is the supreme, universal, and only God, as contrasted with the "national" gods of Egypt and the surrounding nations.

V. Enrichment Suggestions

1. Memorize the ten plagues, in order.

2. Read further about the Exodus in Martin Noth, *Exodus*, Westminster Press; also Dorothy Clarke Wilson, *Prince of Egypt*, Westminster Press.

6
Sinai and the Covenant

I. Significant Questions

1. After the murmuring of the people just out of Egypt, God supplied them with two things "from heaven." What were these?

2. What war-like people did Joshua and the Hebrews defeat on their

way to Sinai?

    3. What were the names of Moses' wife and father-in-law?

    4. What are the three elements, found in three consecutive sections of the book of Exodus, that made up the formal act by which Israel entered into a covenant with God?

    5. What is meant by the statement that the Ten Commandments are mainly "prohibitions"?

    6. What act sealed the covenant between God and Israel?

    7. What was the greatest difference between the tabernacle and the temple that followed it?

    8. What three pieces of equipment were found in the holy place of the tabernacle? What one in the holy of holies?

    9. How did God answer Moses when he requested to see the glory of God?

II. Word Studies

    1. What is the source of the word "manna"?

    2. What is the meaning of the name "Joshua"?

    3. For what was Sinai named?

    4. What is the meaning of the term "decalogue"?

    5. What does "to tabernacle" mean?

    6. Why was the Feast of Pentecost so named?

    7. Why was the Feast of Tabernacles so named?

III. Inspiring Lessons

    1. God will supply our needs (manna and quail) but not necessarily our wants.

    2. Organization is still a great aid in achieving God's work (Jethro's suggestion to Moses).

    3. People need to sense and to be appalled at the holiness and righteous nature of God today as the Israelites were when they witnessed the presence of God at Mount Sinai.

    4. The magnitude of Moses' character is discerned in his constant intercession for rebellious Israel, even to the point of requesting to be blotted out of God's book as a remission of the sins of the people.

IV. Key Concepts

    1. Salvation in the Old Testament, as discerned in God's dealing with

Israel, is as much a matter of grace as it is in the New Testament. Israel became God's people through grace.

2. The distinctive element in the religion of the Hebrews, revealed to them at Sinai, is its highly ethical character, quite a contrast to the pagan religions of the nations surrounding them.

3. The love, mercy, grace, and forgiveness side of God's character seen at Sinai as well as the holiness, righteousness, and justice side of God (Exodus 34:6,7).

V. Enrichment Suggestions

1. Study about the various peaks in the Sinai peninsula, any one of which may have been the one connected with Moses and the giving of the law. See *Biblical Backgrounds* by J. McKee Adams and Joseph A. Callaway, Broadman Press, pp. 42-48.

2. Study about manna in a Bible dictionary.

3. Study some Bible dictionary relative to the tabernacle.

4. Study further the sacrificial system demanded by the Mosaic law, especially the three most important feasts, in a Bible dictionary or *Halley's Bible Handbook*, Zondervan Publishing Co.

7
The Wanderings and the Conquest

I. Significant Questions

1. By what miraculous means did God guide the Israelites in their march from Sinai toward Canaan?

2. What was Moses' invitation to his brother-in-law, Hobab?

3. When Moses begged God for relief from the gigantic task of dealing with such a child-like people, what was God's answer?

4. What two of the twelve spies sent into the land of Canaan brought an acceptable report?

5. What did God have in mind in making the children of Israel wander forty years in the wilderness?

6. What two possible motives were behind the rebellion of Korah, Dathan, and Abiram?

7. What three objects were placed inside the ark of the covenant for safe keeping?

8. What was Moses' three-fold error when he struck the rock at
Meribah in his effort to obtain water?

9. By what method were the people healed of the bites from the
fiery serpents?

10. Where was the land of Bashan?

11. To what strategy did Balak, king of Moab, resort in order not to
have to fight the Israelites?

12. What unethical thing did Balaam do to satisfy his hurt feelings?

13. What unusual request did the tribes of Reuben and Gad make
relative to the allotment of Canaan?

II. Word Studies

1. Where did the valley of Eshcol get its name?

2. Why was Meribah, where Moses struck the rock, so appropriately
named?

3. What is the meaning of "Arnon," a stream entering the Dead Sea
on the eastern side?

4. Deuteronomy has what appropriate meaning?

III. Inspiring Lessons

1. The repulsiveness of jealousy is easily seen in the rebellion of
Miriam and Aaron against Moses.

2. Lack of faith in God, especially when he has proved himself in so
many miraculous ways, can be a cardinal sin (Israel at Kadesh).

3. We should be able to see God and forget the giants, rather than
see the giants and forget God (spies in Canaan).

4. It is possible for those especially called of God to be blind to his
motives and desires while others are able to see plainly (Balaam, the
dumb animal, and the angel).

IV. Key Concepts

1. Majority decisions are not necessarily the correct ones; sometimes
the minority is right (2 as over against the 10 spies).

2. True repentance on the part of God's people always brings forgiveness (fiery serpents).

3. God's called men have a right to proclaim only what God desires
them to proclaim (Num. 22:21-35).

V. Enrichment Suggestions

1. Study the idea of the covenant in another book; for instance, William W. Stevens, *Doctrines of the Christian Religion*, William B. Erdmans Publishing Co., pp. 352-370.

2. Read the book of Deuteronomy in a modern translation.

3. Read about the Ten Commandments. See Jack Finegan, *Let My People Go*, Harper and Row, pp. 117-130, and Page Kelley, *A Nation in the Making*, Convention Press.

8
Joshua and the Conquest of Western Palestine

I. Significant Questions

1. What woman of Jericho befriended the Israelites?

2. Why was it necessary to capture Jericho immediately after crossing the Jordan?

3. What was the condition of the Jordan that made the crossing at that time of the year (month of Nisan) especially miraculous?

4. What four significant events took place immediately after the crossing of the Jordan?

5. In what dramatic manner did God direct Joshua for the taking of Jericho?

6. Why were the Israelites unable to conquer Ai on the first attempt?

7. What did Achan steal and hide?

8. Why was it necessary that the Mosaic Law be ratified, as commanded by Moses? Where was it done?

9. To what deceit did the people of Gibeon resort in order not to be conquered by Joshua and the Hebrews?

10. What battle brought victory in the south of Canaan for Joshua?

11. What battle brought victory in the north for Joshua?

12. What was unusual about the battle in the north against Jabin and his fellow kings?

13. What method was generally used to determine the allocation of the land among the various tribes of the Hebrews?

14. What tribe received cities distributed throughout the land, rather than a designated territory, as all the other tribes?

II. Word Studies

1. What was Joshua's name before Moses changed it to Joshua?

2. Why was the valley of Achor appropriately named?

III. Inspiring Lessons

1. Many people have a tendency not to take God seriously when he issues a command or warns of sin (Achan).

2. Deceit sometimes brings consequences greater than those it intends to avoid (the guile of Gibeon).

3. The misunderstanding of the motive of Reuben, Gad, and half Manasseh at the fording the Jordan should make it very apparent how easy it is for one today to misunderstand.

4. Joshua's challenge to the people and his firm resolve that he and his house would "serve Jehovah" should be an inspiration to modern day Christians.

IV. Key Concepts

1. The covenant that Joshua made with the people of Gibeon is a good example of a covenant between two tribes of people, as over against a covenant between God and his people.

2. There are two incidents in the Old Testament in which time "stood still": Joshua's "sun over Gibeon" (Josh. 10:12,13) and Ahaz's sundial in "turning backward" during the days of Hezekiah (2 Kings 20:10).

3. The "walls" of man always go down before the power of God; spiritual power is always superior to physical power (Jericho).

V. Enrichment Suggestions

1. Study the meaning of "casting of lots" as a form of divination in the Old Testament in a Bible dictionary.

2. Make a map-study of the various tribes and of their locations in the land distribution. See *Biblical Backgrounds* by Adams and Callaway, pp. 96-103 and *Zondervan Pictorial Bible Atlas*, Zondervan Publishing Co.

9
The Judges and Spiritual Decline

I. Significant Questions

1. What were some of the pagan nations surrounding the Israelites and posing a constant danger to them?

2. Why is the period of the Judges sometimes called the "dark ages" of Hebrew history?

3. What were the five perils, or dangers, that confronted the Israelites after the conquest and distribution of the land?

4. What were the five phases of the cycle found in the book of the Judges in connection with most of the judges listed there?

5. Who was Jabin's general, and who was Deborah's general?

6. How did God providentially aid Deborah's army?

7. Why was Gideon threshing wheat in a wine-press?

8. What three signs, or confirmations, did God give to Gideon that he would be with him and help him?

9. Where did the Philistines originate?

10. How does the story of Samson differ from those of the other judges?

11. What kin was Ruth to David the king?

II. Word Studies

1. Who changed Gideon's name to Jerubbaal and why?

2. Why was Abimelech, son of Gideon, known as the "bramble king"?

3. What is meant by gleaning?

4. What is meant by Levirate marriage?

III. Inspiring Lessons

1. Man cannot do things "his way" and expect to prosper and have happiness (Judg. 21:25).

2. Jephthah's rash vow is quite a contrast to Jesus' teaching about simplicity of speech (Matt. 5:33-37).

3. The story of Samson constitutes a supreme example of a wasted talent, or gift, rather than the use of it for God's glory.

4. The powerful influence for good in a righteous life may be seen

in the effect of Ruth upon her daughters-in-law.

IV. Key Concepts
   1. To fulfill his purposes God many times calls the ones we would least expect, as Gideon and Jephthah.
   2. Supreme physical strength and extreme psychical immaturity may be found in one and the same person (Samson).
   3. Even though God's chosen ones may descend to a low moral and spiritual plain, God never forgets them but continues in his providential dealings.

V. Enrichment Suggestions
   1. Study the list of the judges to discover one good characteristic in each.
   2. Inquire of your friends and relatives whether they have ever used the "putting forth of the fleece" approach for making decisions.
   3. Read in the Scriptures concerning the Mosaic Law and child sacrifice (Lev. 18:21; Deut. 12:31).

10
Samuel and Saul

I. Significant Questions
   1. In what two ways may Samuel be classified besides being a judge?
   2. What were the names of the five Philistine strongholds which formed a confederacy?
   3. In what way did the Philistines have a great advantage over the Israelites? Who finally reversed this situation and brought supremacy to Israel?
   4. Why was Samuel an answer to prayer?
   5. Why was the polygamy practiced by Elkanah unusual?
   6. What were the names and the nature of Eli's two sons?
   7. How did Eli react to Samuel's news of doom?
   8. What probably happened to the place called Shiloh?
   9. What kind of a king did Samuel picture to the Hebrews as their future ruler and when did his prophecy take place?
   10. Where did Saul's public anointing take place?

11. What three kingly characteristics did Saul have at the start of his career?

12. What physical miracle did God perform to vindicate Samuel before the people?

13. What was Saul's second great sin and what was the consequence of it?

II. Word Studies

1. Samuel's name means what?

2. Why did Phinehas' wife name her son "Ichabod"?

3. Beth-shemesh shows the picturesque way in which Hebrew cities were named. What does it mean?

4. Why did Samuel name the stone representing his victory over the Philistines "Ebenezer"?

III. Inspiring Lessons

1. Hannah's faith that God would answer her request of him is an inspiration to the Christian of today.

2. There is a danger in honoring the members of one's family before honoring God.

3. Evil thwarts the fulfillment of God's purpose in the world (Hophni and Phinehas).

4. Just as the ark of the covenant had a deeper meaning than to be a "good luck charm", so the Bible today has a deeper significance than being an object that "wards off calamity."

5. Disobedience, suspicion, and jealousy can lead to a wasteful, rather than a useful, life.

6. Youthful ardor, such as that of Jonathan, sometimes accomplishes more than systematic methods.

IV. Key Concepts

1. When one man fails, God always has another to replace him, as David for Saul and Samuel for Eli.

2. Things and people are holy because they belong to God and are set aside to him. He does not wish them to be profaned, as was the ark several times in the Philistine episode.

3. The theocracy (God's direct rule over his people) did not have to cease with the start of an earthly monarchy, if the proper earthly king

were selected.

V. Enrichment Suggestions
  1. Study further about how the tabernacle was built.
  2. Read further about the ark of the covenant and its significance
for Israel.
  3. Read about the manners and customs of the Hebrews.
  For all of these a good Bible dictionary will be helpful, for instance,
Davis Dictionary of the Bible, Broadman Press; *Hastings Dictionary of
the Bible*, Scribners; and the four-volume *Interpreters' Dictionary of
the Bible*, Abingdon.

11
David and the Empire

I. Significant Questions
  1. What relation was there between David's anointing by Samuel and
the Spirit of God?
  2. From what tribe did David come, and from what prominent family in that tribe?
  3. What incident brought David back into Saul's presence after his
youthful days as Saul's armor-bearer?
  4. What effect did the song of the women about Saul and David have
on Saul?
  5. At what two places could David have easily killed Saul but refused to do so?
  6. How did David repay those of his own tribe of Judah who had
befriended him during the days of his "outlaw life"?
  7. Why did Saul make a visit to the witch of Endor?
  8. What did David do as an expression of grief due to the death of
Saul and Jonathan?
  9. What was the "golden age" of Israel's history?
  10. Where did David's second, or public, anointing take place?
  11. Why did Abner transfer his allegiance from Ishbosheth to David?
  12. What finally happened to Ishbosheth?
  13. Why did David need a new capital apart from Hebron?
  14. How long did David rule at Jerusalem over the whole country?

15. After the disappointing news that God would not let him build the temple, what good news did David receive from the Lord?

16. To what extent did David geographically expand his kingdom?

17. What was the probable occasion for the writing of Psalms 51 and 32?

18. What were five disasters that hit David during the last few years of his reign?

II. Word Studies

1. The name David has a significant meaning. What is it?

2. How did Nabal, of Carmel, live up to the meaning of his name?

3. What is the meaning of "Ishbosheth"?

4. Why was Solomon's name appropriate to his reign?

III. Inspiring Lessons

1. David's complete trust in God, as discerned in his words to Goliath the giant, would be a good example to follow in today's world.

2. No matter how formidable the foe in life, God's might and Spirit far transcend the danger.

IV. Key Concepts

1. Man sees the outside; God sees the inside of man.

2. God's house should be at least as fine as our own houses (2 Sam. 7:2).

3. Sin is accumulative, for David's adultery led to attempted deceit and then on to murder.

V. Enrichment Suggestions

1. Trace David's path (on a map) during his "outlaw life" and note the happenings at each place.

2. Study necromancy and soothsaying in the Old Testament in a Bible dictionary.

3. Read David's prayer in 2 Samuel 7:18-29 and compare it with the model prayer of Jesus in Matthew 6:9-13.

12
Solomon and the Temple

I. Significant Questions

1. When was Samuel's verbal picture of a despotic king fulfilled?

2. Solomon's coronation group consisted of what people?

3. Why did Solomon have a deep suspicion that Adonijah's request for Abishag was an act of treason?

4. What four men felt the effect of Solomon's anger not long after he became king?

5. What was Solomon's wise choice, and what was God's answer?

6. What three things were found in the holy place?

7. What was in the holy of holies, and what was it like?

8. What two men of the city of Tyre were helpful to Solomon in the building of the temple?

9. What was the port for Solomon's fleet of merchant ships?

10. What four sources of income, besides taxes, did Solomon have with which to operate his lavish kingdom?

11. What two dangers were working at the disruption of Solomon's vast empire?

12. How did the last part of Solomon's reign compare with the first part?

13. What three foreign opponents brought trouble to Solomon sometime during his reign?

II. Word Studies

1. What does "oracle" mean in 1 Kings 6:23?

2. Solomon's ships sailed to what land for their strange cargoes?

3. For the site of the temple David purchased a threshing floor from what Jebusite man?

III. Inspiring Lessons

1. God's desire to impart to man spiritual and intellectual wisdom has never diminished; the "understanding heart" is available to man today.

2. It is possible for one to start out gloriously in life and end up ingloriously due to tampering with sin.

IV. Key Concepts

1. God is the source of all truth, all knowledge, and all wisdom, not only for Solomon but for everyone.

2. A nation cannot break the first of God's Ten Commandments and fail to pay the price.

V. Enrichment Suggestions

1. Read in a Bible dictionary or encyclopedia about the temple built by Solomon.

2. Read a book about the great men of the Old Testament, such as Rolf Rendtorff, *Men of the Old Testament*, Fortress Press and William S. LaSor, *Great Personalities of the Old Testament*, Fleming H. Revell Co.

13
Israel, Jeroboam to Jehu's Revolution

I. Significant Questions

1. How long did the peaceful era last between Judah and Israel?

2. In what ways did Judah have advantages over Israel?

3. What was the background cause for the split of the kingdom into Judah and Israel?

4. What dynasties proved to be the two strongest in Israel's history?

5. Who made Samaria the capital in Israel?

6. What are the names of the four kings ruling in the house of Omri?

7. Where did Ahab get his wife and who was she?

8. What was being settled in the contest on Mount Carmel between Elijah and the prophets of Baal?

9. What was the cause of Jezebel's extreme hatred for Elijah?

10. What threefold duty was given by God to Elijah at Mount Sinai?

11. Whose vineyard did Jezebel get by deceit and murder?

12. What was Elijah's prophecy concerning the end of Ahab and Jezebel?

13. What was dramatic about the way in which Elisha took Elijah's place as the great prophet in Israel?

14. How did Elijah compare with Elisha as a miracle-worker?

15. For what two reasons was Naaman disgusted with Elisha?

16. What two kings were allies in the second battle of Ramoth-gilead?

II. Word Studies

1. What were the names of the two cities where Jereboam established his golden shrines?

2. What were the names of the three capitals of Israel?

3. Our activities and our words reveal God to others, as is seen in the words of the widow of Zarephath to Elijah.

4. Gehazi's greed, ultimately becoming leprosy, is an apt symbol of the devastation resulting from all sin.

IV. Key Concepts

1. The power of sin to dominate the lives of people is vividly displayed in the selfishness and jealousy of Jeroboam as he led a whole nation into idolatry rather than run the risk of losing his throne.

2. The very simple way God deals with man is seen in Elisha's demand that Naaman dip seven times in the Jordan River to be rid of his leprosy.

V. Enrichment Suggestions

1. Study the "remnant idea" as found in the Old Testament.

2. Investigate the custom of child sacrifice, as seen in this chapter by the sacrifice of the eldest son of the Moabite king.

14
Israel, Jehu Through the Fall of Samaria

I. Significant Questions

1. In what dramatic manner did Jehu learn that he was destined to be the next king in Israel?

2. Why can Jehu be termed a "bloody revolutionary"?

3. Exactly how did Elijah's prophecy concerning Jezebel come true?

4. How did Jehu "strike a blow" against Baal worship in Israel?

5. How was Jehu's "zeal for Jehovah" incomplete?

6. Under what king did Israel reach its height in prosperity and international prestige?

7. What king of Israel broke down the wall of Jerusalem and plun-

dered the temple and the palace?

8. What was the prophecy of Jonah in regard to Jeroboam II?

9. What two great prophets proclaimed God's word in Israel during the time of Jehu's dynasty?

10. What kings were involved in the Syro-Ephraimitic War?

11. Who was the last king to reign in Israel?

12. What was the date of the fall of Samaria and to what king of Assyria did it fall?

II. Word Studies

1. What is the origin of the people called Samaritans mentioned in the New Testament?

III. Inspiring Lessons

1. The Bible lists many ways and opportunities to display a "zeal for Jehovah" besides that of destroying the "enemies" of Jehovah.

2. The influence of a person continues long after his death, as Elisha's miracles did not stop when he died.

IV. Key Concepts

1. God is very patient with his people, not bringing judgment and catastrophe till he has warned many times.

2. God sometimes uses a pagan nation as the "rod of his anger" with which to chastise his specially called ones.

V. Enrichment Suggestions

1. Make a study of Tiglath-pileser, or Pul, and his achievements in a Bible dictionary.

2. Read further about the prophet Amos. See Introduction to "Amos" in *The Broadman Bible Commentary*, Vol. 7.

3. Read further about the prophet Hosea. See Introduction to "Hosea" in *The Broadman Bible Commentary*, Vol. 7.

15
Judah, Rehoboam Through Ahaz

I. Significant Questions
  1. How many dynasties were there in Israel? in Judah?
  2. The break between Israel in the north and Judah in the south came at about what date?
  3. Who invaded Judah during Rehoboam's reign, taking much booty?
  4. For what is Asa noted besides his military conquests?
  5. What king was the first to set up a system of religious schools throughout his realm to teach the people the laws of Moses?
  6. What king in Israel and king in Judah established peace and good relations between the two countries?
  7. What was peculiar about the death of Ahab?
  8. What was Micaiah's advice to Ahab and Jehoshaphat?
  9. What was Jehoshaphat's tragic business venture?
  10. What two kings did Jehu kill and how did he accomplish this?
  11. What aunt and uncle secretly reared the little son of Ahaziah till he could be placed upon the throne?
  12. What happened to Athaliah?
  13. What happened to Joash after the death of Jehoiada, the priest?
  14. What king of Judah was so evil that his own people chased him out of his country and killed him?
  15. What kind of a king was Ahaz? Describe his activities.

II. Word Studies
  1. What is the other name for Petra, capital of the Edomites?
  2. What is the meaning of the phrase "till he was strong" (2 Chron. 26:15)?

III. Inspiring Lessons
  1. The evil and idolatrous life of Jehoram, successor to Jehoshaphat, is one of suffering and tragedy, thus showing the extremely high price of sin.
  2. Many times in the Old Testament a prophet of God rebuked a good king for an unholy alliance with an evil one, reminding us of Paul's admonition to Christians in 1 Corinthians 6:14 to 7:1.

IV. Key Concepts

1. The providence of God is seen in his control of things so as to move progressively toward the end he has chosen. This is easily discerned in God's leading of kings like Asa and Jehoshaphat and of prophets like Hanani and Micaiah.

2. Sin is seen in the Old Testament as a violation of the righteous nature of God, for his nature becomes the objective standard, or norm, by which sin is judged. Any activity, such as idolatry or apostasy, which thwarts God's purpose to save man to a high moral order, is sin.

V. Enrichment Suggestions

1. Read further into the fertility cults and the Baal worship of the people of Canaan, the neighbors of the Israelites.

2. Damascus has one of the oldest continuous histories of any city of the world. Read about this city of ancient Syria.

16
Judah, Hezekiah Through the Fall of Jerusalem

I. Significant Questions

1. Whose reign was a bright interlude between the reigns of two evil kings?

2. What was the relationship between Hezekiah and the prophet Isaiah?

3. Who was king in Jerusalem when Samaria fell to Sargon II of Assyria?

4. What was the great engineering feat described in the Siloam Inscription? Describe it and tell of its purpose.

5. What Assyrian king met catastrophe at the hands of the Lord outside Jerusalem in 701 B.C.?

6. What does tradition say happened to Isaiah the prophet?

7. In what year did Nineveh, capital of Assyria, fall to the Medes and Babylonians?

8. What was unusual about the finding of "the book of the law of Jehovah" in the temple in 621 B.C.? Explain the significance.

9. Jeremiah the prophet was highly influenced by what book of the Old Testament?

10. When did Jeremiah begin his work?

11. Where and how was Josiah killed?

12. What was the relationship between Jehoiakim and Jeremiah?

13. Where did Nebuchadnezzar defeat Pharaoh Necho, thus bringing all of Assyria, Syria, and Palestine under Babylonian control?

14. What was the date of the first deportation of Hebrews to Babylon?

15. Why did the priests, prophets, and people want to kill Jeremiah?

16. What was the date of the second deportation? The third deportation?

17. What did Jeremiah advise the captives in Babylon by means of his letter?

18. What finally happened to Zedekiah?

II. Word Studies

1. Why was Hezekiah's tunnel named Siloam?

2. Name the four great eighth-century prophets, each of which has a book of the Bible bearing his name.

3. What are the Hebrew names of Shadrach, Meshach, and Abednego, Daniel's three friends?

4. What Babylonian name was given to Daniel?

III. Inspiring Lessons

1. Hezekiah depended heavily upon Jehovah with the help of Isaiah; and conditions in the land were greatly improved over those during the reign of wicked Ahaz, thus showing that God's way of life brings far greater happiness and well being than a godless one.

2. Though Manasseh had a change of heart late in life that made him endeavor to set straight all the corrupt and abominable deeds of approximately half a century of reigning in Jerusalem, he was unable completely to restore conditions to their previous state. It is difficult to remove all the scars of sin.

IV. Key Concepts

1. Deism, the belief that God created the world and then withdrew, leaving it to develop itself, as well as the belief that God has given no revelation to man, is seen to be false and heretical with a reading of the Old Testament.

2. The omniscience of God is clearly apparent in Old Testament prophecy. Every "thus saith the Lord" of the prophets is grounded in the all-knowing of God.

V. Enrichment Suggestions

1. Read the poem "The Destruction of Sennacherib" by Lord Byron and then read the account in 2 Kings 18:13 to 19:37.
2. Study further the great prophet Jeremiah. See Clyde T. Francisco, *Studies in Jeremiah*, Convention Press.

17
The Captivity and the Restoration

I. Significant Questions

1. Approximately how many Israelites were deported altogether to Babylon?
2. What book of the Bible very graphically pictures Jerusalem in its ruins and desolation?
3. What kind of a life did the Hebrews experience in the Babylonian captivity?
4. What was the twofold religious crisis that the Hebrews faced in the captivity?
5. What did Jeremiah advise the captives in exile in his famous letter to them?
6. What does tradition say happened to Jeremiah?
7. How did the Jews get started speaking Aramaic?
8. What was one very beneficial effect of the Babylonian exile upon the Jews?
9. In what date did Babylon fall to the Persians?
10. How did Cyrus the Great break with the traditional way of dealing with captured people?
11. How many people in all do scholars estimate returned to Palestine in the three migrations?
12. What were four factors that encouraged the Hebrews to return to their homeland?
13. What was the main objective in the first return?
14. What is the significance of the Feast of Purim?

15. What was the date of the second return to Palestine and who led it?

16. What were the conditions in Jerusalem and Judah at the time of the second return?

17. What was the date of the third return and who led it?

18. What was accomplished soon after the third return?

II. Word Studies

1. What is the meaning of "synagogue"?

2. What is the difference between the terms "Jew" and "Hebrew"?

3. What is the meaning of the term "proselyte," as used by the Jews and as used by Jesus in Matthew 23:15?

4. What is the meaning of Pur, from which Purim comes?

5. Malachi is an appropriate name for a prophet. What does it mean?

III. Inspiring Lessons

1. Just as the materialism and prosperity that the Israelites encountered in Babylonia posed for them a temptation to draw them away from a close relationship to Jehovah, so materialism and affluence threaten us today.

2. The strict adherence of Daniel and his three friends to their personal ideals was recognized and admired by those in authority above them, thus leading to their being placed in positions of responsibility. So it is today.

3. Nehemiah's pious, courageous, and noble spirit, as well as his defiant stand against all that he found wrong in God's sight, is an inspiration toward Christian living.

IV. Key Concepts

1. The prophet Ezekiel made the Israelites realize that God could be worshiped in Babylonia as well as in their homeland many miles away. The idea of national gods was ruled out in the Old Testament.

2. Sometimes God used a pagan with which to fulfill his purpose in the world. Cyrus, king of Persia, is called God's "shepherd" and God's "anointed."

3. God's providence, or his design being fulfilled in the world, is apparent in the book of Esther as he protected the Jews.

V. Enrichment Suggestions

1. Investigate the rise of the synagogue as an institution of the Hebrew people. See *The Centuries of Decline* by B. A. Sizemore, Convention Press or some Bible dictionary.

2. Find out what you can about Judaism in a Bible dictionary and *Christianity and World Religions* by Luther Copeland, Convention Press, pp. 79-95.

18
Hebrew Prophecy and Poetry

I. Significant Questions

1. What effect did a prophet's call from God have on his message?

2. What king did Elijah denounce face to face? What king did Nathan denounce?

3. What did God command the prophet Jonah to do?

4. Why is the book of Jonah one of the greatest missionary books in the Old Testament?

5. With what three prophets of the Old Testament were the schools of the prophets associated?

6. At what point do many people have an erroneous idea about prophecy?

7. What six books of the Old Testament are considered books of poetry?

8. How does Hebrew poetry differ from poetry in English and other modern languages?

9. What are the four varieties of Hebrew poetry? Give an illustration of each one by naming a book of the Old Testament.

10. What book of the Bible is probably read by more people devotionally than any other book?

11. Who is called "the sweet singer of Israel"?

12. What is the theme of the book of Job?

13. The name of what man is associated with Proverbs more than any other?

14. Who does tradition say wrote the book of Ecclesiastes?

15. Who is the traditional author of Song of Solomon?

16. What is the theme of the book of Lamentations?

II. Word Studies

1. Name seven other terms that are used in the Old Testament to refer to the prophets.

2. What is the term applied to statements in the Old Testament concerning a coming of a Messiah?

3. Why is a prophet more a "forthsayer" than he is a "foreteller"?

4. What is meant by the term "parallelism" as it is used relative to Hebrew poetry?

5. The word Ecclesiastes has what meaning?

III. Inspiring Lessons

1. God still calls and commissions "forthsayers" today with which he delivers his message to humanity.

2. It is just as impossible to "run away" from God today as it was for Jonah.

3. Christians rob themselves of great spiritual comfort and strength when they fail to read and meditate on the Psalms.

4. Many pitfalls and heartaches in life could be avoided by reading and applying the wisdom of Proverbs in daily living.

IV. Key Concepts

1. Prophets, priests, and kings constituted the three classes of men in Israel through whom God revealed himself.

2. Even though the Old Testament speaks of a coming Messiah who will bring light to a sinful and chaotic world, another great act of God, the incarnation, was necessary for that light to be seen and experienced by man.

3. One of the greatest elements in the relationship of redeemed man with a loving God can be expressed only in song, as is discerned in the Psalms.

V. Enrichment Suggestions

1. Look into some good books on the prophets of Israel and Judah, for instance, Kyle M. Yates, *Preaching from the Prophets*, Broadman Press.

2. Read about the book of Proverbs. See Introduction to "Proverbs" in *The Broadman Bible Commentary*, Vol. 5.

3. Read about the book of Psalms. See Introduction to "Psalms" in

The Broadman Bible Commentary, Vol. 4.

4. Read more about the messianic passages in the Old Testament in *Halley's Bible Handbook*, Zondervan Publishing House, pp. 387-401.